A VOYAGE TO THE INTERIOR

A VOYAGE TO THE INTERIOR

THE PAINTINGS OF

GARY M. JAMES

WITH ADDITIONAL PAINTINGS BY

ALEXANDER JAMES

and including "Art at the Interface"

First published in the UK 2016

ISBN 978 -1- 85457-0888

Published by: Clinical Press Ltd., Redland Green Farm, Redland, Bristol, BS6 7HF, UK.

www.clinicalpress.co.uk

Contents

Foreword

Everyone remembers their first sighting of a Gary James. James is an artist without precedence. A creator of unique visions that in my opinion pay no homage nor draw inspiration from any painter who has gone before. That is perhaps one of the rarest statements I can make about an artist. It's almost impossible for a painter living in the modern era where one is constantly immersed in images of supposedly relevant contemporary art to remain true to an intellectual template that solidified at an early age. There is a freshness in James' work, a beguiling innocence that somehow enlivens my spirit, pervading even his most complex paintings. It reminds me that not all visual art that is memorable needs to evolve out of an art institution blessed by the appointed mandarins of the contemporary art world. I'm hugely relieved that the art of Gary James exists. It's akin to a vigorous breath of fresh air in a stuffy room.

When I first viewed Gary's paintings I was retrieved to my past, as keenly as if by sniffing some long forgotten odour, into the times when I would successfully appeal to my parents that I was not well enough to go to school. The day would be spent reading Rider Haggard and Kipling, happily inhabiting a bedroom festooned with images of tribal people in East Africa, views of Kilimanjaro and delicate biplanes taking smiling people to tented camps under baobabs. Pure Gary James. Its images such as those that initiated my lifelong love affair with Africa – a landmass fractured by the aftershocks of the slave trade, boundaries drawn up in Brussels by people who had never stepped foot on the continent and now with many self-imposed wounds. Happily Africa's vastness is also a land of valid undamaged societies full of wise elders, impish boys and girls and mysterious rites and relics. It's a continent inhabited by the mind of Gary James. Gary resides for years in his imaginary River Market. Through his beautifully constructed paintings and gorgeous carved frames we become intimate with the lives of all the inhabitants. How I would love to live there! Delicate balustrades and colourful carpets drying in the sun on warm cliffs that no doubt are reflecting the voices of happy people enjoying life in a most lovely nook somewhere in Africa. The fact that it doesn't exist outside the mind of this extraordinary artist is, after spending some time with his work, almost impossible to believe. Such is the clarity of Gary James' imagination.

I am thrilled that this book is finally being published. It brings together in one volume most of the major works spanning a mature artist's career. Gary works very slowly. His technique and the complexity of the subject demands that. Each frame alone takes him more time than most contemporary artists would take to paint an exhibition! It has long been a frustration to both the artist and myself that we have been unable to gather all his most profound works together from the various collections where they hang so that people can enjoy the extraordinary breadth of Gary's vision. To a large extent his paintings are sequential, each unwrapping the story a little more. This publication succeeds completely in telling a tale which has evolved over decades.

Mark Read
EVERARD READ ART GALLERY

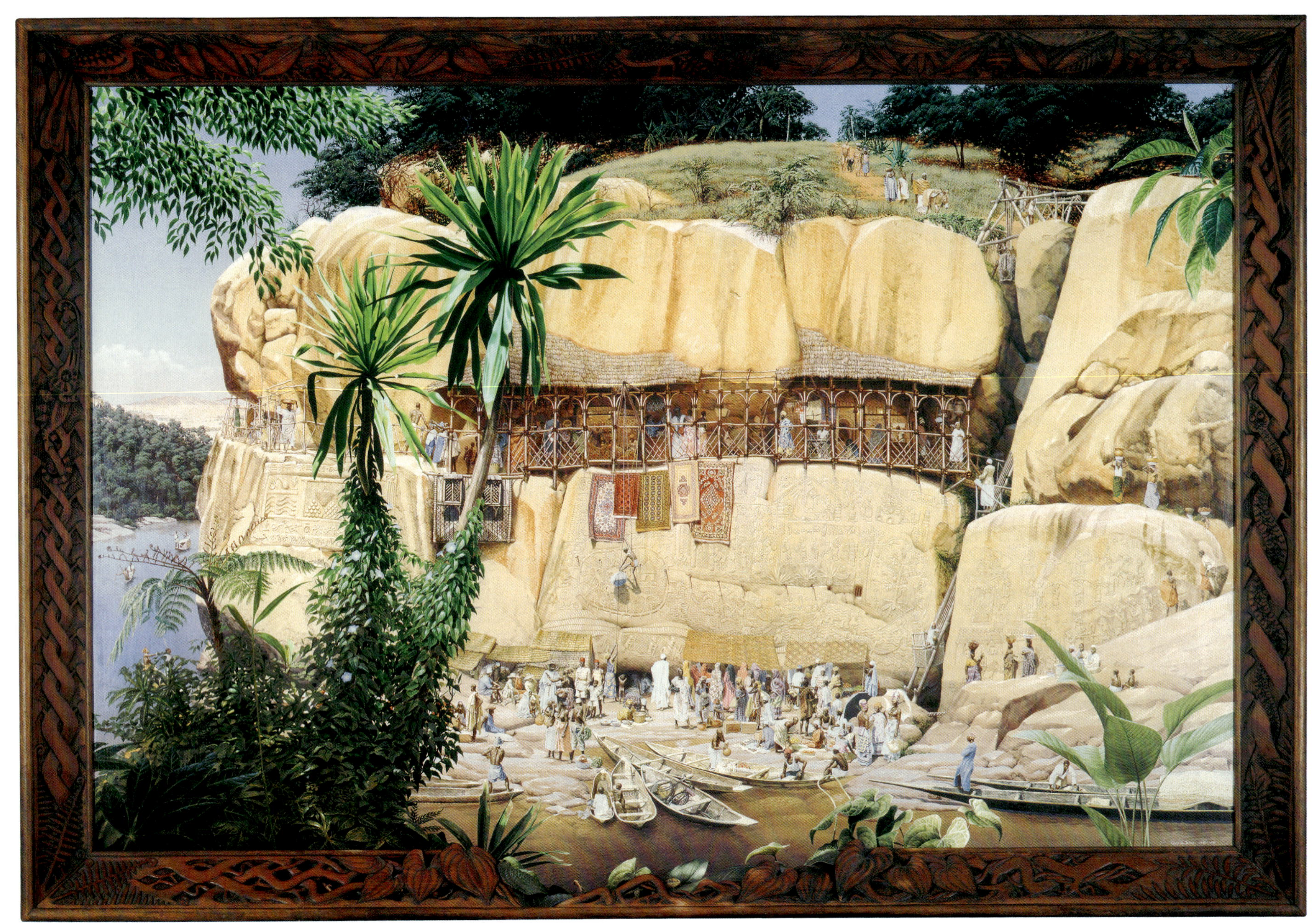

River Market (see pages 46 to 51)

Introduction

"Wait until someone decides to write a book on you of their own volition" counselled my brother Nick sensibly on learning of my intention to begin work on this book. "And wait for hell to freeze over first" I countered, given my tenuous position in the British fine art scene. No, if my presence on the art scene was to be registered at all, I was going to have to do the job myself.

The snags were two-fold. First, having realised quite early that the world was stuffed full to the gunnels with nice, modest paintings done for a ready sale, I concluded that it needed no more from me. In what time I had for painting I would concentrate on producing just a few "epics" a year. Then when I turned full time painter I found that my innate tendency was to put more and more work into fewer and fewer paintings rather than to increase output. Instead of the one or even two exhibitions a year mounted by some painters of my acquaintance, it looked as if one a decade was going to be pushing it. I wasn't about to flood the market, that was obvious.

Then there was the problem of falling between the two main camps in contemporary art, the new art establishment of the so called "cutting edge" or "avant-garde" to whom anything that looked like art probably wasn't ... and the academies, hitherto bastions of traditional art, who initially accepting my paintings, began to find them too innovative in quite the wrong way. Since all my work now goes abroad virtually straight from easel to purchaser via the dealing gallery, I find myself amongst those who make a living from paintings never seen in Britain – and that hurts a bit.

"You should worry" say friends to me, "you're laughing, why bother with Britain?" Well, I was brought up as a colonial and colonials were always supposed to retain an affection for "The Old Country". In Britain though, there is no equivalent of the Wild West legacy that in America has folks queuing to buy Wild West art. Our "Wild West" was the colonies – and the least said about them the better it seems now. However, for better or worse they did put Britain all over the world map and left a profound mark on those of us fortunate enough to have experienced life on "the pink bits" of empire. And that is what I decided to draw on.

But don't expect to find in my paintings a faithful exposition of the colonial life, or even the wildlife come to that. Colonialism did have its shortcomings (as did the Wild West), whilst the legions of "jumbo" and "big cat" painters headed me right off the game trails in spite of an early fascination. Besides I left Africa at about the age at which many of the latter were coming to it, so my imagination had already been forming on that continent and it was my launch pad not my landing.

Time and distance lend licence as much as enchantment and invention is an imperative in my work. The view from my conservatory studio in springtime, over garden, park and wooded hills could be breath-taking. But it was here, all around me and I had no need to recreate it in paint. Besides I had no wish to be dictated to by the view.

I have never been able to give a succinct answer to the question "what sort of painting do you do?"
In execution perhaps " pre-Impressionism" about covers it. And if that sounds positively historic it is worth bearing in mind that nothing ages faster than "modernism". The art that lasts is figurative art, the visual equivalent of written language. It is the interplay of ideas with skills in the use of that language that can give one wings - to past, present or future.

As for the settings, here they are of an Africa just over the horizon – the bit you haven't seen yet. The time is set by the most expressive choices of transport and the costumes before the all pervasive influence of Westernisation.
Though travel can play its part these could be described as the "ripping yarns" of a studio artist. Those who on occasion took them for scenes from real settings have looked in vain for the dashing brushwork that befits such reinterpretation – for the seduction of suggestion rather than miniaturist detail. Here though, in creating an alternative "reality" that increasingly makes use of a sculptured frame to interface with our real three dimensional world, the aim is to lose the surface rather than celebrate it.

This book is not intended to be a full autobiography, though .....

Part 1 starts with a brief account of the Kenyan upbringing that acts as the "pilot light" to the oeuvre. Nor is it a story book as such, though narrative is a great source of imagery and each painting may contain its own subplots fitting into a theme. It is rather the record of a body of work otherwise unseen as a body.

Part 2 is in the form of an illustrated CV, the better to "cut to the chase". However before we do that...

Part 3 contains a selection of the paintings largely done in the 1970s, the artist's "ranging shots".

Part 4 deals with the contentious issue of the frame and the door it opens to "Interface Art".

Part 5 contains the main paintings of the "Voyage to the Interior" theme and variations. The latter part portrays in some detail the making of a painting and its frame and includes a map of the Rivermarket series.

Part 6 introduces a small selection of the paintings of son and fellow Voyage Artist, Alexander James.

Acknowledgements

To my brother Nick, for remembering bits that I didn't.

To my wife, Paulette for suffering the same refrain for so long. (A novel would have been so much quicker).

To Edward Dowden (painter), who set my course to … Ray Harris Ching (painter) … who set me on course to the splendid Everard Read Gallery of South Africa – and particularly Mark Read, with whom the bucks start.

Also particular thanks to Paul Lawrence and Mark Dyer of Carnival Digital Graphics in Bristol, UK, who steered this project into the 21st Century... St. Paul and St. Mark for the digital era. Also Paul, Lois and Mark of the amazing polymath Goddard family and my delightful daughters-in-law, Mandy and Linda and Jane Bertini for their patient and unstinting input. Likewise to Andy Vowles of Robbins Timber in Bristol, for his unfailing patience over the years dealing with a pair of pernickety painters.

My grateful thanks to you all

Gary M. James

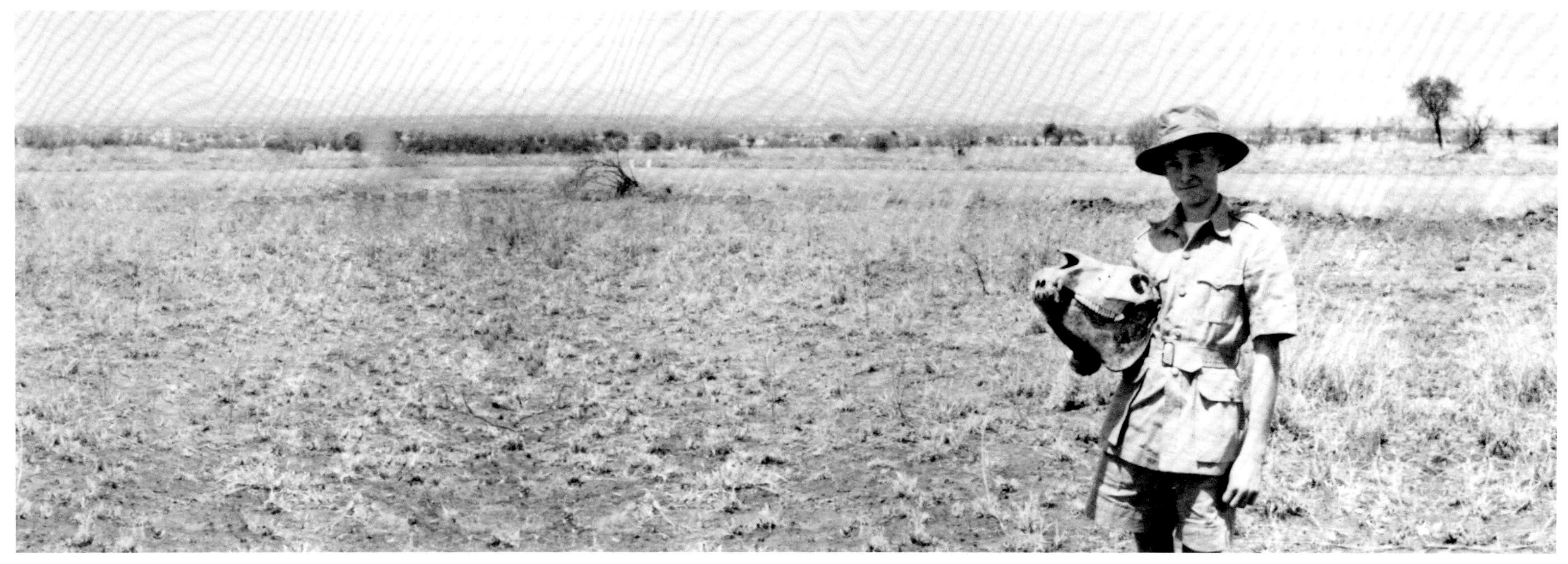

The artist, aged about twelve, Standing in M.M.B.A., ("Miles end miles of blerry Efrica")

Part 1 The Source

"Come friendly bombs and fall on Slough…" poeticised John Betjeman…. and lo, along came World War II, and they did. Thankfully they missed the small block of flats opposite the park where the infant artist, baby brother Nick and parents Doris and Leslie lived. As an engineer Dad's was a reserved occupation, though it often took him away on war work.

In 1948, the war safely over, Dad – no longer extracting magnesium from sea water or designing flame throwers and mortar mounts, now worked for the engineering subsidiary of the international coffee dealing firm Naumann Gepp Dorman. By them he was posted to Nairobi in "The Colony & Protectorate of Kenya" as builder/manager of a factory manufacturing aluminium structures for the ill-fated ground nut scheme and the coffee industry.

And so we flew in a Lancaster bomber derived York transport from the new wood-shack and canvas Heathrow Airport – from darkest rationed Britain to brightest, widest Africa. Life now for an impressionable six year old became a kaleidoscope of strange new sights, smells, sounds and races, shaken up by four new bungalow homes in the first year. The first was corrugated iron on brick piles near an army camp where the last post was sounded each night to the lowering of the flag and polo played in the evenings. The lion skin rug on the sitting room floor of the next, complete with snarling head, had been shot out in the kitchen garden where I now caught exotic butterflies. The memory of the third, a chalet in the grounds of a grand house, was seared into me by the hot poultices slapped onto a boil the size of a quail's egg on the back of my neck.

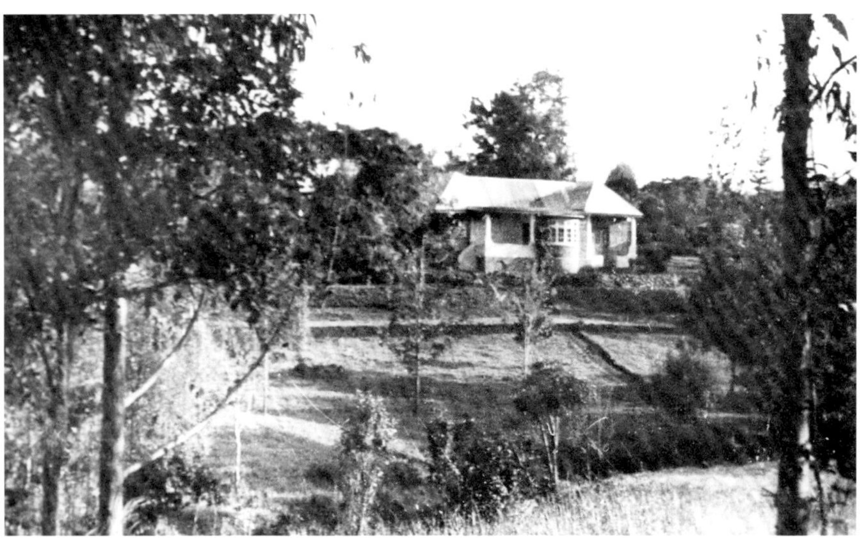

The house in the Kirichwa Kubwa Valley seen from the far side of the garden

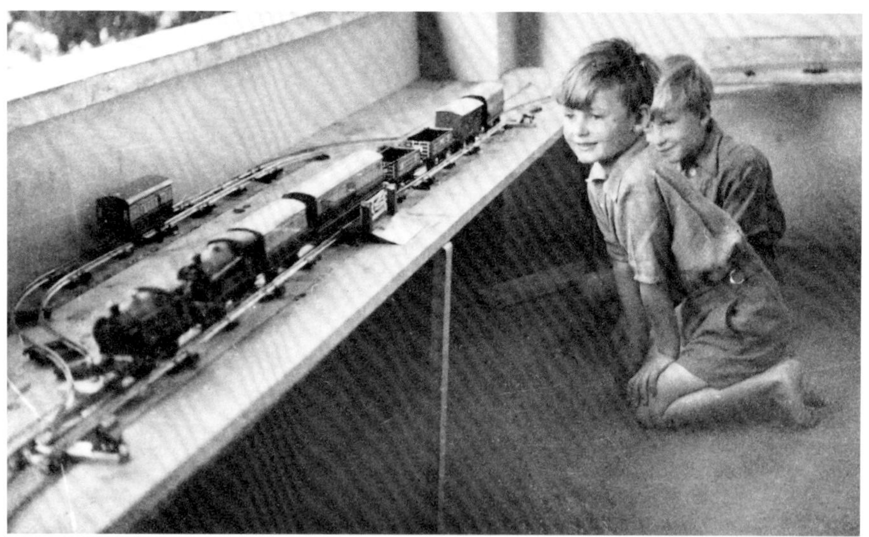

Brother Nick and the author (behind) enjoy a Christmas surprise on the verandah, c 1950

But in the fourth we settled for the next five years – a bungalow with a two acre garden down in the valley of the Kirichwa Kubwa River. This, like Baroness Karen von Blixen's river a few miles away, ran down from the Ngong Hills and divided our garden in two. Just a chain of rock pools sprayed with oil against mosquitos in the dry season, it was a thundering brown torrent in the long rains carrying bushes and trees with it.

After a year at the larger Nairobi Primary School my brother Nick and I attended the local Kilimani Primary School. Its uniform, for the boys, was khaki bush shirt and shorts obtained from Ahmeds in Nairobi, tailors to the "white hunters" and actors on location for such films as "Where No Vultures Fly" and "West of Zanzibar". But more important to me always than school sports and education were the childhood crazes. Stamp collecting,, now virtually extinct as a childhood occupation, was all consuming then, and I suspect that it was the ornamental themed borders around many colonial stamps that subsequently led to my taking the issue of framing seriously. Likewise the dioramas at the then Coryndon Museum in Nairobi, with their dimensional interplay – of say, a warthog in real leaf litter against painted backdrop lit by push button.

TV only came to Kenya years after Nick & I left the country. So a trip to the cinema was a special treat off which we kids would live in the imagination for months or even years. The latest Eagle comic had a similar effect and thus inspired we made things – incessantly. Tin, wood, aluminium scrap, cardboard, branches, bamboo and papier maché, all were used in the production of miniature "galleons", bows and arrows, "horse pistols", suits of armour and lances (for use on bikes), puppets and home made cap guns. Also buggies and a none-too buoyant raft for the river. Our mother's nail scissors were ruined when used to cut up tin cans, teeth were used as pliers and my legs and fingers still bear the scars from the use of broken bits of razor blades. Eventually, somewhat desperately, we were bought a boxed, junior tool kit for Christmas – and looked at it nonplussed. What were you supposed to do with this?

Occasionally there were after work drives out to the Nairobi Game Reserve in our canvas topped Standard Eight – to park in the midst of an odiferous pride of lions. Driving back again we would wonder at the long, thin lines of grass fires in the gathering dusk. Then the BBC's relays of "Children's Hour with Uncle Mac" on the wireless before bed, cicadas zinging outside and a hyena whooping over the valley. Early safaris were made on business, to Uganda or Tanganyika (now Tanzania) in the work's Ford van. Mum and Dad sat up front in the cab, Nick and I and assistant Makutsi sitting on cushions and spare wheel in the open cage back collecting dust.

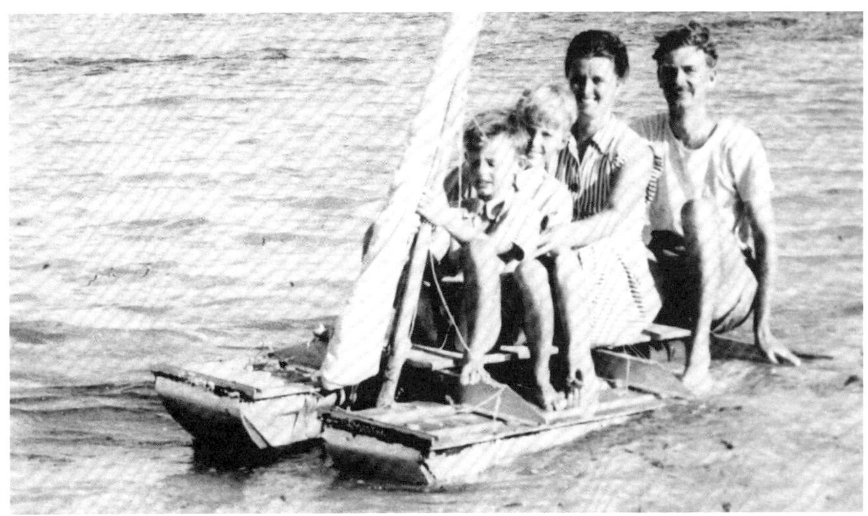

The family afloat (just about) on Dad's homemade aluminium pontoon raft

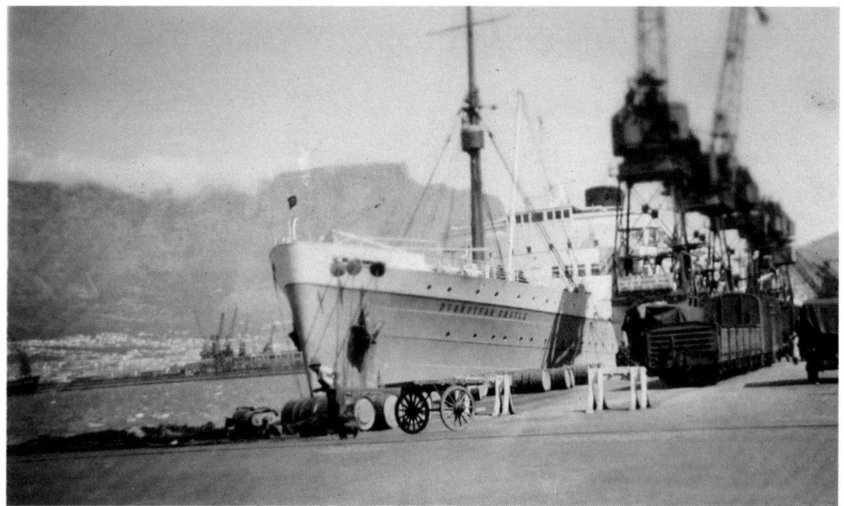

The Dunnottar Castle,
snapped on a "Box Brownie" beneath Table Mountain, Cape Town.

Once a year, before we hazarded the pot holes and ankle deep dust of the Mombasa road, we would take the "Lunatic Line" down to the coast on holiday. As the sun went down over the plains the call to the train's dining car was sounded by a steward on a small xylophone down the corridor. A three course meal was served on white linen amongst marquetry panelling lit by bracket lamps and we would return to find bunks made up in our compartment. At Tsavo halt the sound of soft African voices and the glow of hissing tilley lamps passing beneath the wood slat blinds would rouse us momentarily. Here in 1898 the two Man Eating Lions of Tsavo had held up the laying of the line for months as they devoured the workers, until finally being shot.

A coral reef fringes much of the Kenyan coast and behind this, with its unceasing soft roar of breaking waves, our hotel would be a group of palm thatched "bandas", set amongst bush and palms. Hot water was provided by a log fire beneath an oil drum and the outside toilet a "long drop" referred to irreverently as "the chapel in the moonlight". We slept under a single sheet and mosquito nets – and bats in the rafters, and learned to swim amongst the fishes in an Indian Ocean with the chill taken off by the sun. How strange now to reflect that at the time we were totally unaware that just sixty years before Great Grandfather John James had chased slavers in a cutter up some of the creeks we crossed over now when he was serving in the East Indies Squadron of the Royal Navy.

In 1952 came "home leave". Sailing from Mombasa on board the Union Castle ship M.S. Dunnottar Castle, we called in at Tanga, Zanzibar, Dar es Salaam, Beira, Laurenço Marques – and were joined by relatives in Durban for the trip on round the Cape via East London and Port Elizabeth to Cape Town. Our visit coincided with the third centenary of the arrival of the Dutch settlers under Jan van Riebeeck, and riding the cable car to the top of Table Mountain we were fascinated to be told that anyone able to lift with one hand a gold brick then on display could keep it. Nobody did.

Then our passage to St. Helena, out in the Atlantic was prolonged by a storm that threw a young boy from his top bunk smashing his femur. Tragically he subsequently died of pneumonia, Nick and I witnessing his burial at sea "distracted" by ice creams. And Nick had nearly preceded him overboard in the same storm. In a deck chair race round the rear deck I pushed him into a bollard – and he remembers hanging through the rails looking down at the screws churning below.

Then on St. Helena we never did make it to Napoleon's exile home as our ancient tourer shed a wheel. Eventually our plank and canvas swimming pool was packed away preparatory to docking at Tilbury, Port of London. What a change of view from our cabin porthole after Table Bay!

And now Britain turned me into an Anglophile. Six months of touring the relatives in a staid pre-war Austin; lit up department stores and double decker buses reflected in the wet, blackened streets; "Magic" Grandpa's conjuring tricks and tales of his days in the Royal Flying Corps. Visits to a circus and the "Spot-Light Tattoo", caravanning in Cornwall with Polperro's smugglers' tunnel, the enchanting Emmett Railway at the Battersea Funfair....and the mysterious cabinet in Grandma's four poster bedroom that opened up onto a small grey screen...our first taste of television – Rob Roy MacGregor knee deep in grey heather. Britain was a land of magic.

Eventually we returned via the Mediterranean and the Suez Canal, 1st class on the maiden voyage of the SS Uganda. (Thirty years later the Uganda served as a hospital ship in the Falklands War and Nick then serving in the RAF and bound for home as Officer in Charge of the returnees, caused a stir when it was learned that not only had he sailed on the ship's maiden voyage but 30 years later he was on this, its last before being scrapped!)

The return to reality was not smooth. The Mau Mau Emergency had been declared in our absence and up-country friends now packed guns on their hips. Never an absorbent scholar and having missed several months at school I found myself having to stay down a year. Dad now had home guard duty and was conscripted into the Kenya Police Reserve. This furnished him with anecdotes for the tennis club – a colleague slapping his sten gun down in mounting their safari truck and blowing half the roof off, and modesty maintained on dawn raids when looking for arms by frisking the giggling Kikuyu ladies with a mine detector. Mum was left in charge during these absences armed with our small .22 Beretta automatic – though her practice with this had not inspired confidence. Head averted, eyes tight shut and finger in ear she shot everything but the target. The Emergency was no laughing matter though, least of all for the African populace caught between the Government forces and the Mau Mau who killed far more of their own than white settlers.

School lunches were now taken at safe houses, sitting at trestle tables out under the pepper trees. And then problems at work exacerbated by the Emergency meant that Dad lost his job. Mum, a secretary at the East African Tourist Travel Association (where she had to redirect American tiger hunters) now became principal bread earner – until Dad found a government job as a factory inspector and then Labour Officer. He now drove around in bush jacket and Land Rover, inseparable pipe clamped twixt his teeth.

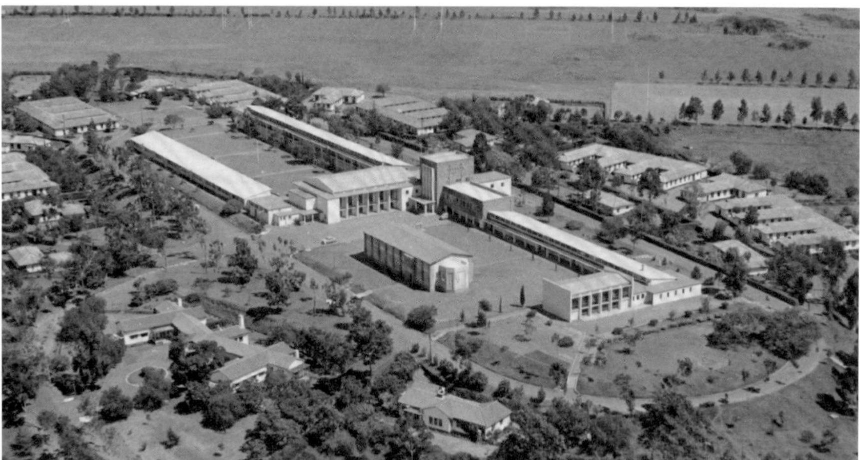

The Duke of York School, Nairobi. Tuition block surrounded by "Brooklands"

And with that came a move from our river valley home to another bungalow on a ridge overlooking coffee plantations north of Nairobi. And that meant boarding school for Nick and I. Nick went to Nairobi Primary and I to the Duke of York School for boys, on the edge of what was then "the Kikuyu Reserve". The search light that flashed through my bedroom window at home, from a Mau Mau suspects detention camp down the road, now flashed from a watch tower with armed Askari at the barbed wire perimeter fence, through the windows of a bolted and sandbagged dormitory. The school had an armoury for its Combined Cadet Force, which would have been a tempting target for gangs often armed with home made guns that used door bolts and inner tube rubber as firing mechanisms.

The extensive school grounds were still half bundu (bush), ideal for secret smokers' dens – and supposedly the odd Mau Mau dugout. Hyraxes serenaded us with their screams at night, sharp-eyed "shite-hawks" swooped from way up in the blue to snatch our buns at break and a leopard might cross ones path to the tuition block at night. Snake collecting was a popular hobby – worn under the shirt during lessons, along with the customary sheath knife – and surprising an attractive lady history teacher when one peeped out at her. Then a vulture with a sick sense of humour took to watching the cross country runners, those not used to the 5,000 foot altitude, as they puked and passed out in the undergrowth.

Educationally I continued to perform like a low energy light bulb. Cadets turned me off from any thoughts of a military career – and in Kenya's one

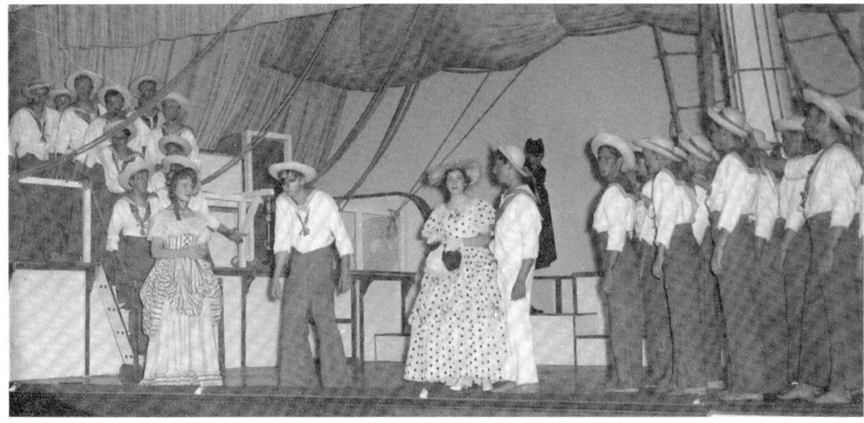

Dick Deadeye (with "Richard III" hunch) realises that he has forgotten his lines.

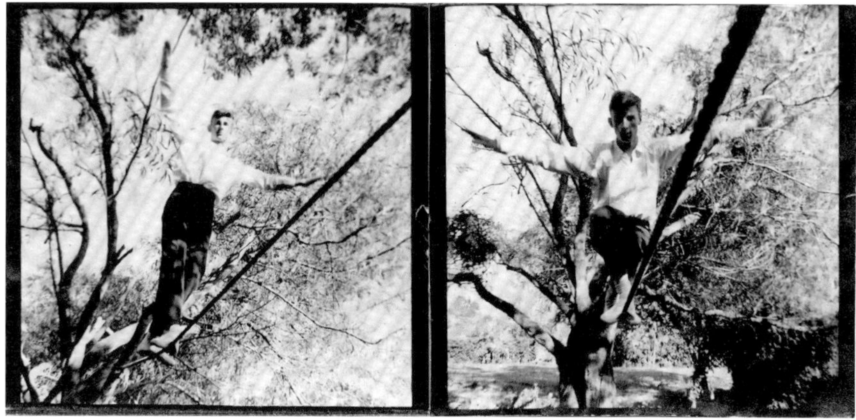

Practice on the tightrope. Home processed photos taken by Nick.

true religion – sport, I turned a devout agnostic. My kicks came from making and drawing, not inflated leather – and here at least the school pressed the right buttons. An early interest in cartooning saw me drawing "funnies" in the school's news sheet, the "Brooklands Baraza" (Brooklands – the drive encircling the tuition block, Baraza – Swahili for a meeting or meeting place). In the art club I got to know Richard Leakey, subsequently the famous palaeontologist and then as skinny as I was, when I did what I was convinced was a better drawing of his dad Louis's "Nutcracker Man" that had featured in the "Illustrated London News". And with my chum Laurie Slade (cousin of Julian Slade of "Salad days" fame then taking Britain by storm) I became stage struck – set painting, programme designing, prop making and occasionally acting and singing. During a performance of H.M.S. Pinafore, in which I was the ship's villain Dick Deadeye, and in front of an audience that included the Governor of Kenya and my parents in the front row, I had an almost "out of body" experience – one that I would not care to repeat. Dick Deadeye has a number in which he sings between and against the chorus – and in the middle I suddenly realised I could not remember what came next. Then, with mind numb in shock I realised that I was singing on auto-pilot. Thank heavens for all the rehearsals.

Home was now a bungalow on the slopes of the extinct Menengai Crater overlooking Lake Nakuru, famous for its flamingos. Here, whilst recovering from a bout of malaria, I stretched a rope between two blue gum trees – and began my hobby of tight rope walking. (I subsequently put this to use at various fêtes back in England).

In 1957 we were on home leave again, this time via Aden and the Suez Canal, a year after the Suez Crisis – rusting hulks in all directions on the central lake. Then my school days were brought to an abrupt end when our school became a refugee camp for Belgians who had driven across the continent from a Congo in revolt. After a nightmare drive they were in a sad state and Nick remembers one car with a machine gun poking through its knocked-out rear window.

By then we were living back in Nairobi and I secured a brief volunteer period of "work experience" at the Donovan Maule Theatre in town. This was the one professional theatre in East Africa and I became unpaid assistant to the stage designer Bill Piggott. Furnishing the set for George Bernard Shaw's "Candida" – an Edwardian drawing room, we borrowed an ornate cabinet consigned to the MacMillan Library when Karen von Blixen departed the country forever. With Bill's carpenter assistant Philip Kakui I held onto the cabinet for dear life in the back of the theatre's open van... And then fifty one years later, when introducing my side of the family to Kenya I was delighted to meet this cabinet again – Karen's jewel cabinet back in her house where it belonged.

Then, in September 1960, it was "out of Africa" for me too – though I did return for summer holiday's "home leave" in the other direction in 1962.

And thus was the long trail for my future career as a painter lit.

Part 2 "Out of Africa" ... a CV

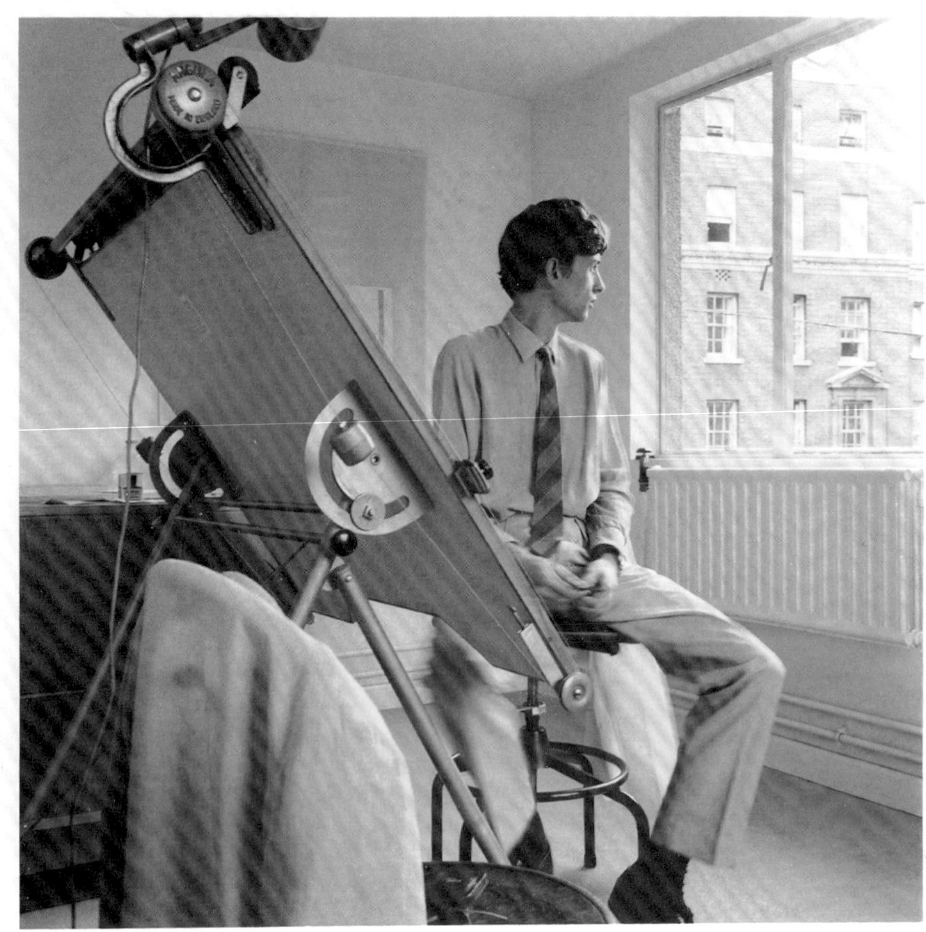

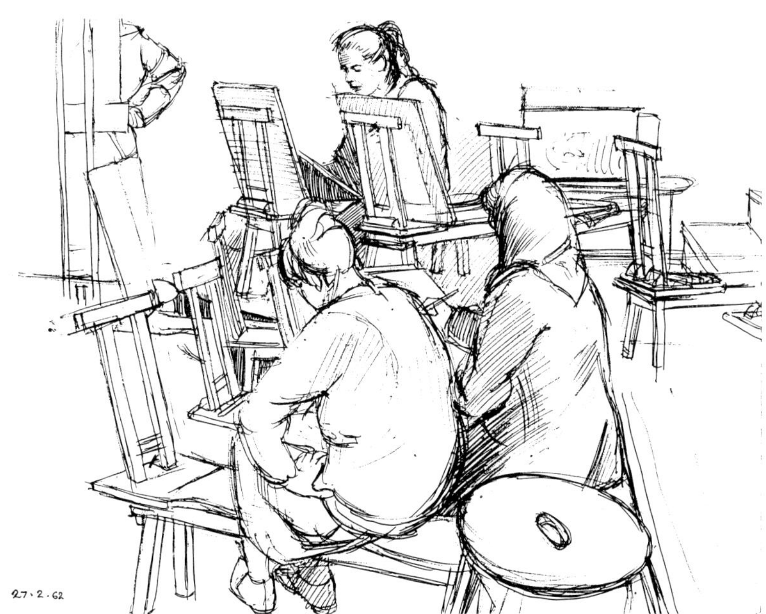

1960 Student at St. Martin's School of Art, London, specialising in illustration.

Craftwork: Wood engraving under Clifford Webb.

Sculpture: under Philip King, (later Sir Philip King, President of the Royal Academy).

In the later 1960s life drawing became "un-fashionable" in many art schools and one northern councillor was heard to say "We're not going to subsidise sex on the rates".

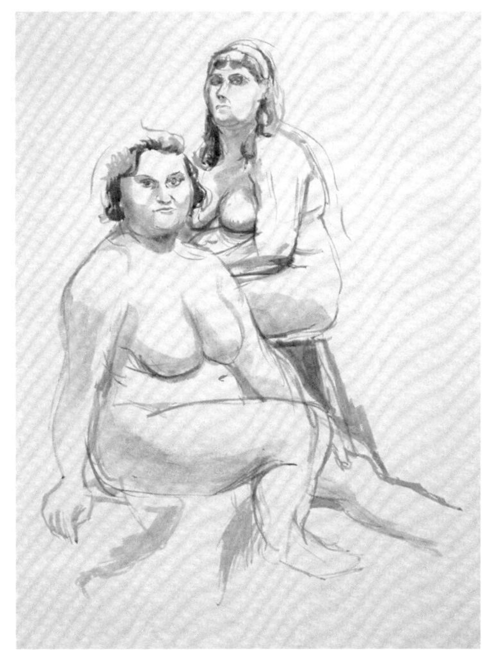

"Sex on the rates"

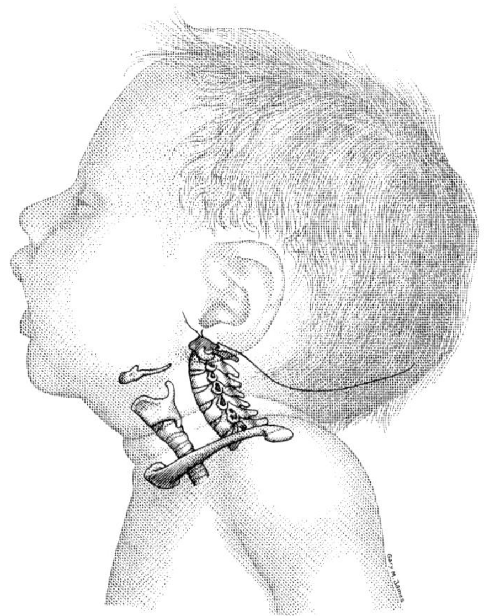

(1994)

1964 One of three students on the eighteen month course in Medical Art, run by the Medical Artists' Association of Great Britain, focussed on six London teaching hospitals. Based at the Central Middlesex Hospital under Irene Prentice of fondest memory.

Little known as a profession, of small numbers, medical art could claim to be as old as medicine itself with Leonardo da Vinci an early luminary! In brief the profession produces visual (and physical) aids for teaching medicine. Before the advent of computers this included drawing in the operating theatre and morgue or anatomy room, book and lecture illustration, modelling, animation, exhibition work, cartoons and statistics. About the only thing I never did as a Medical Artist was bronze casting.

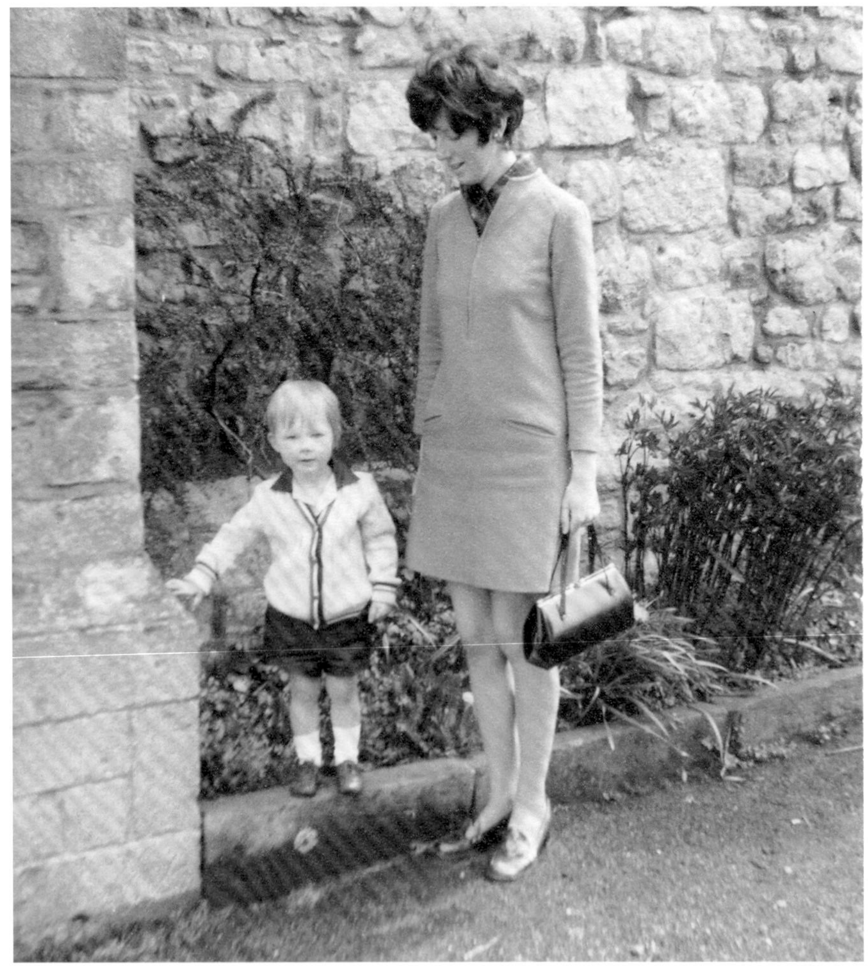

Paulette, with son No. 1 (1968)

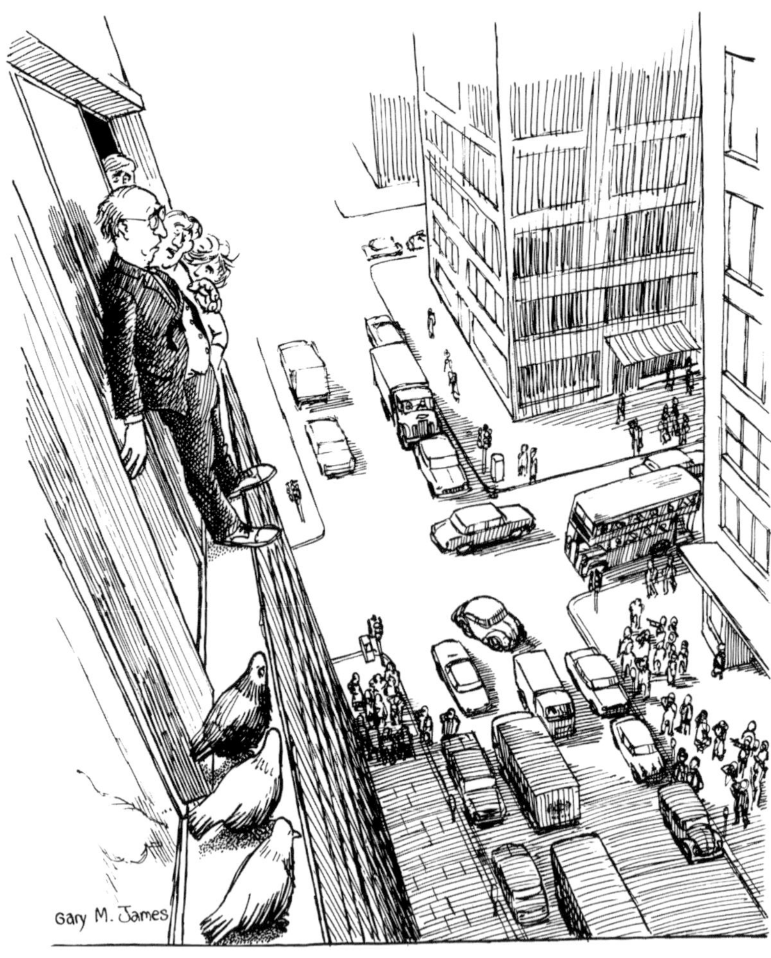

"When I was learning my parents just shoved me off."

1965 Married Paulette Easton. We met at a Toc H* "Mobile Action" meeting in a tin shed on Tower Hill and subsequently had two sons – Patrick ("Patch") born 1967 and Alexander ("Alex") born in 1969.

*(Toc H = "Talbot House" – a good works & fellowship movement founded as a halfway house behind the trenches in the First World War)

1966 I became the Medical Artist at the University of Bristol. After almost succeeding, I suspended attempts to boost income by getting cartoons into Punch Magazine and in 1969 took up the brush instead.

Cartoons continued to be much in demand in the medical work.

Investigation | Therapy

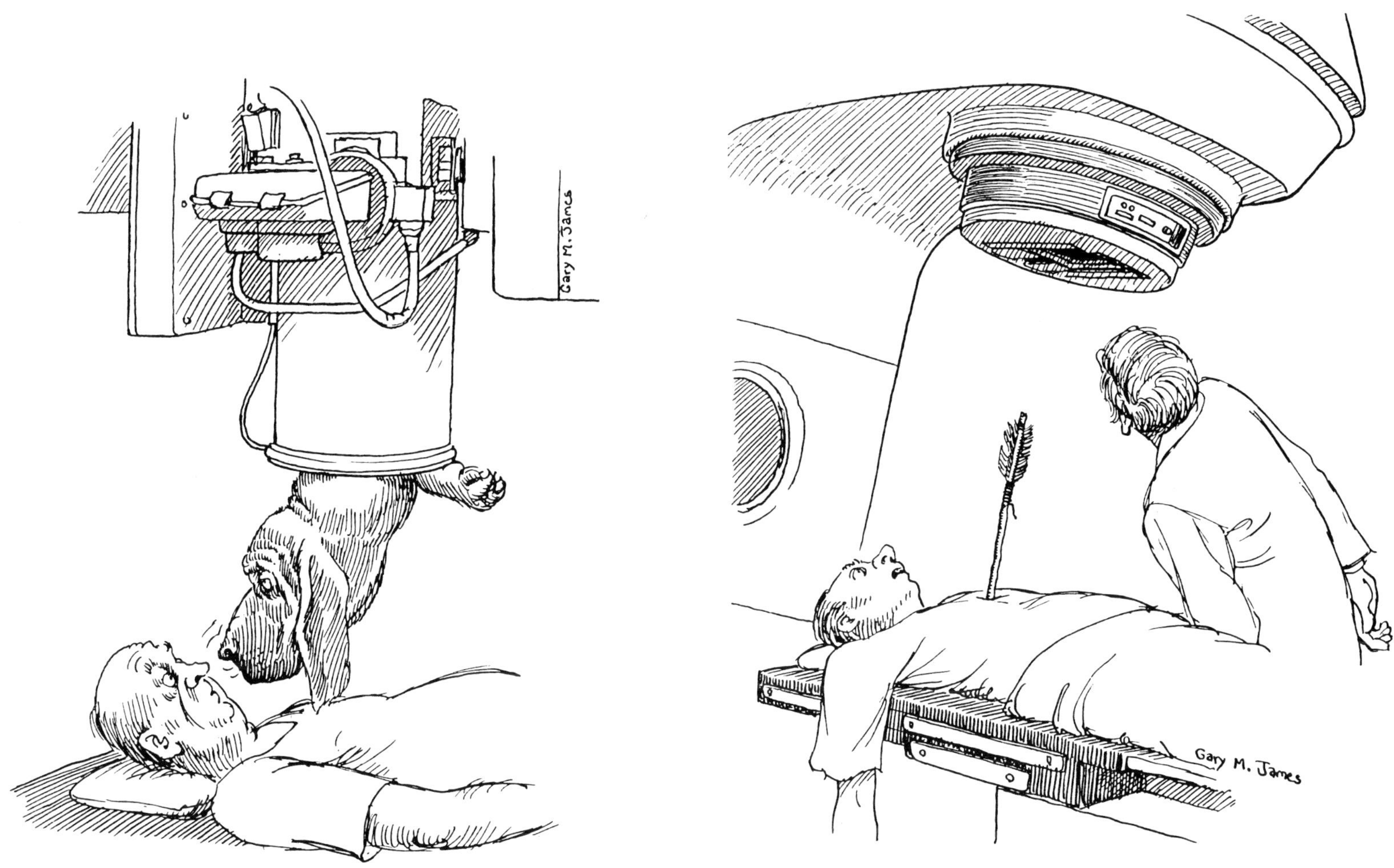

Radiology for investigation and therapy

1969

2nd son! Alexander Edward born.
Future Voyage Artist.

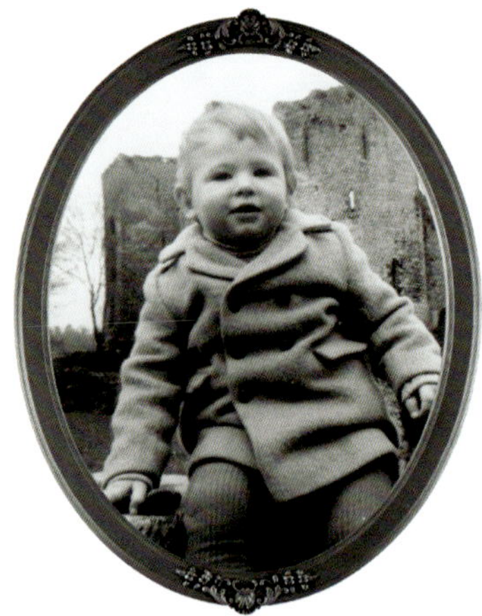

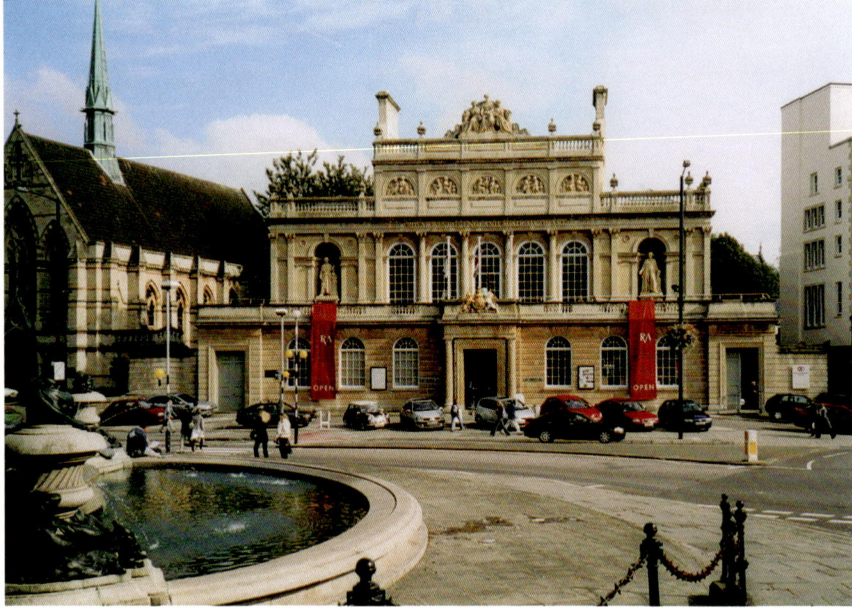

1970 to 1980 Book illustration commitments allowing, an average of one painting per year hung at the Royal West of England Academy annual Autumn Exhibitions.

1977 Small one-man exhibition of paintings at the Bristol City Museum & Art Gallery.

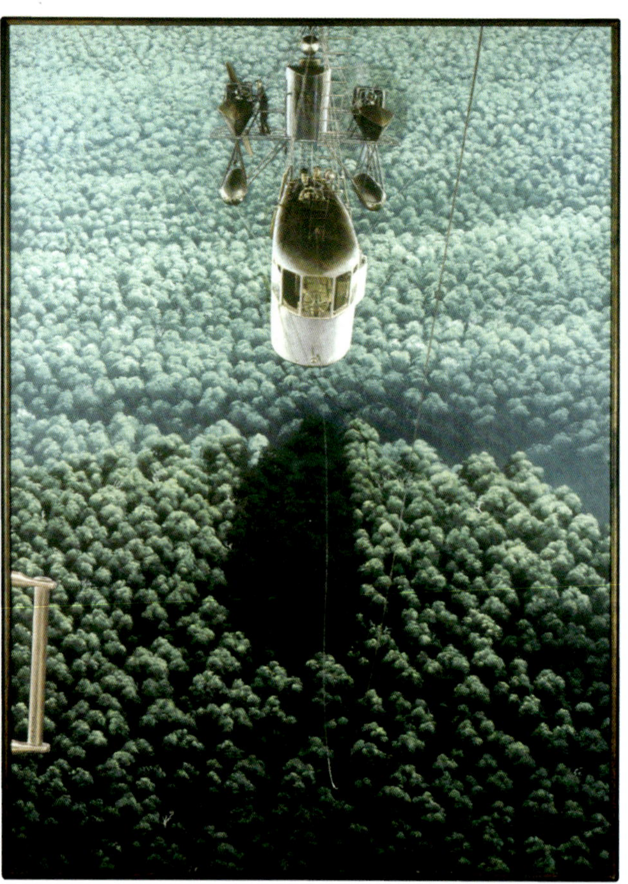

1980 First hang in the Royal Academy's Summer Exhibition – "Captain Maltravers' Voyage to the Interior".
Published in the "RA Illustrated and TV Pick of the Show for the presenter Russell Harty (see also page 23). This painting was the first of my "North Sea" airship series.

Hangs at the RWA now became intermittent, my work found incompatible by the hangers who found my "giant miniatures" in carved frames stuck out like sore thumbs in a mixed show, unless hung in isolation.

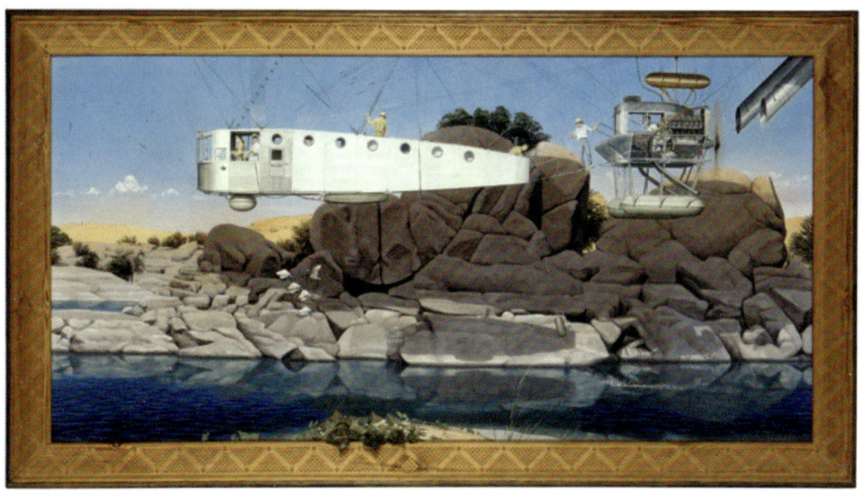

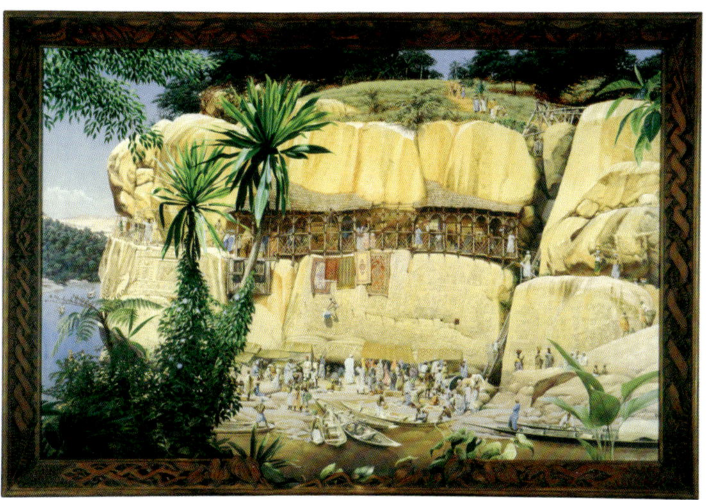

1981 Two paintings in the Royal Society of British Artists Annual at the Mall Galleries: "Zimbabwe" (p. 22) and "An exploratory prod" (p. 24). Subsequent size restrictions make this an unrepeatable exercise.

1984 Two paintings carefully isolated in the RWA's Autumn Exhibition. (pp. 34, 35 & 36, 37).
"Voyager at Jupiter", 4′ x 6′ goes on display at the Royal Observatory, Herstmonceux Castle, East Sussex, until the Observatory moves in 1988. (p. 25).
About now I decided to concentrate on the African Theme and to show "N.F.S." (not for sale), stock piling against an eventual commercial show.

1986 By "North Sea" up the Nile (above and pages 42 & 43) at the Royal West of England Academy, hung in the entrance.
This painting was the TV pick of the paintings for the critic presenter of fearsome repute, Derek Robinson, in his ITV programme on the Academy.
The "North Sea" airship (page 40) was adopted as the artist's magic carpet of choice.

1987 "Kuba Kubwa" hung at the RWA. (pp. 38 & 39)

1989 "River Market", 4′ x 6′, at the RWA Autumn Exhibition (in the entrance again).

1990 "River Market" at the Royal Academy Summer Exhibition and in the "RA Illustrated", attracts the largest, continuing crowds that we had seen at a Summer Exhibition. The Telegraph gives it two whole column inches and the Times dubs it (ironically) "a genuine Academy lunacy". Answering letters and phone calls for months. (See pages 46 to 51).
Participate in annual exhibitions run by the artist Edward Dowden in Bradford on Avon, Wiltshire, for the next six years.

November - A visit to Egypt results in "The Egyptian Timescale", the key to 10,000 years of history with illustrations and maps. Published by Clinical Press 1997, reviewed in "Egyptian Archaeology" and "KMT". Stocked by the British Museum.

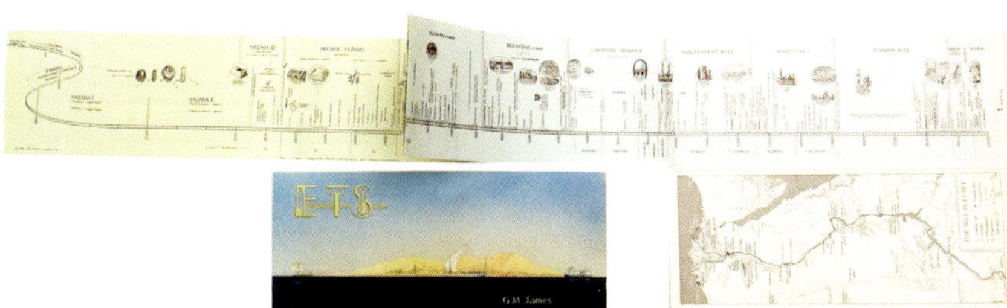

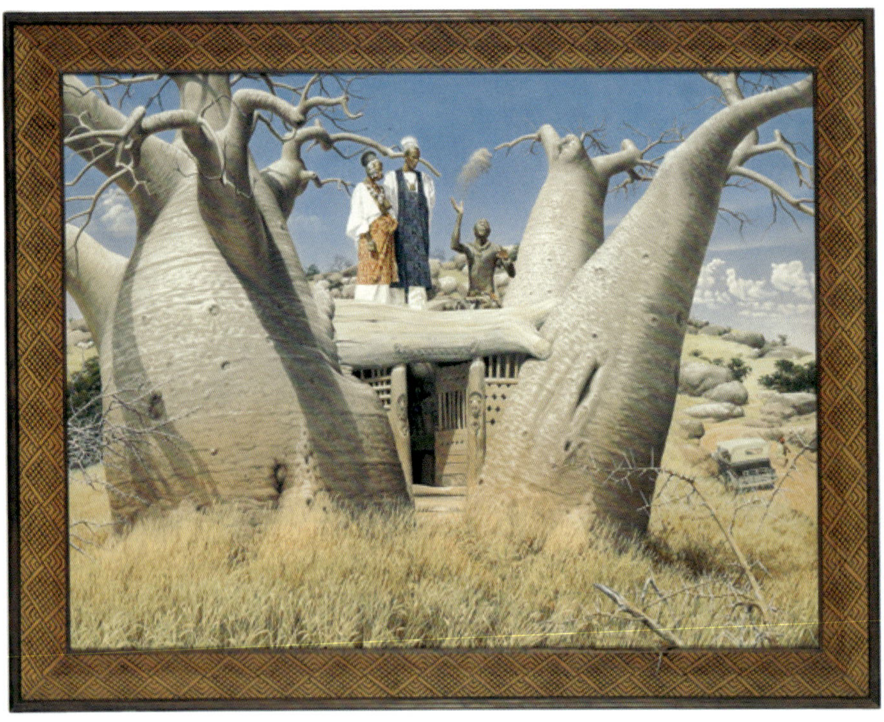

1991 "Forecast", 3′ x 4′, third hang in the RA Summer Exhibition. Published in the "RA Illustrated" my last hang at either Academy. At Varnishing Day warned by another exhibitor that now that a group of abstractionists had been made RAs it was all up for fine detail figuration like ours ... "Conceptual Art" was in and we were out. (pp. 54 and 55).

Paris in the spring.

Father dies.

1992 Visits to Istanbul and Tunisia.

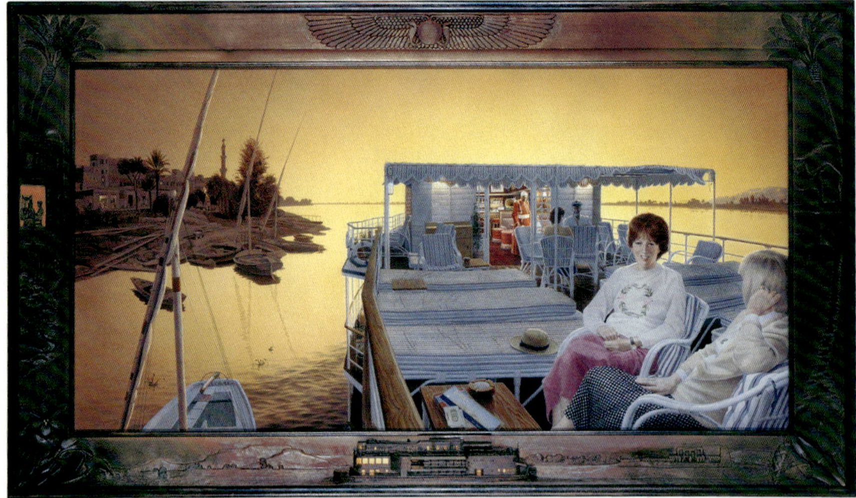

1993 Nile cruise – and painting of same name. (p. 31)

1995 At an Edward Dowden Exhibition meet the doyen of wildlife painters, Ray Harris Ching, who ...

1996 ... introduces my work to Mark Read of the Everard Read Gallery of South Africa.

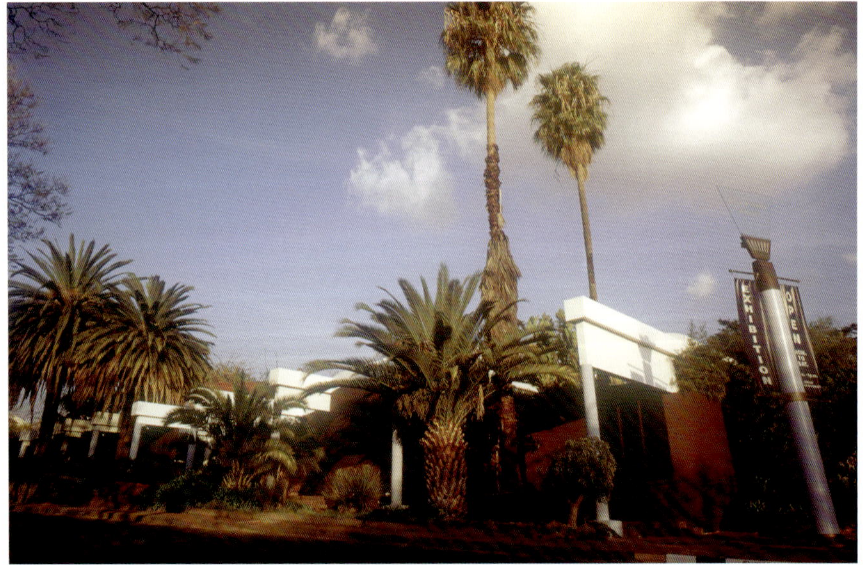

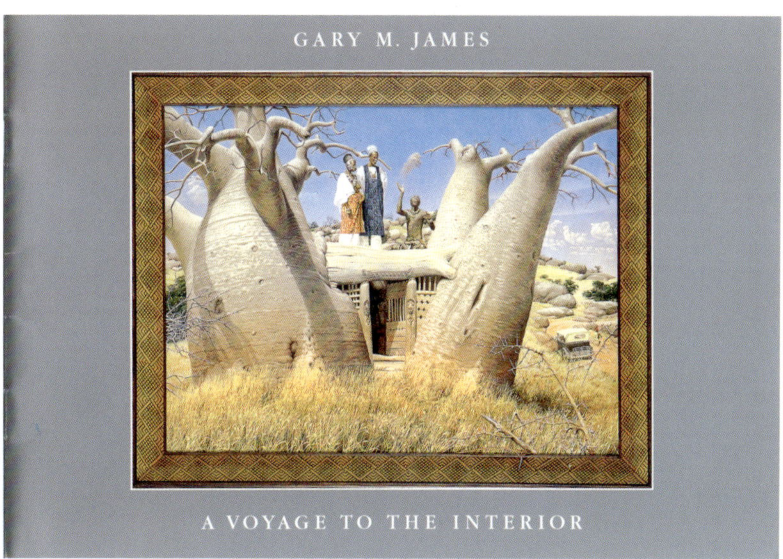

1997 My first substantial one man show at the Everard Read Gallery, Johannesburg. Private View televised by HTV in the UK. The Everard Read Gallery is one of the largest commercial galleries in the Southern Hemisphere, with four galleries and six sculpture courts built around a c.1900 house and set amongst palms, bougainvillea and jacarandas. It has to be one of the most attractive anywhere. More importantly for myself, as an artist, it had an international clientele of Afro-centric tastes with the wherewithal to support a one-a-year painter. News of the show even penetrated a cousin's tennis club. A locker-room first?
The proceeds from the show provided income sufficient for several years. Cast off from medical art. Visit Corfu with older son and daughter in law. Younger son married.
Thereafter paintings wing their way south for solo sales. However ...

1999- 2000 Take time out to mark the Millennium with "The British Time Scale" – a fold-out sweep of 500,000 years of the island/peninsula's history. Thumbnail drawings of artifacts, architecture and technology set against timelines for Roman, English, Scottish & Welsh rulers with fold-out maps, climate and population curve ... not to forget, the Empire. Published by Clinical Press, principal stockists the British Museum. (See in the adjoining column and on the next two pages...)
"The British Time Scale" is nearly two metres in length, has fifteen maps of Britain and one of the British Empire and Commonwealth combined.

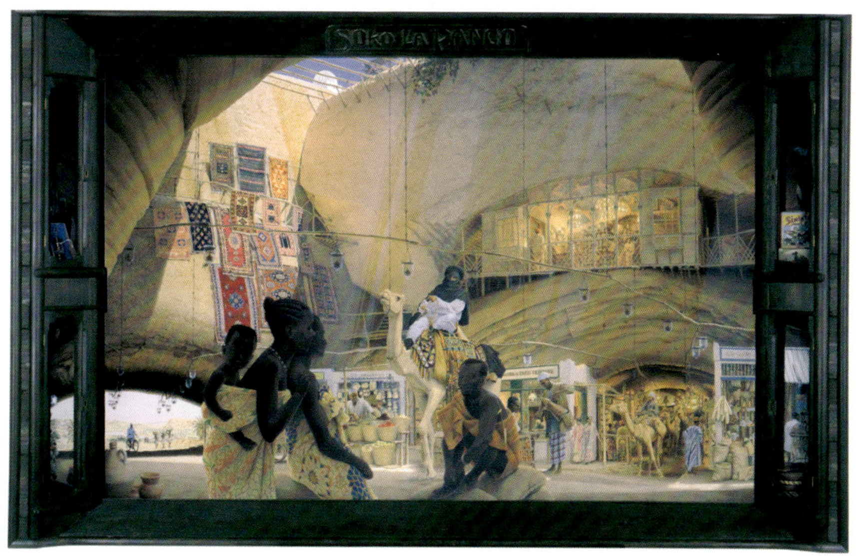

2001 "Soko la Pango" (Cave Market), 4′ x 6′8″, shown at "Art London" before sale at the Everard Read Gallery, earning its artist a sum equivalent to almost three times the RWA's commission on all its exhibitions of the same year. (pp 62 to 69).

2003 Invited to show in the Bath Society of Artists' Annual Exhibition at the Victoria Gallery, "Nile Cruise" wins the public ballot – the artist's first art prize since taking "1st Prize for Imagination" at the Kilimani Primary School, Nairobi, fifty three years before. (pp.12 and 31).

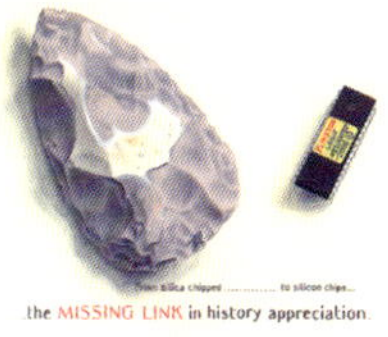

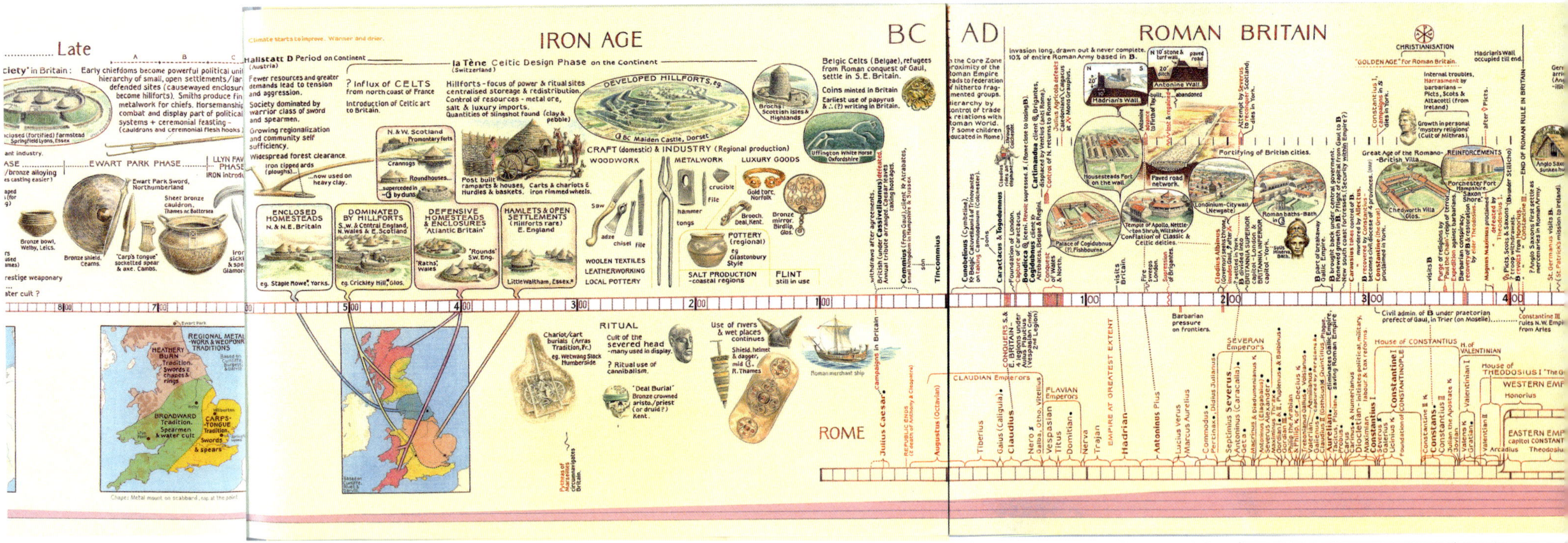

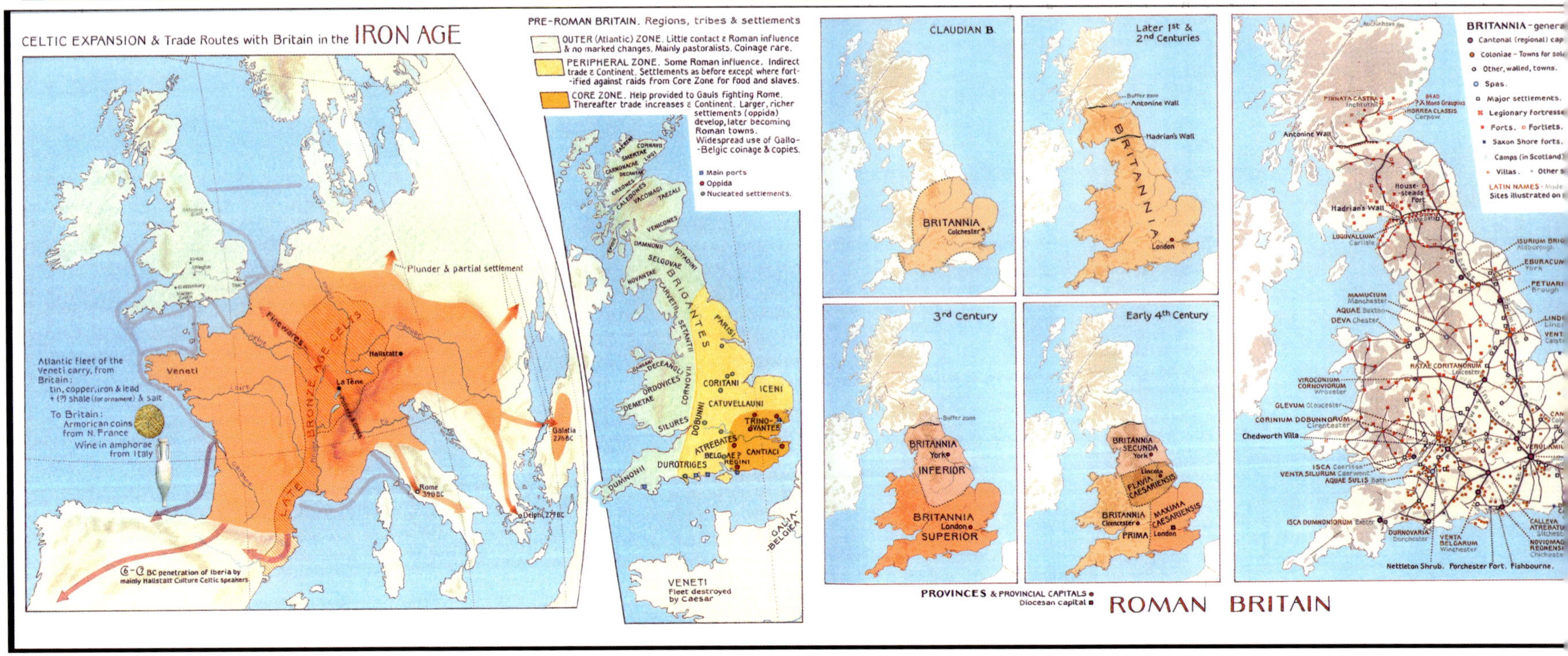

500,000 BC

to

2000 AD

British Timescale (194 cm by 18 cm) published 2000, (Clinical Press Ltd.)

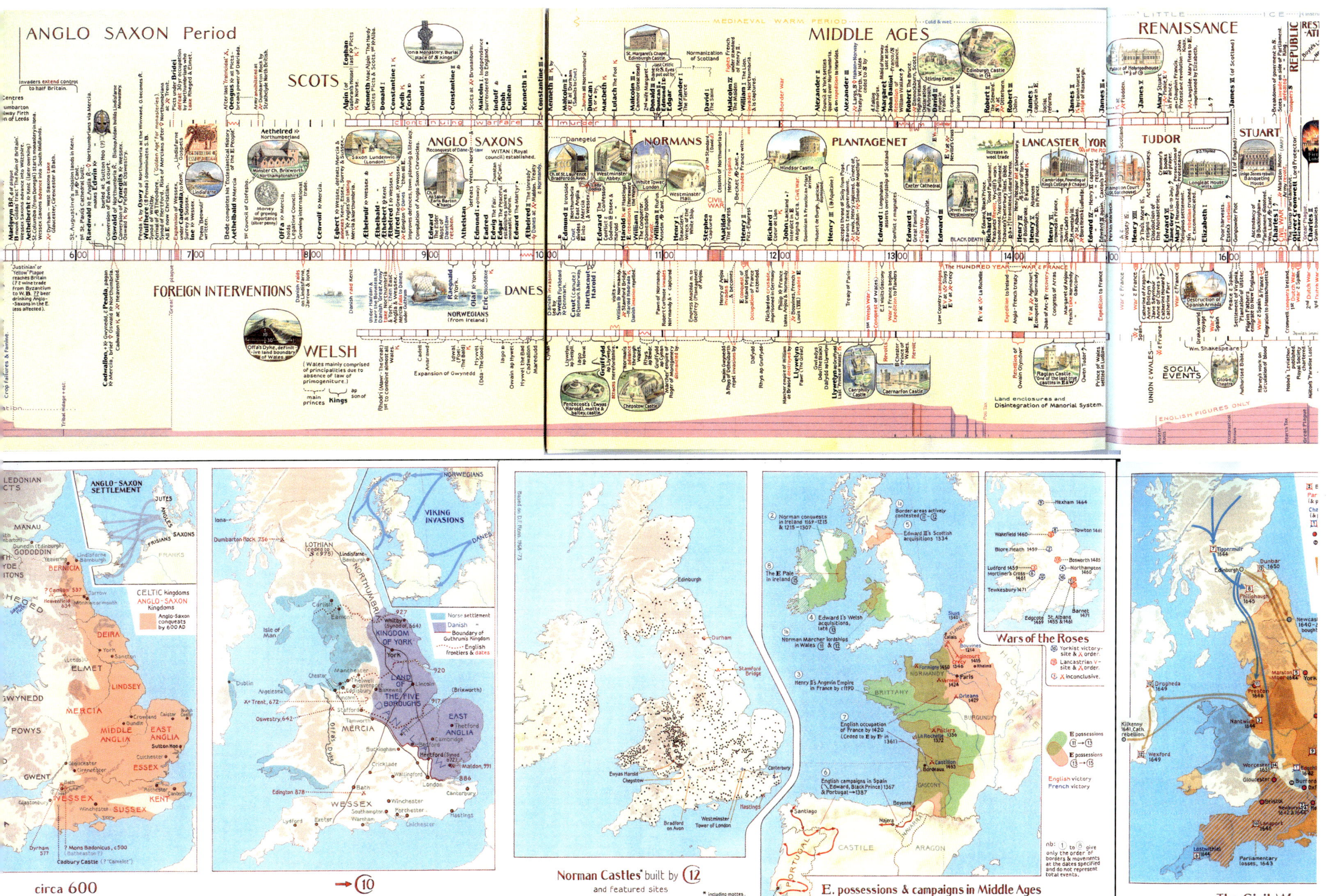

Only part of the Timescale is shown above at 50% of the actual size. The full timescale is nearly two metres in length.
Available from www.clinicalpress.co.uk

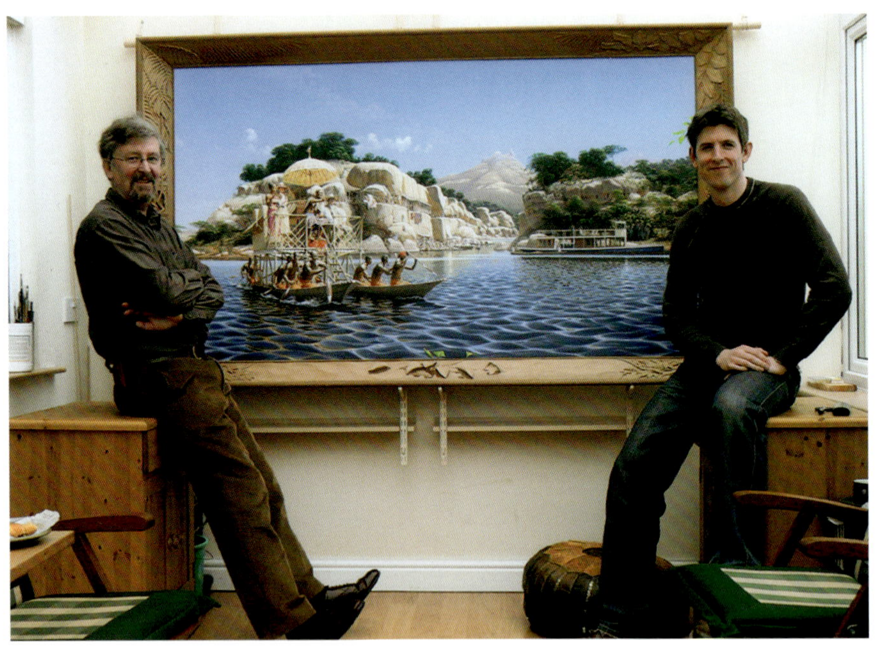

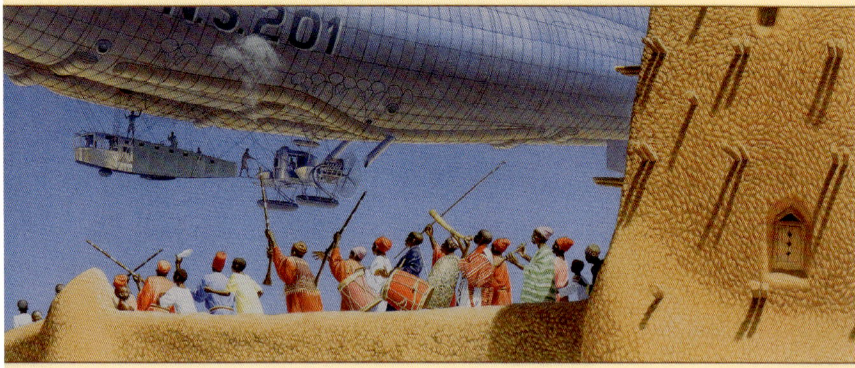

2005 Joined by younger son Alexander, the other artist in the family, to form Voyage Art Ltd. This move proves to be of immense value to both of us, allowing Alex's already strong natural talent to develop and even reintroducing the prospect of putting on the occasional (joint) exhibition. Born into the genre and with his own visits to Africa, North, Central and South, he also develops new techniques.

2008 Spring. Our first joint exhibition at the Everard Read Gallery, "A Voyage to the Interior – continued", gets in safely just before the international banking crisis.
A power cut at the private view has guests examining the paintings by torch, candle and cell phone light – an entertainment in itself. Then a safari up near the Botswana border provides useful reference.

2009 Mother dies.

2011 Tour of Kenya for our family party of eight.

2013 Our 2nd joint exhibition of ten paintings at the Everard Read gallery in this their centenary year.

2016 CIRCA Gallery opens in London: a partnership between Everard Read Galleries, South Africa and John Martin Gallery, London. "The Story of Nusu-nusu" (Gary M James) and "Fading Light" (Alexander James) exhibited at CIRCA (see pp 114 and 136).

Part 3: The 1970s – Some "Ranging Shots"

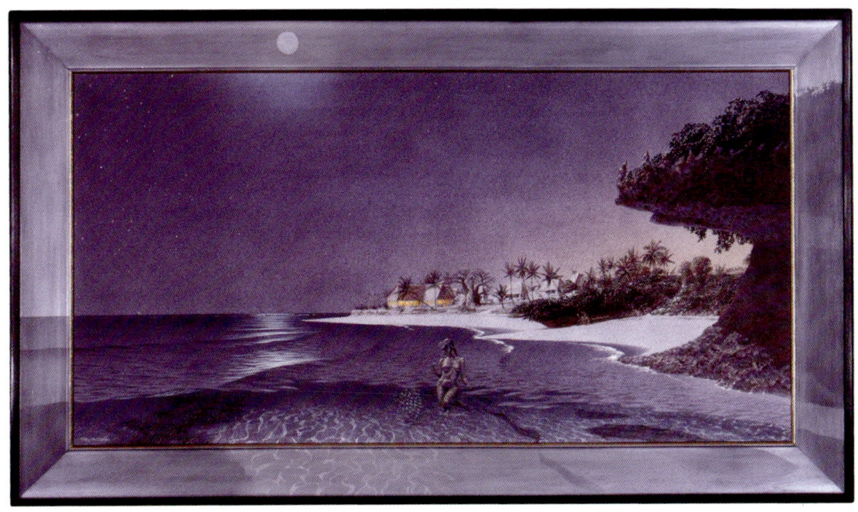

Blue Moon and Bandas 3

Acrylics, 80 x 141 cm framed.

A return to the theme of my first serious oil painting of 1969. Revisited by request in 1990 and contained in a frame inspired by club-house movies – that spread over bar, bottles and stools before being corralled onto the screen.

That I never achieved more than near misses with my cartoons in Punch (at that time my Bible) was largely due to my preferred subject matter – the nascent space industry. At that time a Punch drawing of space might look like a firework label or contain aliens of the variety that would sport TV aerials on their heads. With others from Bristol University and the Aerospace industry however I was a member of the British Interplanetary Society and took what lay beyond the bubble biosphere rather more "seriously". Then Punch preferred to receive about ten jokes in pencilled form from which they might select one to be worked up. Since I saw the humour as emerging from the expression of the finished drawing it occurred to me that I might be thinking more like a painter than a joke-smith. And unlike Punch with its acceptance rate of one in ten – once you were a regular, every person with a little spare cash was a potential buyer ... weren't they? ... And the painting took hold.

Then, working amongst medical researchers rather than art circles I developed my own methods of painting, which owed as much to the lab as the studio. I laid-in backgrounds using sprayers homemade from aluminium and coronary artery catheter, shaved back with scalpels and used racks of bijou specimen jars in place of a palette.

There is a pronounced whiff of science fiction (and occasional fact) running through my 1970s and along with my methods perhaps I was seen as having a certain novelty value at the RWA – providing I could be safely quarantined.

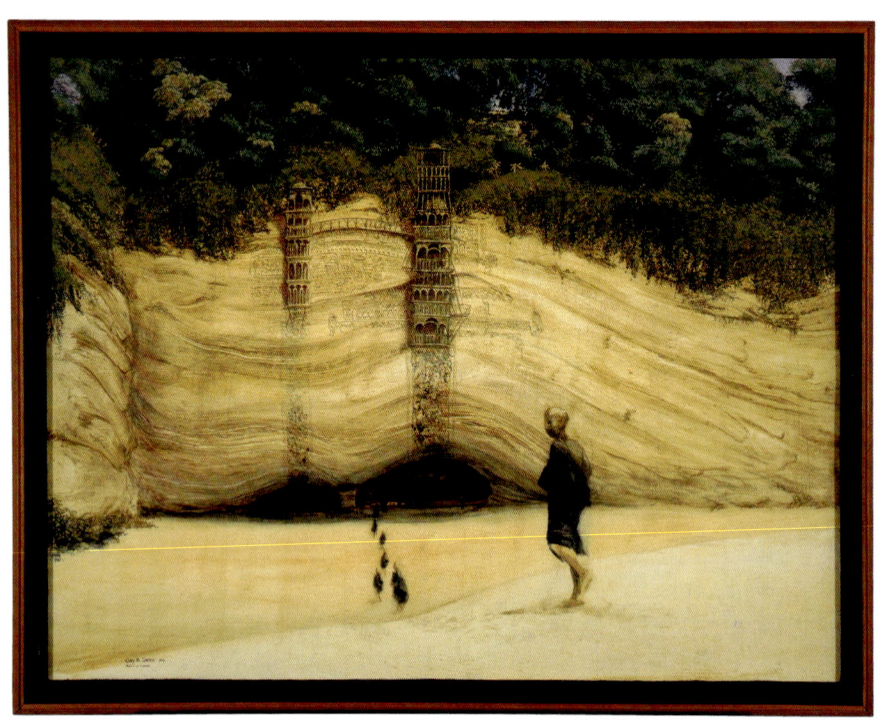

Tomb of an elephant
Oils, 81 x 107 cm, 1970

Exhibited: Royal West of England Academy, 1971
Bristol City Museum & Art Gallery, 1977

An impression derived from the twilight zone between waking and sleep.

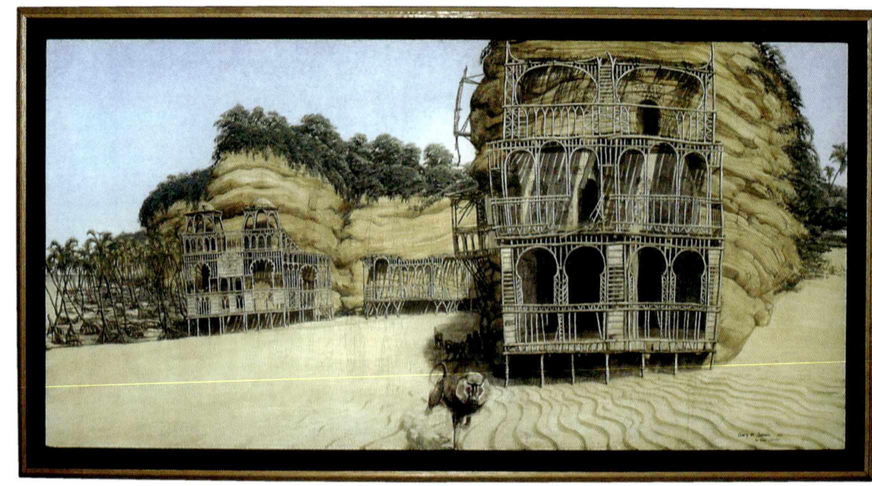

Ape House
Oils, 61 x 122 cm, Summer 1970

Exhibited: Royal West of England Academy, 1970. Sold from a gallery in St. Ives

Gained me the distinction of being "borrowed from" when a later hang at the RWA featured my cliff-hanging structures copied straight – but with a languorous girl in place of my baboons.

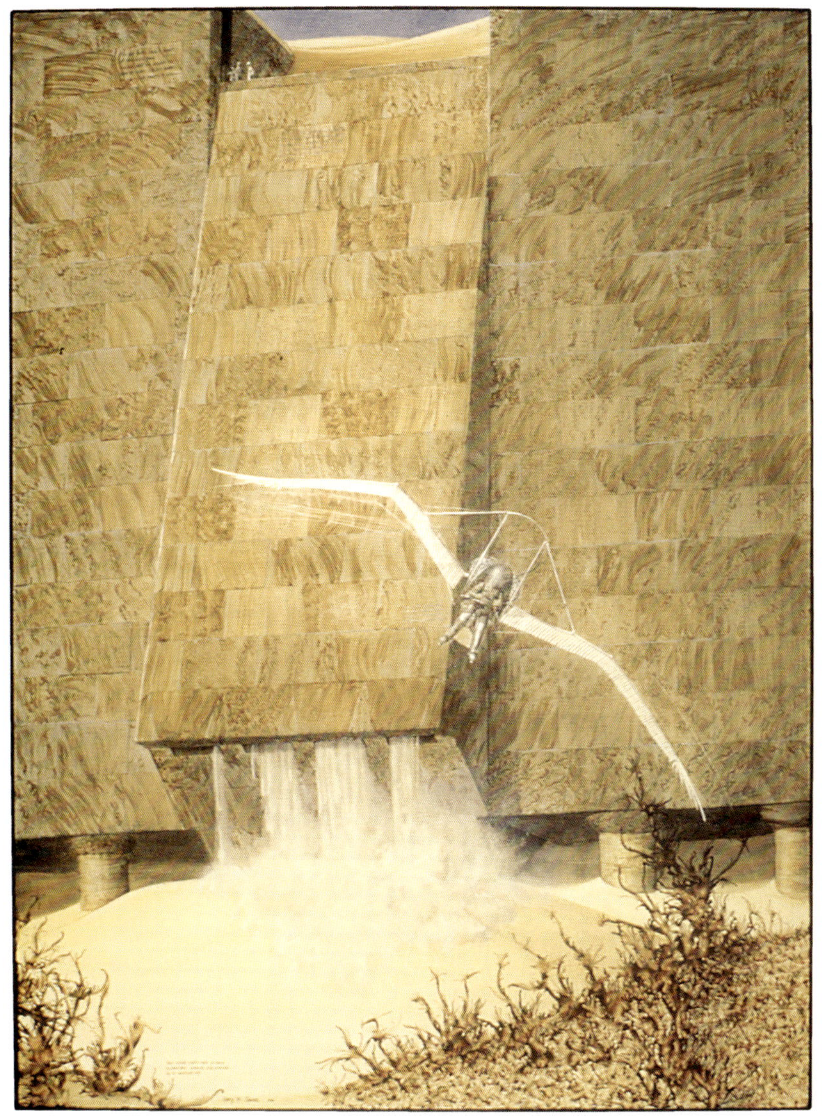

Ornithopter and Sandvents

Oils, 122 x 91.5 cm, 1970

Exhibited: Royal West of England Academy, 1970

A giant dyke holds back the dust of a nuclear blasted landscape, ornithopters used to service shutes that funnel off dust from older layers. In the foreground – "mutant veg". The ornithopter's wings are slatted to reduce drag on the upstroke.

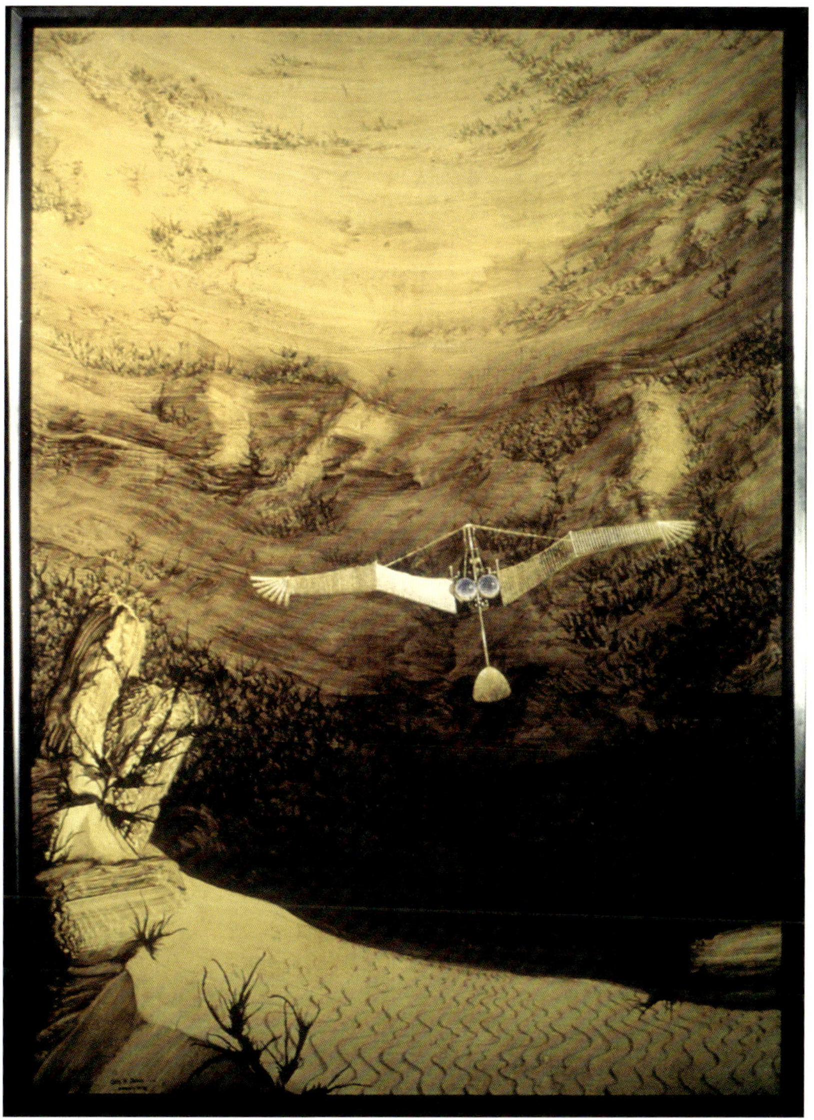

Ornithopter at a Rift's edge

Oils, 122 x 91.5 cm, 1971

Exhibited: Royal West of England Academy, 1972

Recalls the swifts swishing past one's head down into the caldera of Menengai Crater, Nakuru.

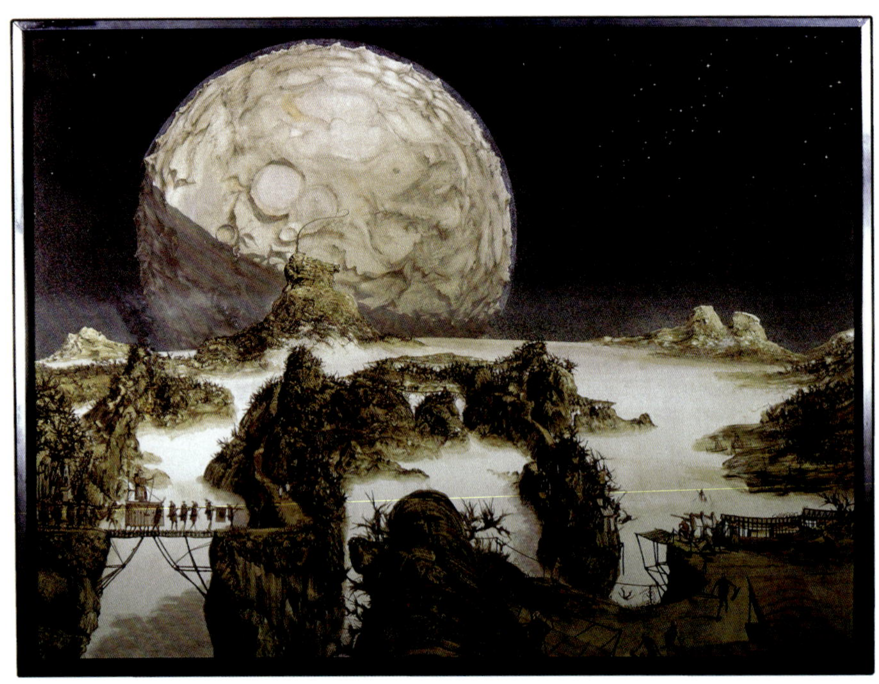

Royal Sport of the Centrifugal Twins

Oils, 91.5 x 122 cm, 1972

Exhibited: Royal West of England Academy, 1972

A cartoon strip in one frame. Arthur C. Clark, shown a slide of this one, said that my hills reminded him of the central hills of Sri Lanka. Did this image, with its fanciful bridge spun out between planets trigger his 1979 novel "The Fountains of Paradise"? I shall never know.

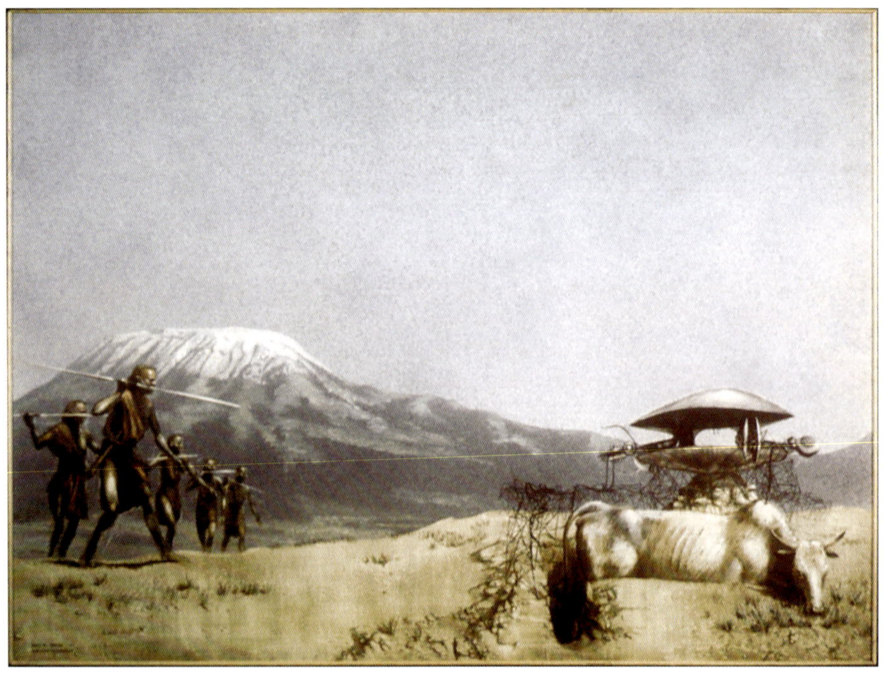

Confrontation of a Vivisectionist

Oils, 91.5 x 122 cm, 1973

Exhibited: Royal West of England Academy, 1973

Thirty years later I learned from one of the hangers, Ian Black RWA, that this painting had been the subject of an unspoken conflict between himself and the then President of the RWA, Donald Milner. Milner hated it ("well it had no trees") and took it off the wall, placing it by the door for consignment to the stock-rooms. Whereupon Ian hung it again ... and Milner again removed it. And Ian hung it again ... and ... Anyway Ian's was the last move – and it sold, so there!

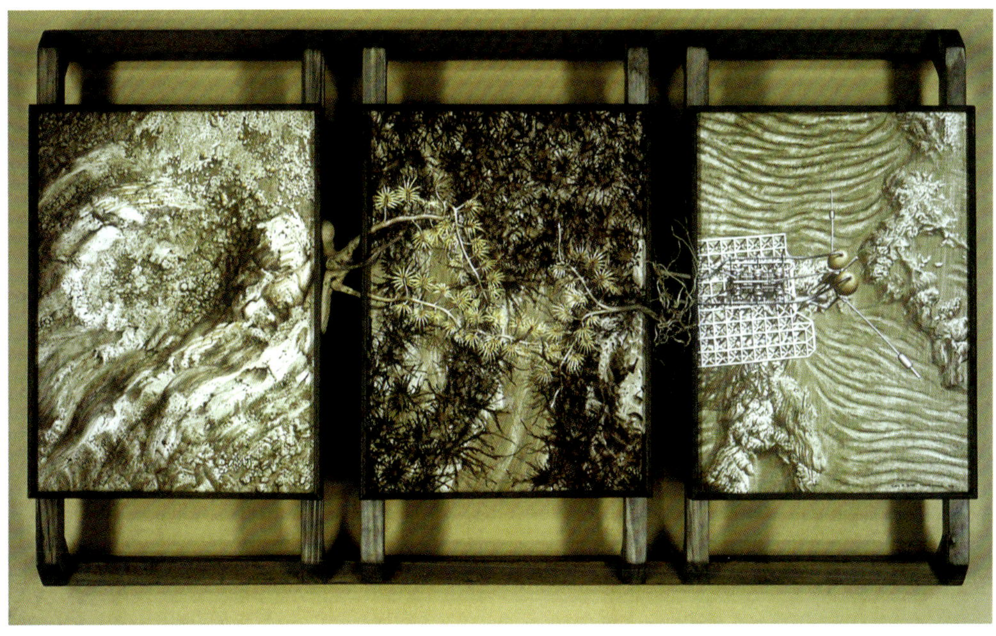

Three Frame Process (Triptych)

Oils, 45 x 76 cm overall, 1974
Exhibited: Bristol City Museum & Art Gallery, 1977

My first "interface" work, in which roots interwove over and into three small panels representing mineral, biological and technological phases.

Turned down for exhibition at the RWA it was eventually found in the sculpture stack room …

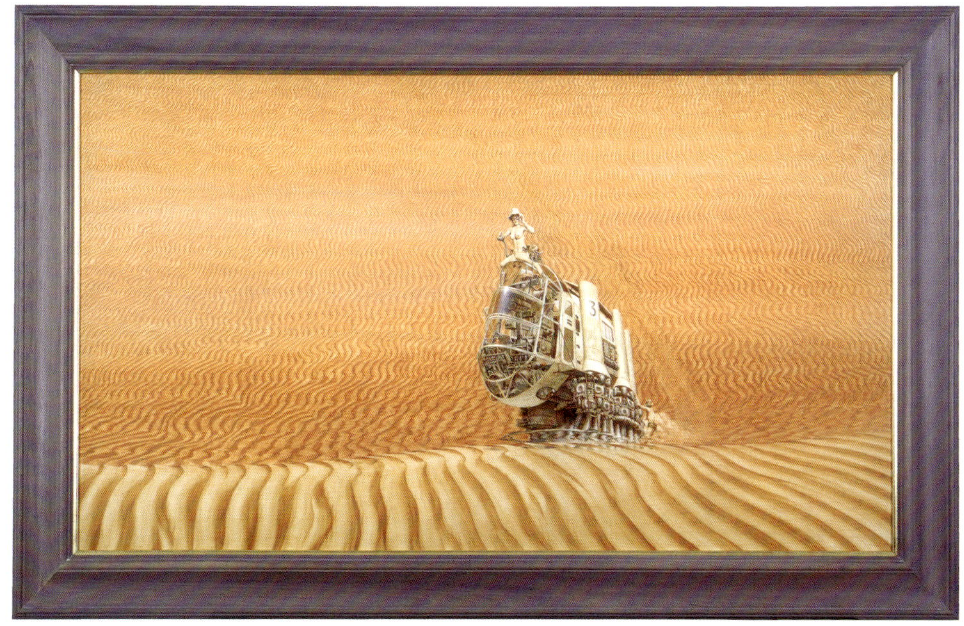

A high seat on the canopy crossing the erg

Oils, 61 x 107 cm, 1975
Exhibited: Bristol City Museum & Art Gallery, 1977

… And no, I had neither seen the film "Barbarella" nor read "Dune" then.

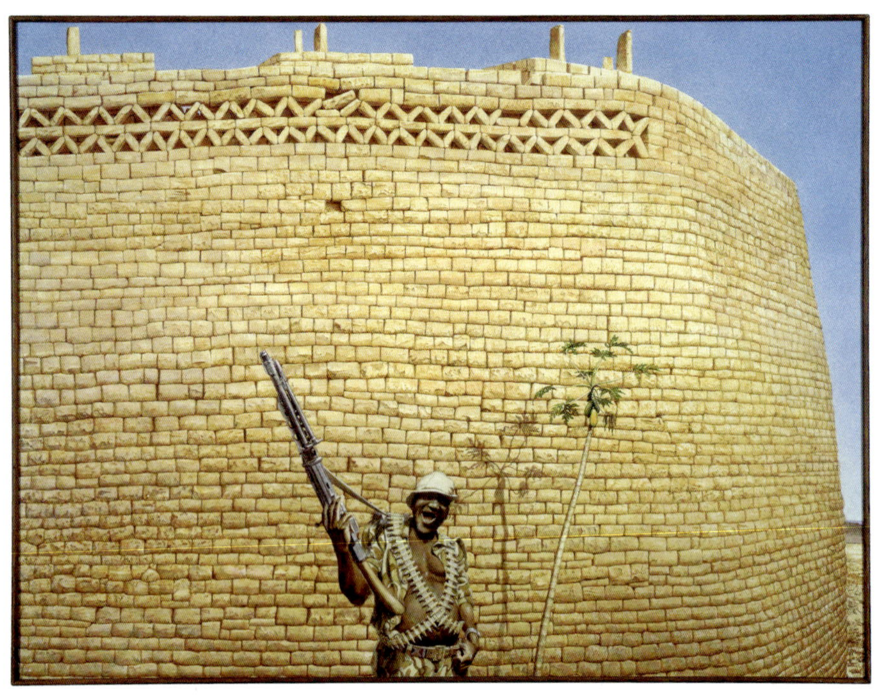

Zimbabwe

Oils, 91.5 x 122 cm, 1975/76
Exhibited: Bristol City Museum & Art Gallery, 1977
Royal Society of British Artists Annual at the Mall Galleries 1981

Painted at the height of "U.D.I." or Unilateral Declaration of Independence in the then, Rhodesia. The ruins of Great Zimbabwe were then regarded as the symbol of black African resistance to white minority government.

The pawpaw "tree" appears in fond remembrance of the colonial breakfast.

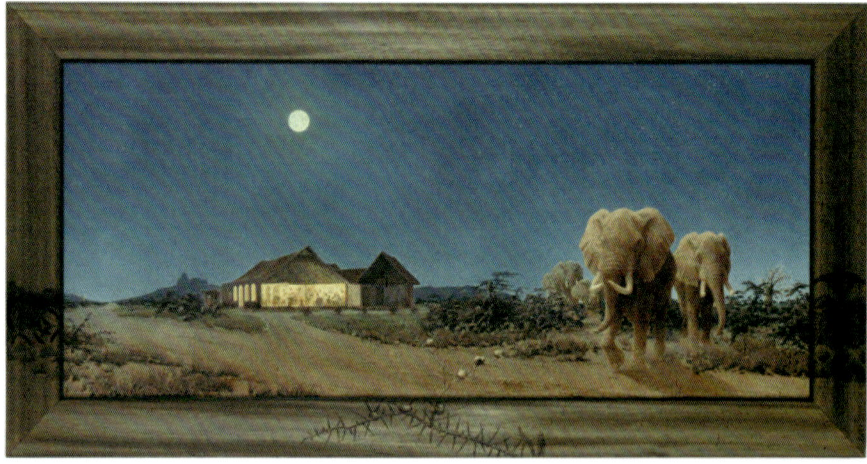

Night Passage

Oils, 56 x 128 cm, 1977
Exhibited: Bristol City Museum & Art Gallery, 1977

Loosely based on "Mac's Inn", favoured watering hole on the 300 mile drive between Nairobi and Mombasa. The artist's family are featured within enjoying a "Tusker" lager.

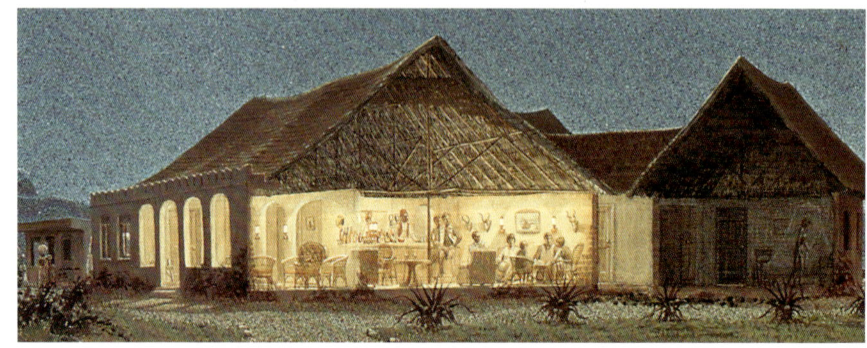

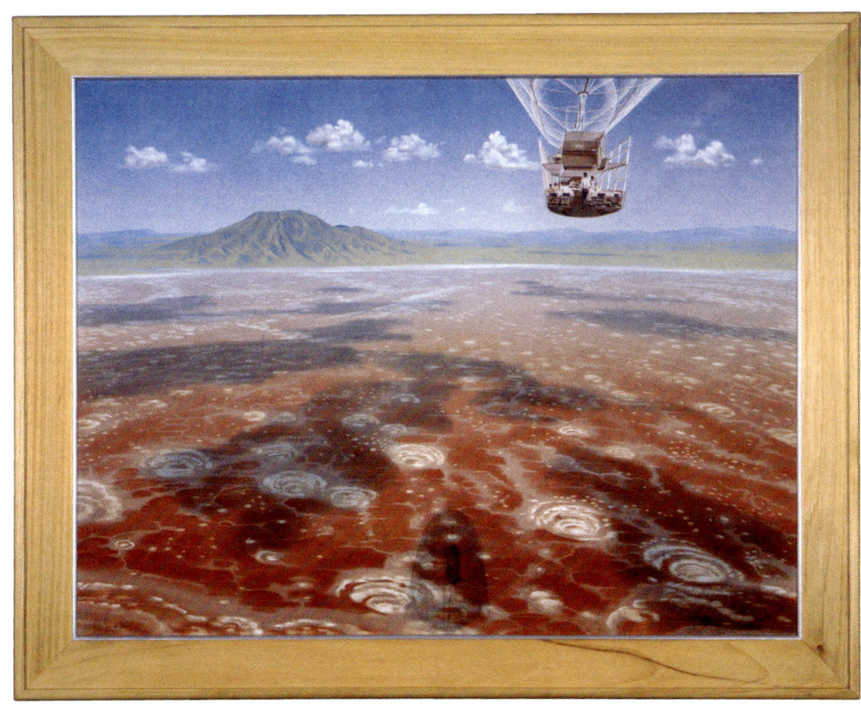

Flight over a soda lake
Oils, 91.5 x 122 cm, 1977

Since painting this view of Lake Natron in Tanzania, hot air balloons have been popping up everywhere in Africa.

My airship here purports to be a hybrid, gaining extra lift to its helium gas bags from the "greenhouse" heating of the air in its transparent outer envelope. And boy, does it need it here! One (soda-white) Christmas at Lake Magadi near here we had to give a hasty burial to a whole gorgonzola cheese that had melted in its box in the boot of the car.

One would not want to land on this lake, or the caldera of the still active Ol Doinyo Lengai (the Masai's Mountain of God) on the far side. The algae staining the lake pink is the only organism that survives such high soda concentrations. It also gives its colouring to the flamingos that filter feed off it when breeding on this lake.

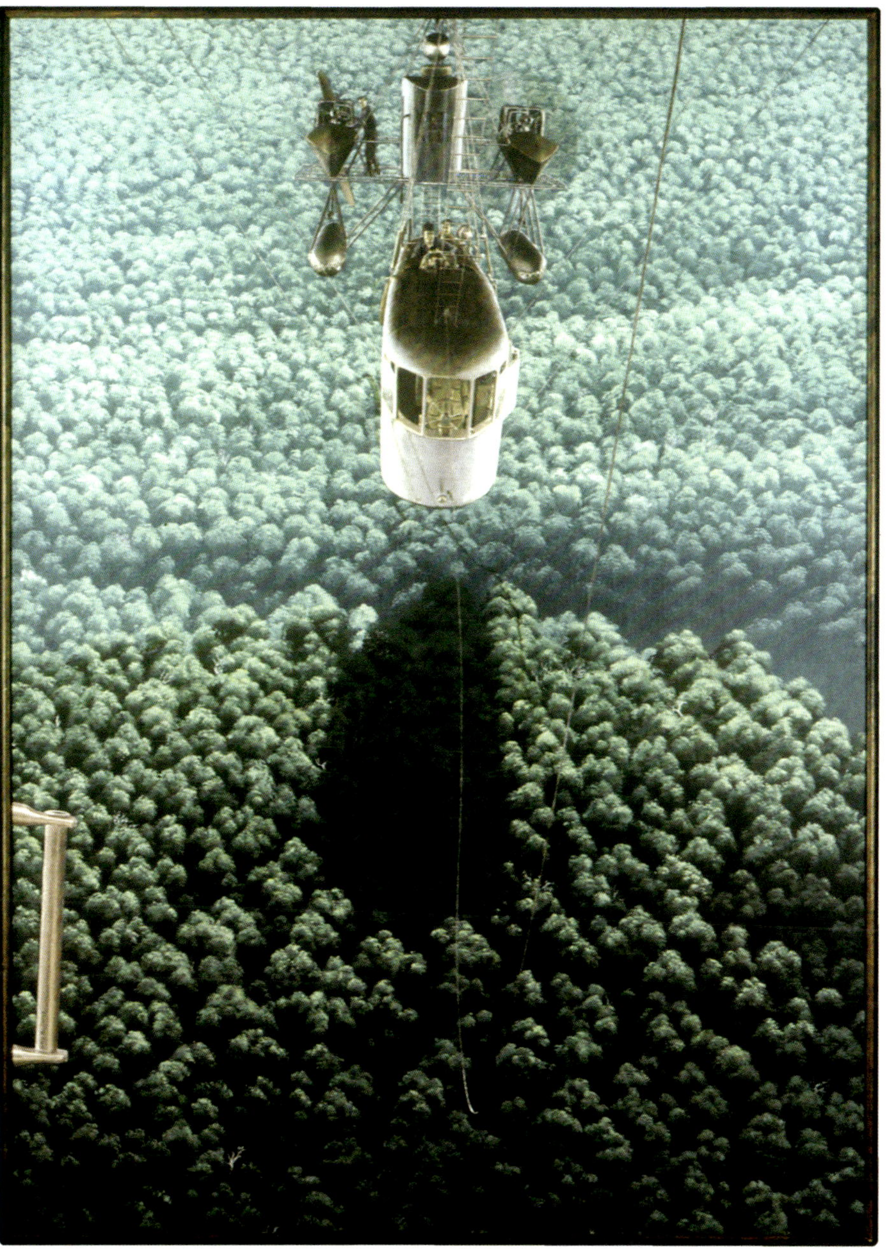

Captain Maltraver's Voyage to the Interior
Oils, 122 x 96.5 cm, 1977
Exhibited: Royal West of England Academy, 1977,
Royal Academy Summer Exhibition, 1980 (see notes page 10).

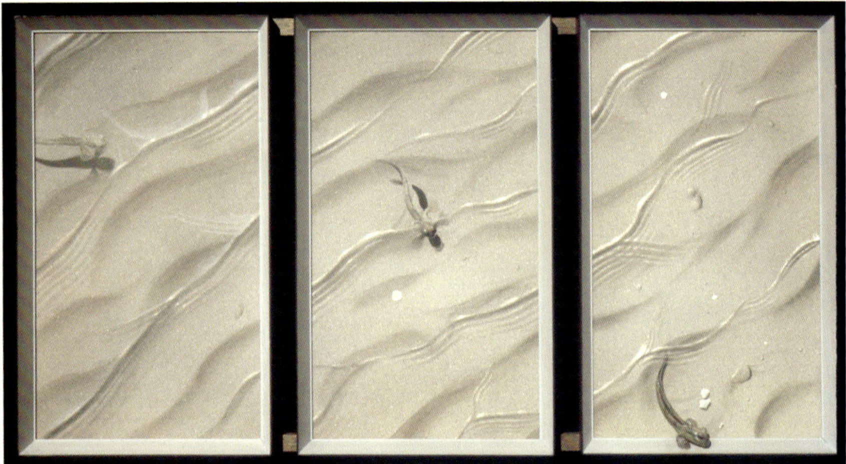

Mudskipper (Triptych)

Oils & acrylic resin, 63.5 x 122 cm overall, 1978

A second interface work. The amphibious mud skipper makes a particularly apposite subject for a painting in which the air/water interface also represents the dimensional interface.

In panel 1 the mudskipper swims beneath the paint and frame. In panel 2 its protruding eyes, modelled in acrylic resin and Perspex, pop above the surface and in panel 3 the whole fish pops out onto the frame leaving only its tail trailing beneath the paint/water.

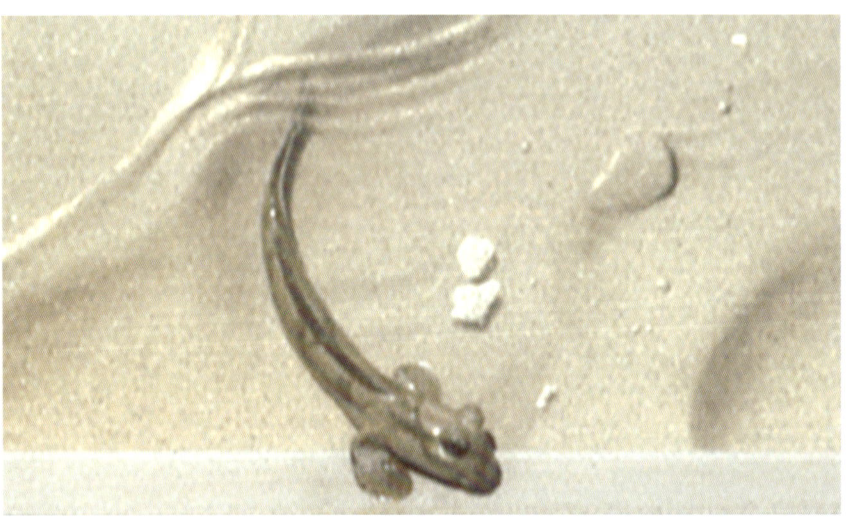

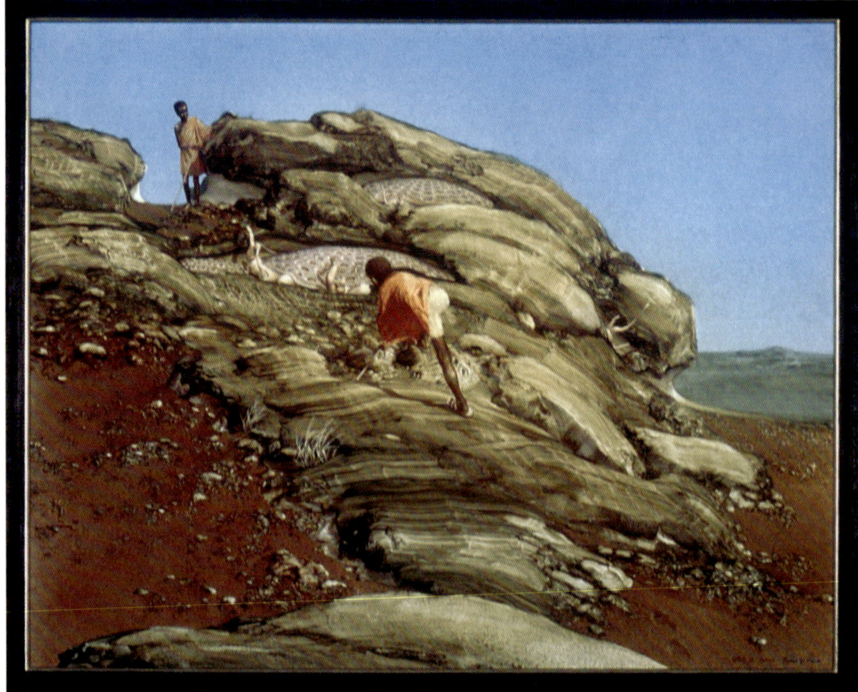

Fumbo ya mawe (an exploratory prod)

Oils, 96.5 x 122 cm1978

Exhibited: Royal West of England Academy, 1978
Royal Society of British Artists, Mall Galleries, 1981

Is it animal, mineral or vegetable? Two Africans visiting the RWA, on being asked by an attendant, ventured that it was a fungus that grew in parts of Africa, albeit much enlarged – "a useful source of water when cut open". A new one on the artist, to whom it was just a sculptural invention.

"Fumbo ya mawe" – Swahili for "Mystery of the rocks" is the title given by the artist's father to this, his favourite painting at the time.

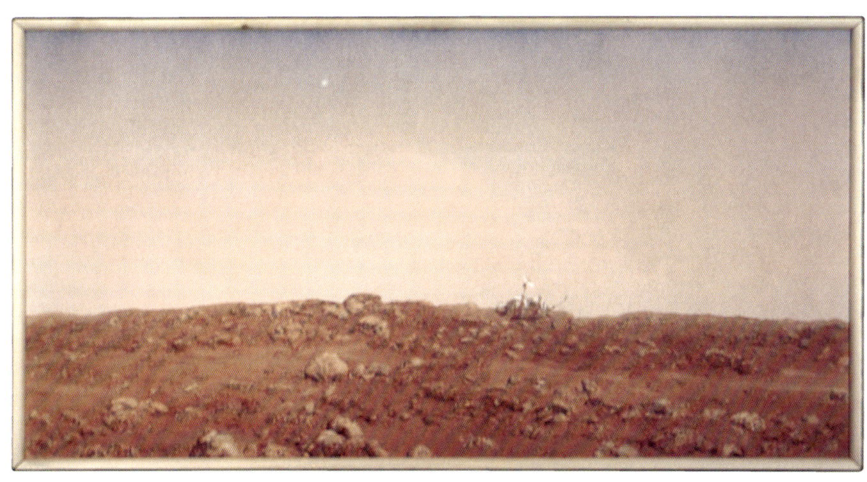

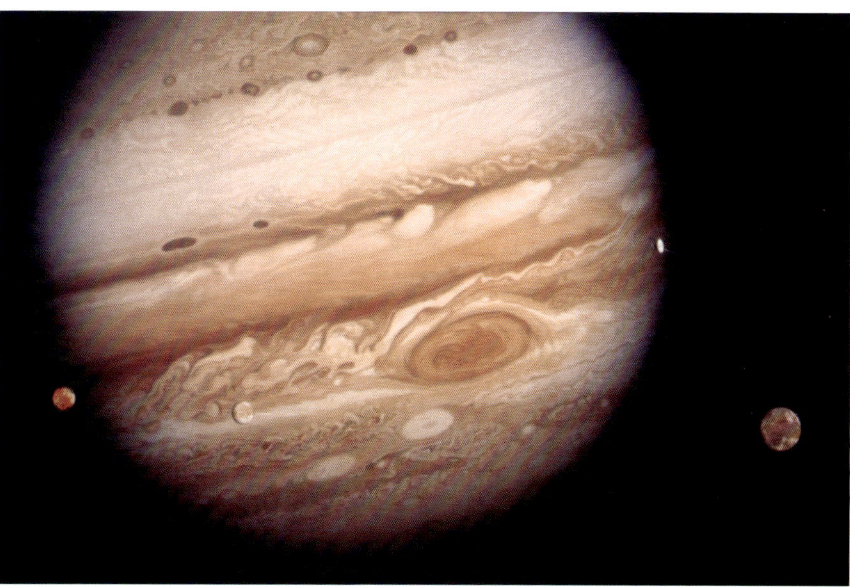

Early Settler (Viking soft lander on Mars)
Oils, 61 x 122 cm , 1979

Published as cover painting for "Life on Mars? : The case for a cosmic heritage" by Sir Fred Hoyle and Professor Chandra Wickramasinghe (Clinical Press Ltd.).

Voyager at Jupiter
Oils, 122 x 183 cm, 1980

Exhibited: Royal Observatory, Herstmonceux Castle, East Sussex, 1984-88

Moons left to right: Io, Europa & Ganymede. Voyager spacecraft at limb of Jupiter, above and to right of the Great Red Spot.

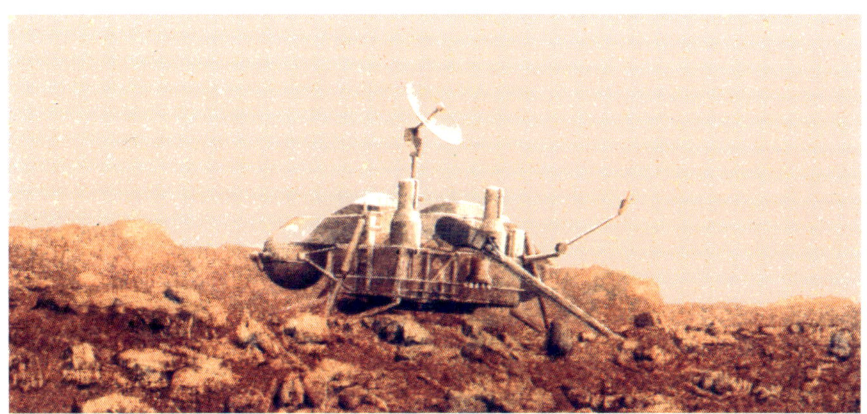

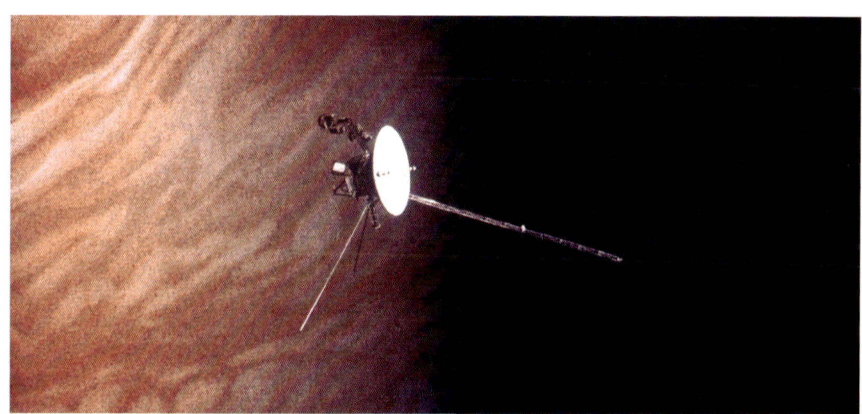

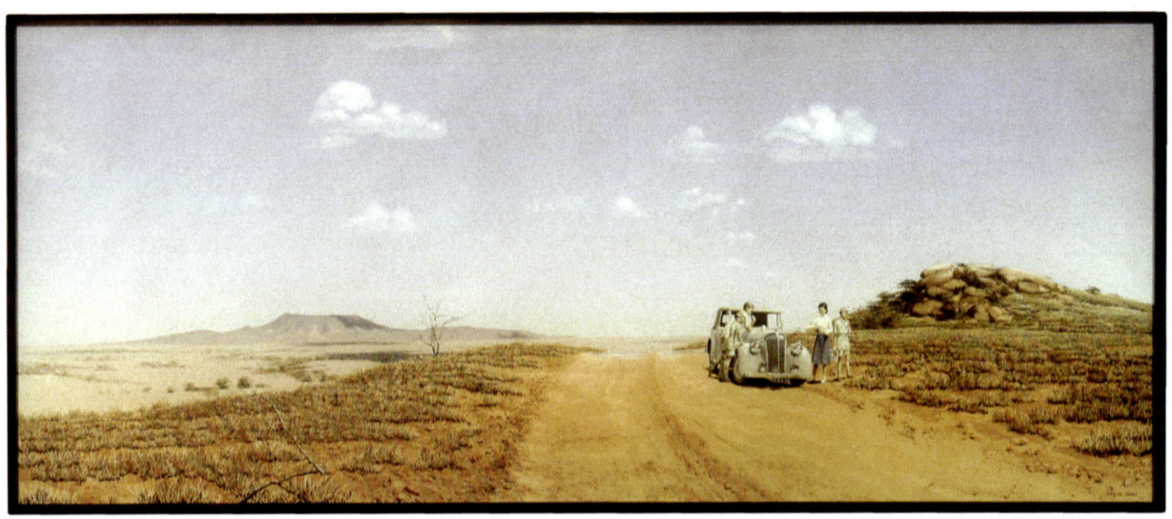

Kilimani (on the hill)

Oils, 61 x 152.5 cm, 1981

Painted for the artist's parents and representing the family at large in our Standard 8, touring a composite version of Kenya, c 1950.

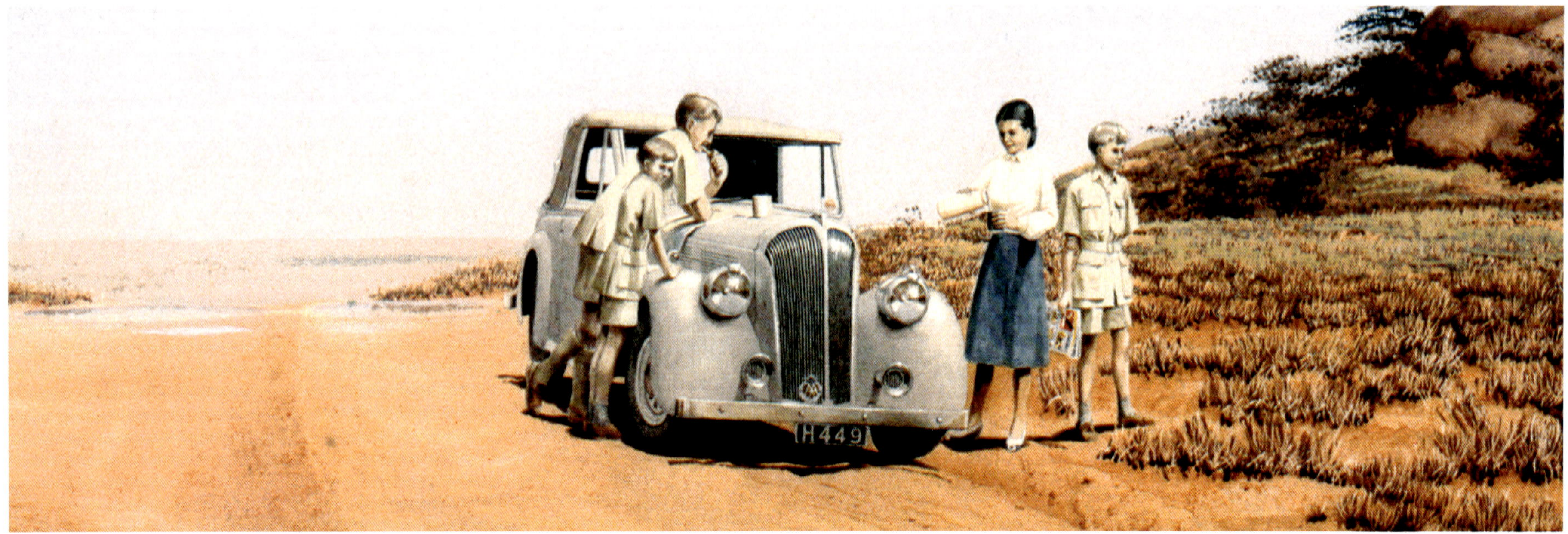

There will now be an intermission as we discuss art at the interface in Part 4

Part 4: Art at the Interface ....

...A splendidly pretentious sounding title perhaps, but one that nevertheless means just what it says.

Sculpture has been described by one wit as "what you back into when looking at a painting". But what if that sculpture were used to draw you into that painting? Artists paint and artists sculpt, why not bring both together in a symbiotic relationship?

This has been done before of course, most notably as icing on the architectural cake of stately home and church or in museum dioramas. When used in the context of a painting itself however the mistake is to place three dimensional elements within the painting itself.

Except in rare cases (such as "Mudskipper", p. 24) 3D and 2D do not mix. Apart from lighting issues, the 3D is in our space not the implied space of the painting.

Being in our space sculpture lacks its own separate context. Naked David stands unabashed amidst clothed tourists sizing up an unseen Goliath in an unseen landscape. And in galleries around are painted landscapes carefully separated from our space by three dimensional frames. When so many of these frames can be quite deeply moulded it seems a mystery that more artists have not made the obvious connection of leading from the one into the other.

The binocular vision that gives us our perception of depth diminishes with distance. So unless the painting is a life sized portrait or purports to bring its subject into our space the dimensions can be catered for using linear and aerial perspective. The frame on the other hand is in our space and can either be ignored as usual or embraced for all the possibilities it presents. It is safely peripheral to our view and with care can become a bridge to both worlds ... so much more than "just a frame".

Of course there has been a long standing fashion of dispensing with a frame altogether – as if to take a swipe at bourgeoise values – and incidentally saving on time, money and effort. Then to most artists who do have a frame it is an afterthought – something to stop the canvas from fraying at the edges perhaps whilst signalling a change in perception and an enhancement in value. After all how often does the frame get a mention in exhibition catalogues or Art History – this 3D link to the past in our space? How many historic frames have been lost simply because they "didn't go with the furniture"?

So, what are the options available in opening our horizons to include the frame? Beyond its use as non specific enhancement one might categorise various approaches thus:

CUSTOMISING

1. Painting the frame. The simplest option for a painter. Juxtaposing with complementary colours as Seurat did or enlivening with designs such as the "barge-board" decorations used by Philip Sutton RA.
2. Decorating with carving appropriate to the subject as distinct from stock mouldings. Generally done by craftsman framers.

INTERFACING

3. Extending the painting out onto the frame in the manner favoured by contemporary painter Pamela Crook RWA. This can 'draw the viewer in', particularly when she uses trompe l'oeil effects. A particularly skilful variation on this are the marquetry frames of Kit Williams of "Masquerade" fame, in which he extends the image onto the frame in inlaid wood veneers, or marquetry.
4. Carving. This can function in ways distinct from just decoration. It can be used to extend a narrative beyond the constraints of linear perspective, adding features "out of shot" or in a different time frame. Or in a formal way it can simply extend the view.
5. Then we have true dimensional interfacing. In this carving meets and interleaves with the subject of the painting via careful overlaps and trompe l'oeil painting to impart a sense of "being there".
6. Using a blend of any or all the above.

One can well appreciate the resistance in some quarters to such "gimmickry". All I can say to such a charge is 'if you haven't tried it don't knock it'. You might surprise yourself. Of course ever since the Impressionists got out into the fresh air the emphasis in painting has been on dexterous brush-work, as like as not producing a painting in a sitting or two, or maybe even a week! In that context the thought of spending weeks, or even months on the frame would be utterly preposterous.

For the 'high-definition' studio artist however interfacing can change the whole game up a gear or two. Trompe l'oeil painting, hitherto just a way to show off your skills, here comes into its own as "synchromesh" between the dimensions, whilst the painter gets to exercise his sculpting skills and the purchaser gets two works of art for his or her money.

It is important though to accept the frame for what it is and to turn its limitations to good account. The magic in "The Lion, The Witch and the Wardrobe" lies within the wardrobe being just that – a wardrobe. Here though, since we can't actually step through into our "Narnia", it has to step out to greet us.

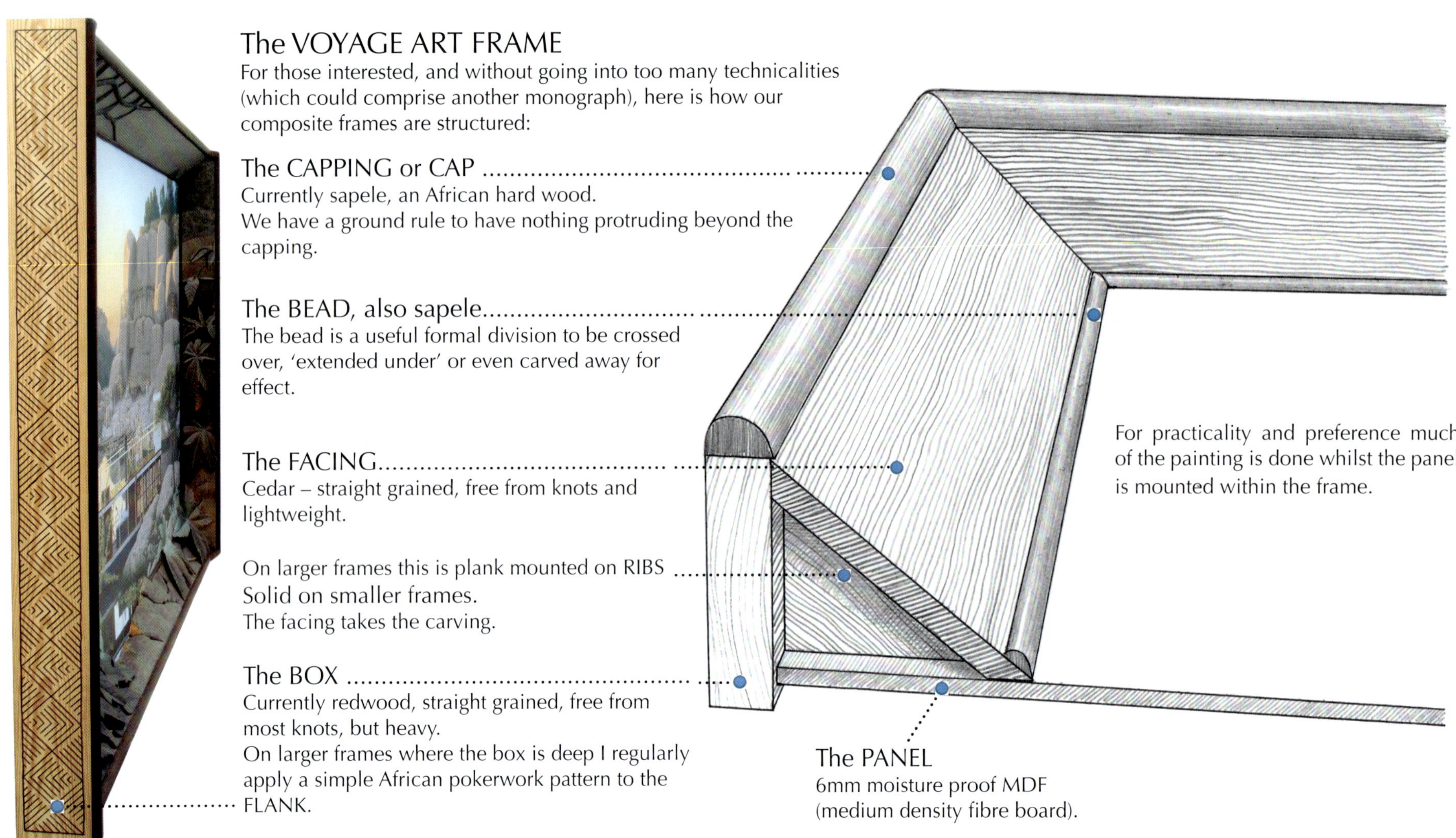

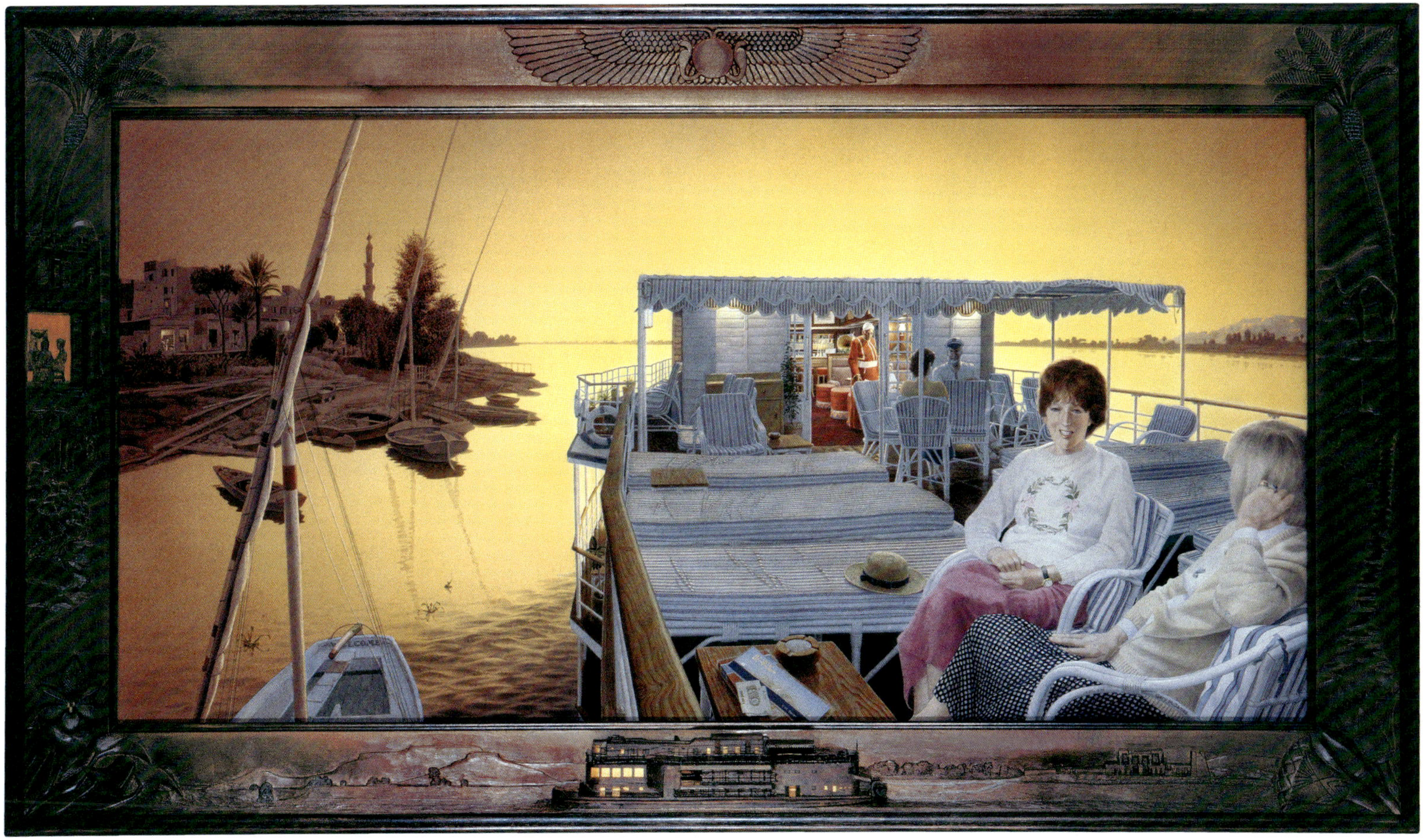

Nile Cruise

80 x 141 cm framed, 1993/94

Exhibited: Victoria Art Gallery, Bath, with the Bath Society of Artists, 2003.

(Notes p. 13)

This painting depicts the artist's wife, Paulette, on board the converted paddle steamer "Royal Memphis", 1993. The frame detail illustrates the use of bas relief carving/modelling to extend the narrative:

Approaching Thebes — The Royal Memphis — The temple of Kom Ombo

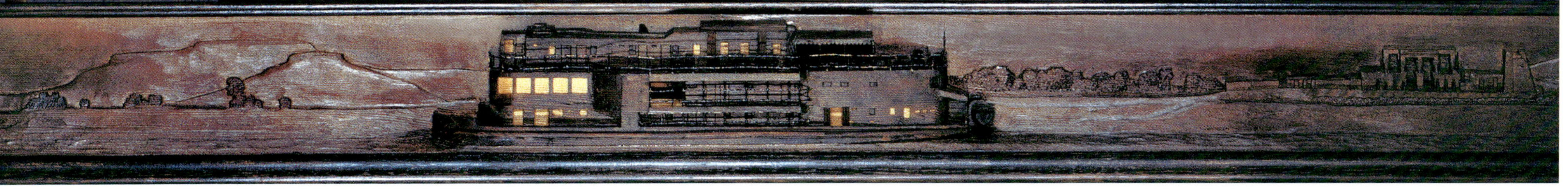

Contents of Part 5
A VOYAGE TO THE INTERIOR
Paintings by Gary M. James

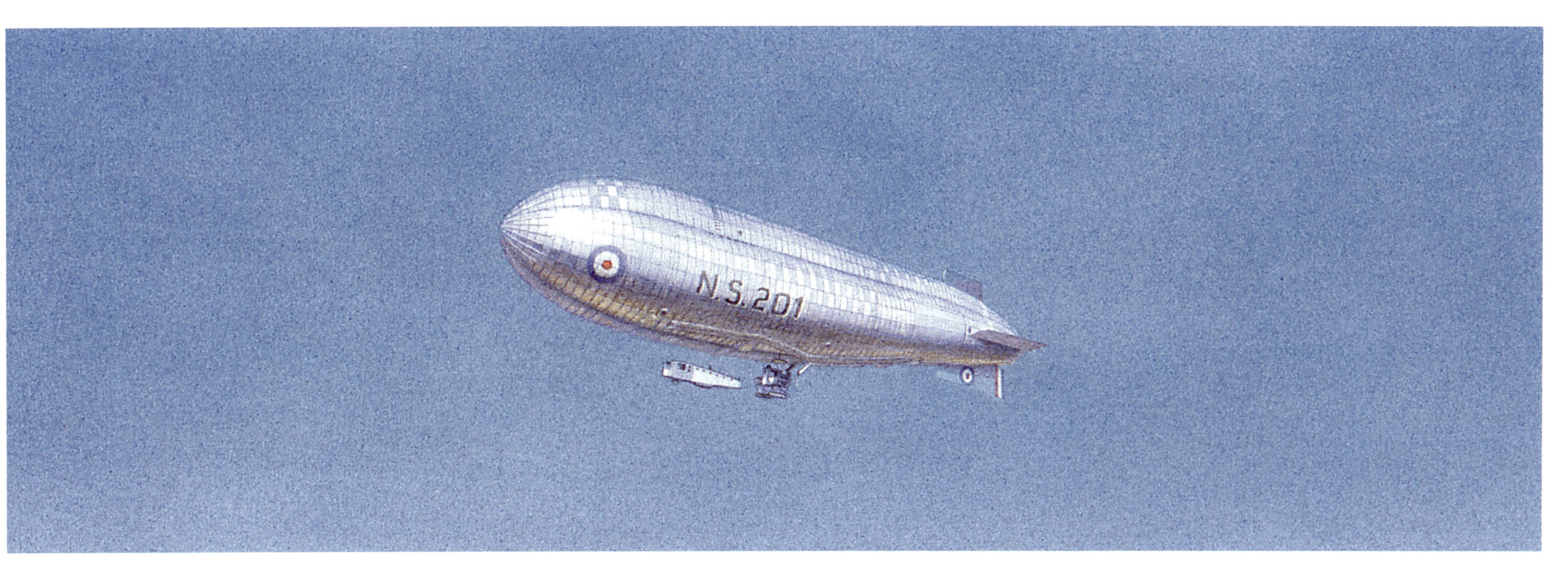

Part 5: A VOYAGE TO THE INTERIOR

Course set ....

(Use of a large magnifying glass when viewing some of these images may add to the immersive experience)

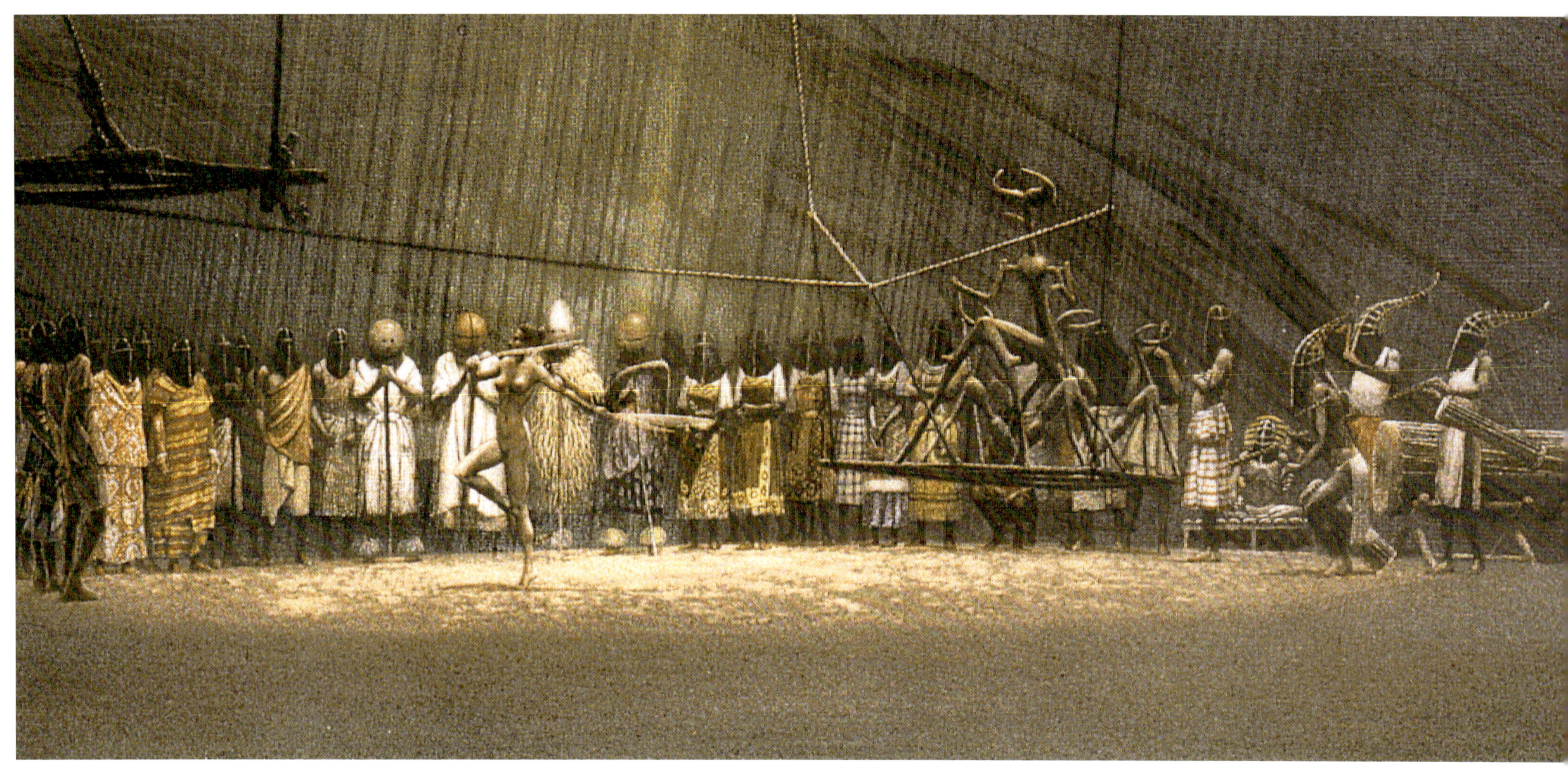

Nameless Rites
Oils, 91.5 x 122 cm 1980 & 1984

Exhibited: Royal West of England Academy, 1984
Bath Contemporary Art Fair, 1993
Everard Read Gallery, Johannesburg, 1997

The rites are just that – nameless, so don't ask. The dancer may bring to mind Josephine Baker and her Danse Sauvage in 1920s Paris, but this lady doesn't overdo the squinting.

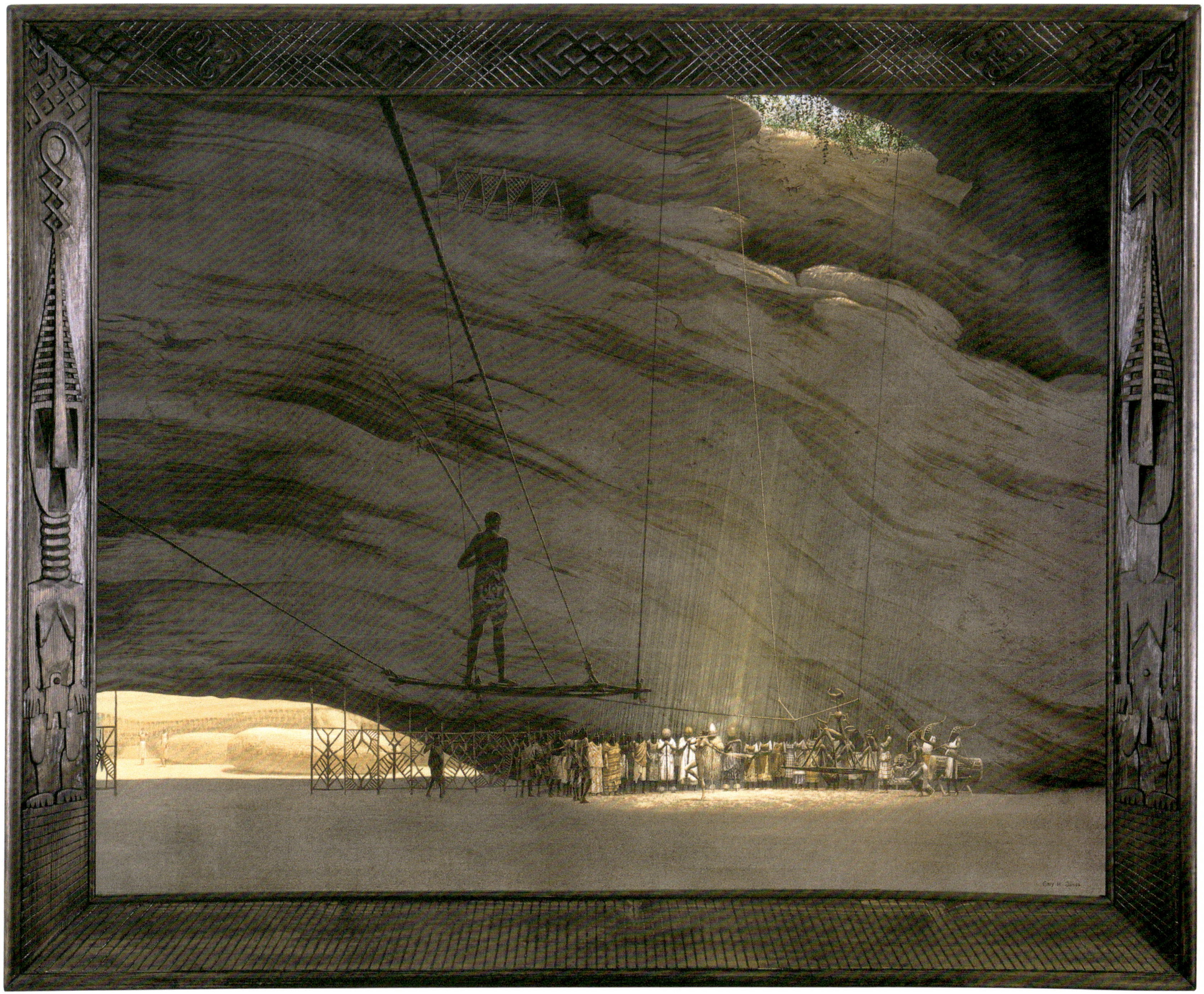

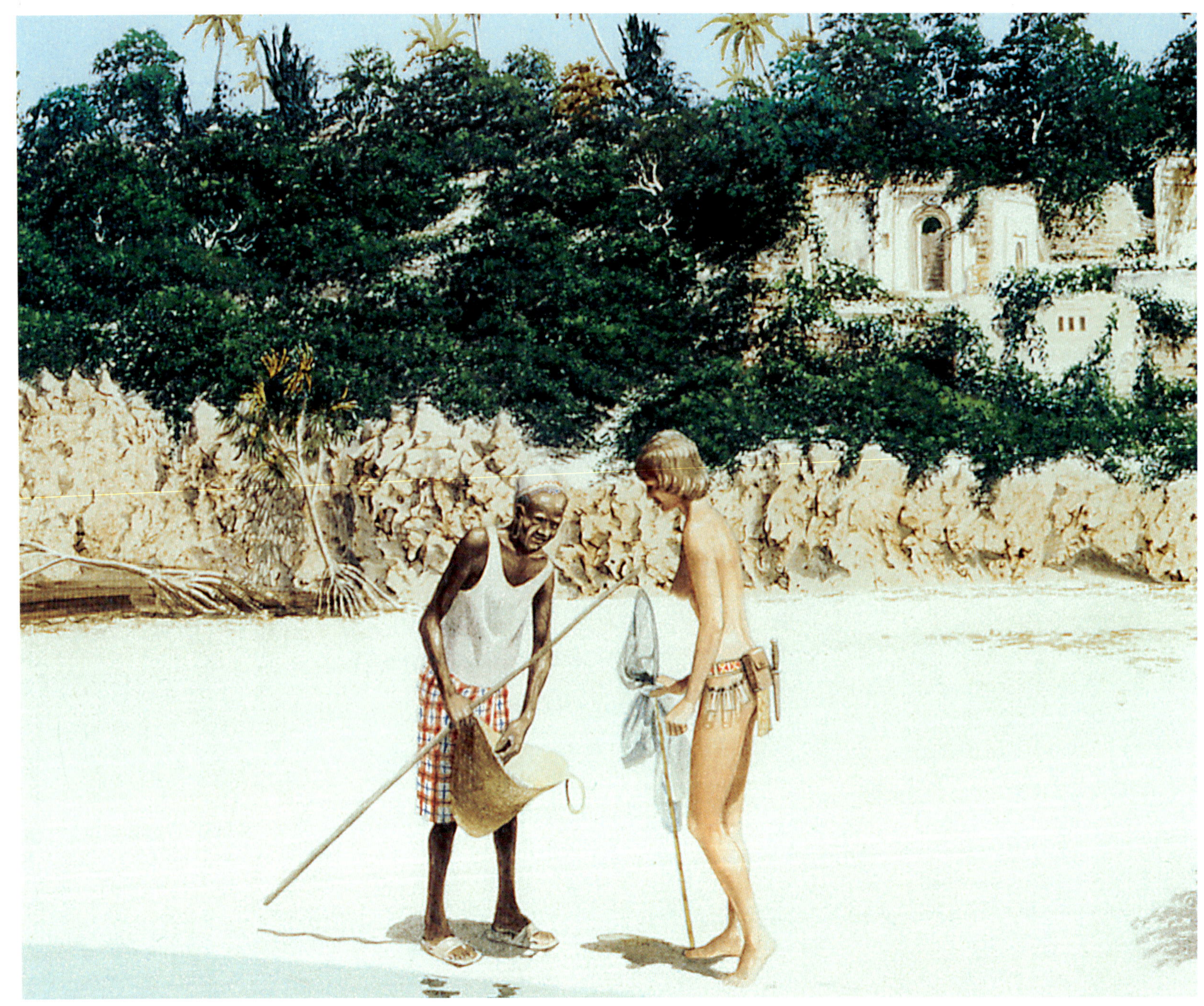

The Entomologist and the Prawn Salesman 2

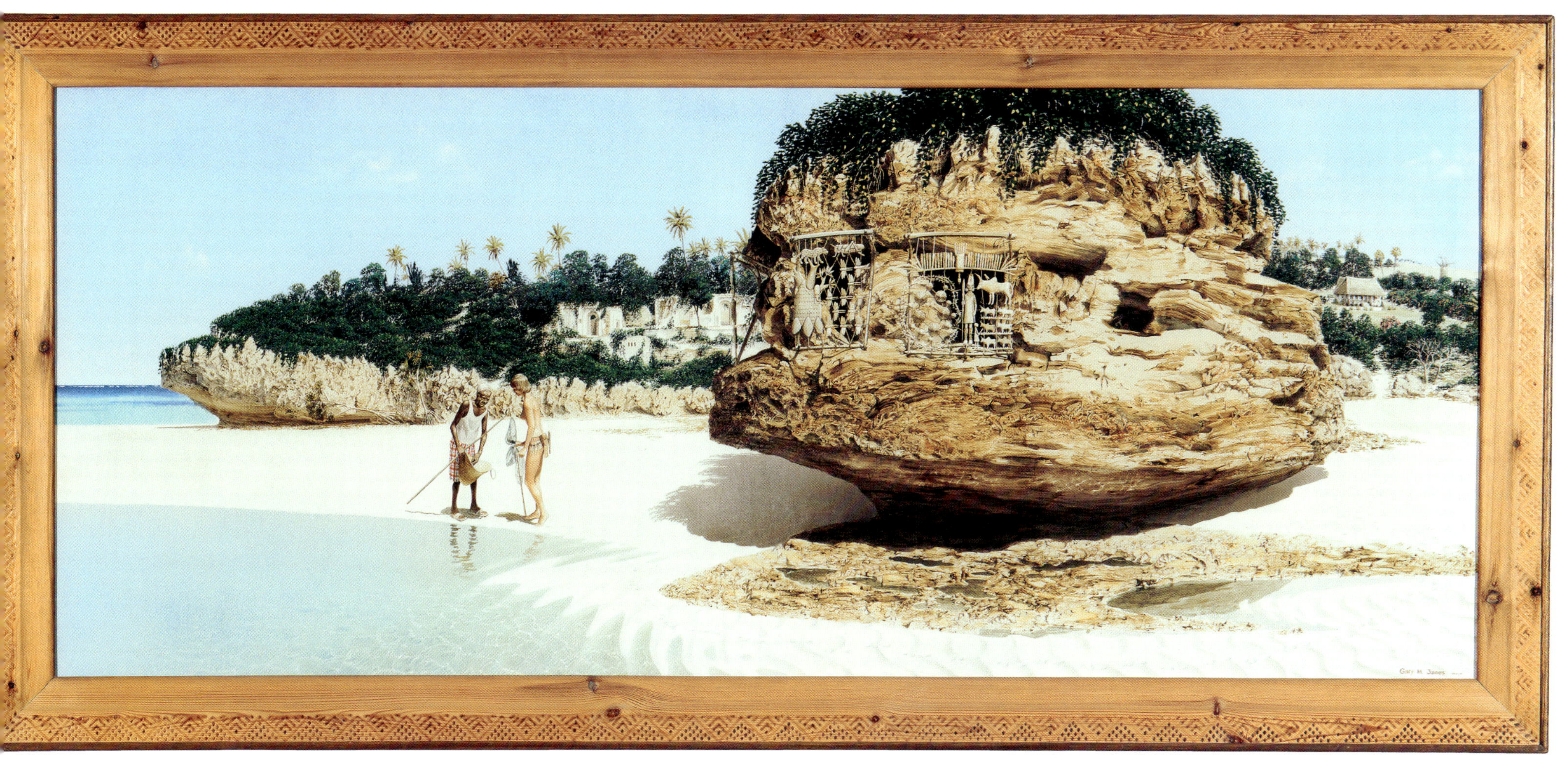

The Entomologist and the Prawn Salesman 2
Oils, 61 x 152.5 cm 1984

Exhibited: Royal West of England Academy, 1984
Everard Read Gallery, Johannesburg, 1997

A return to a subject first painted in 1976.
Remember that scene in Ian Fleming's "Dr No" when James Bond meets the attractive shell collector emerging from the sea, wearing just an army belt and sheath knife.....? Read by the artist at an impressionable age when holidaying on a similar coral coast.

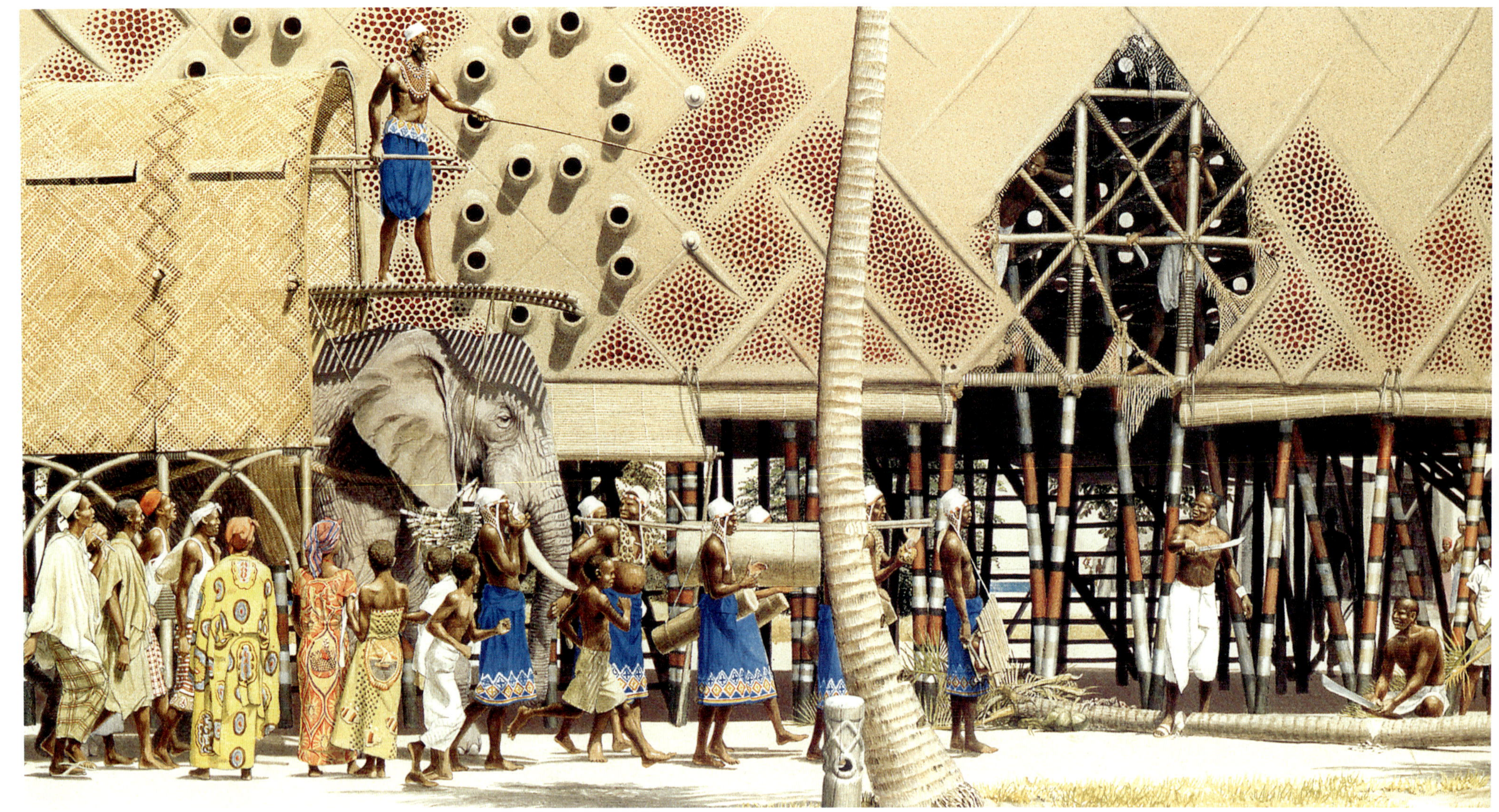

Kuba Kubwa (Swahili - "Big Dome")
Oils, 91.5 x 122 cm, 1984/85
Exhibited: Everard Read Gallery, Johannesburg, 1997

A baraza (meeting) hall, inspired by the shell of a sea urchin. The skeleton is a frame of mangrove poles lashed together, up and over in "lines of longitude and round about in lines of latitude". Diagonal bracings of sisal rope stiffen the structure and coir matting stitched over these is coated with clay. A raised platform stands centrally with five staircases mounting to it. From the platform five banks of open framework seating rake up to the equator in crinoid symmetry. Tubular vents over the staircases provide light and air. Would it work? Who knows? This structure is an invention of the artist!

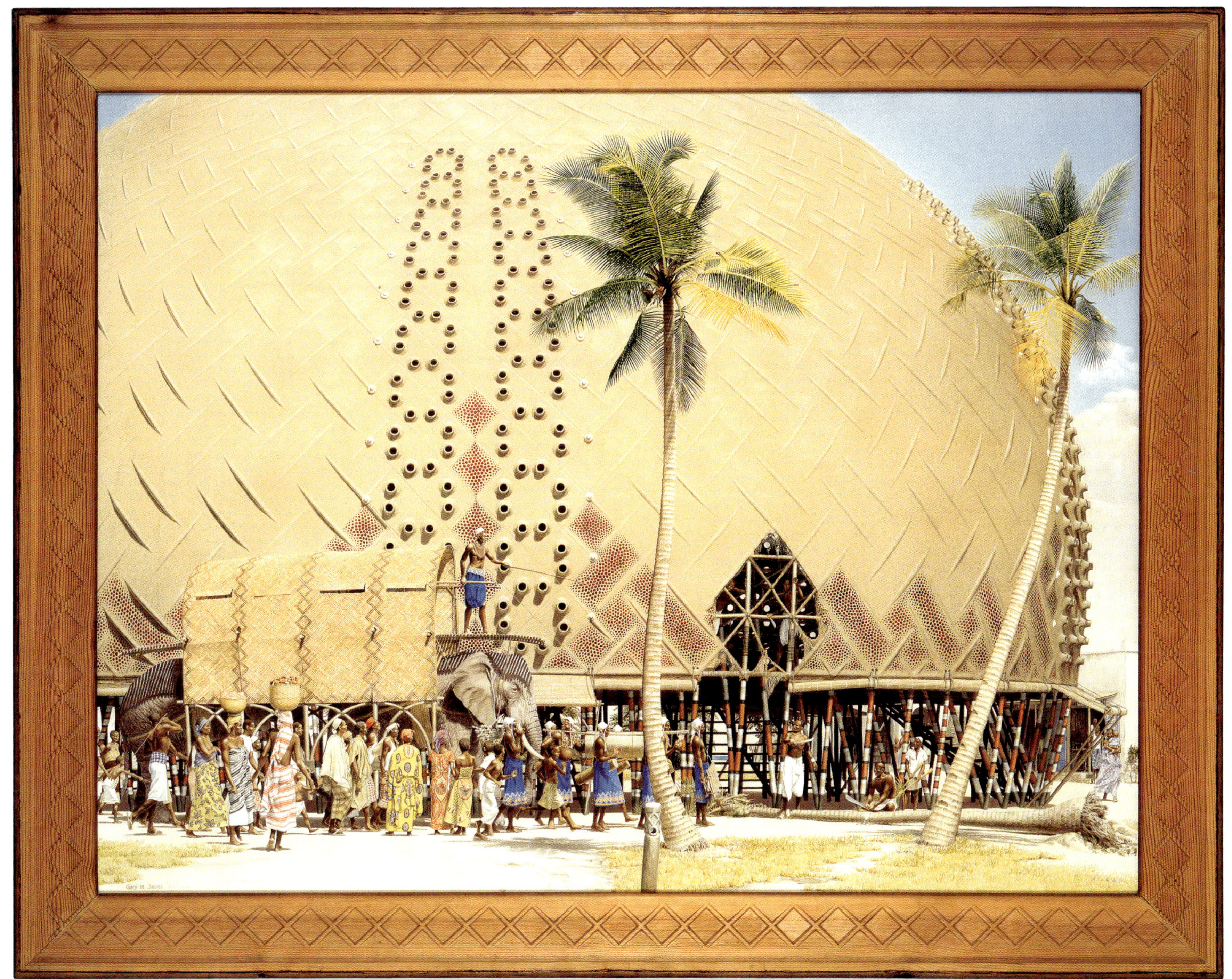

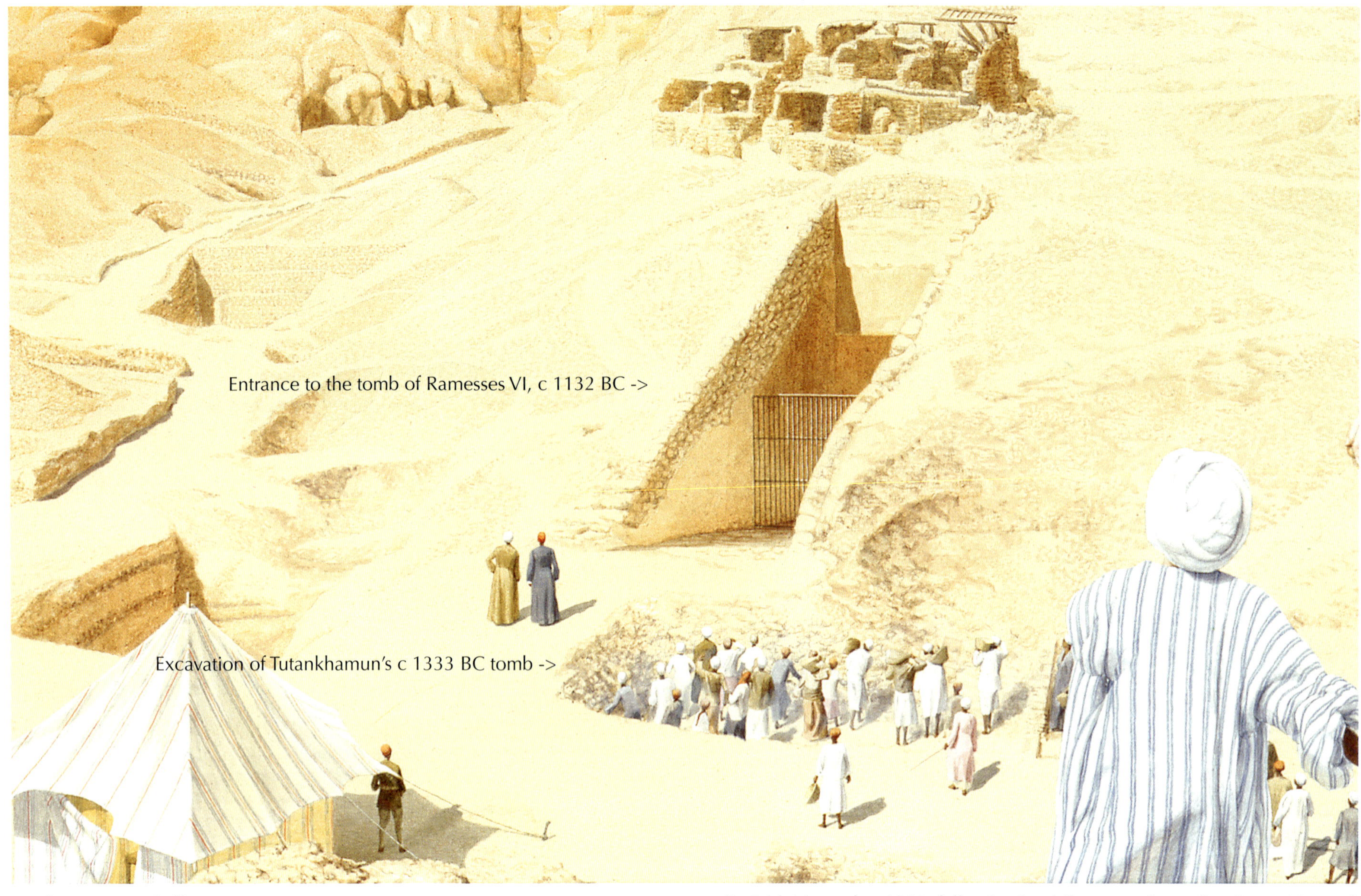

An interrupted dig
Acrylic, 91.5 x 122 cm

1992/93

(Taken out of chronological order and inserted here for narrative purposes).
Exhibited: Everard Read Gallery, Johannesburg, 1997

On 24th November 1922, following Lord Carnarvon's recall to Egypt, Howard Carter's backfill securing the dig was removed and the tomb of Tutankhamun entered.

Subsequently there was an attempt to gate crash the party by landing a biplane nearby, and here the artist gate crashes history with an airship seventy years after the event.

Winged Solar Disc

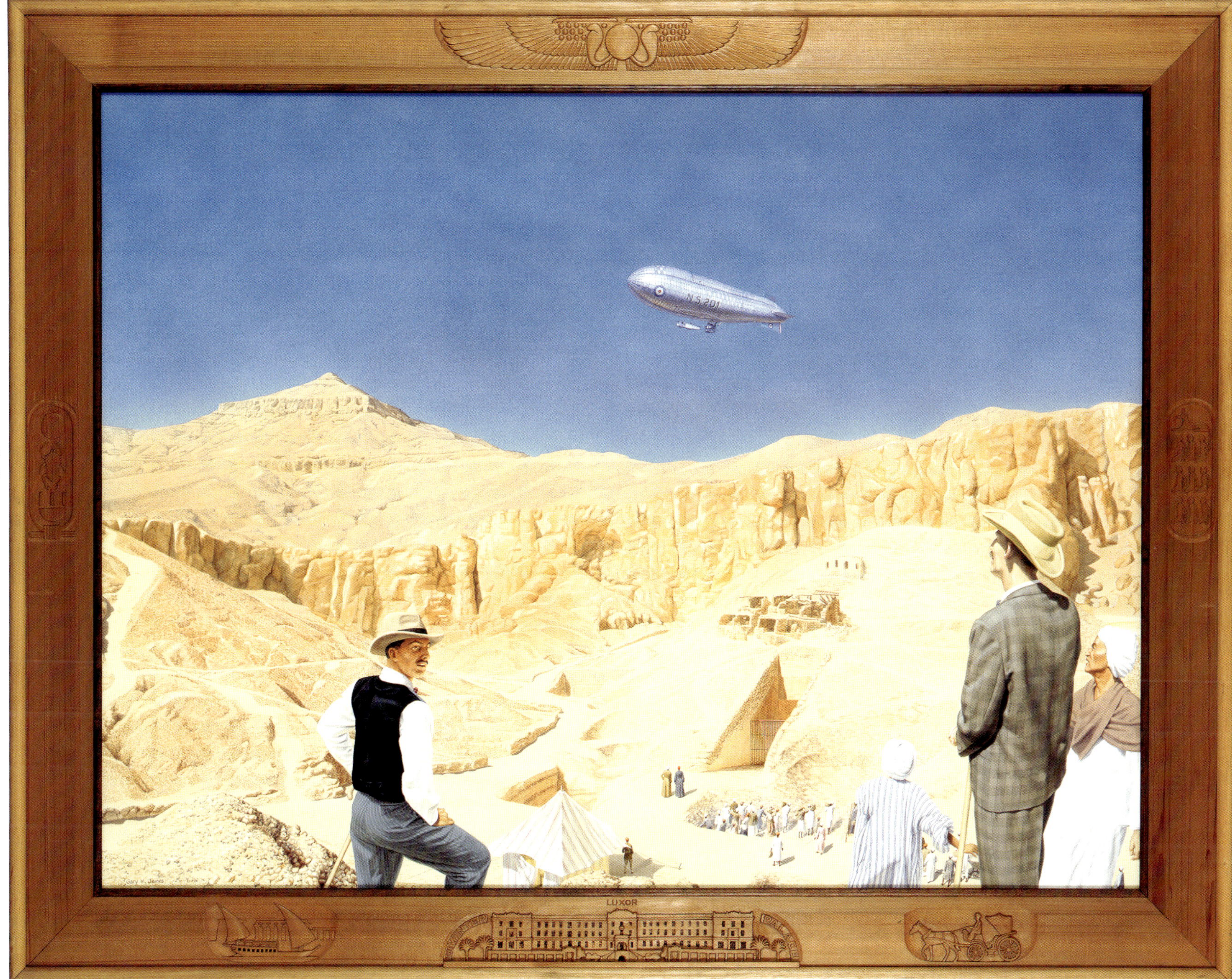

Tutankhamun cartouche

Necropolis Seal

On the Frame: A dahabeyah passing Luxor Temple

Winter Palace, Luxor – Watering hole Of Howard Carter & Lord Carnarvon

A calèche

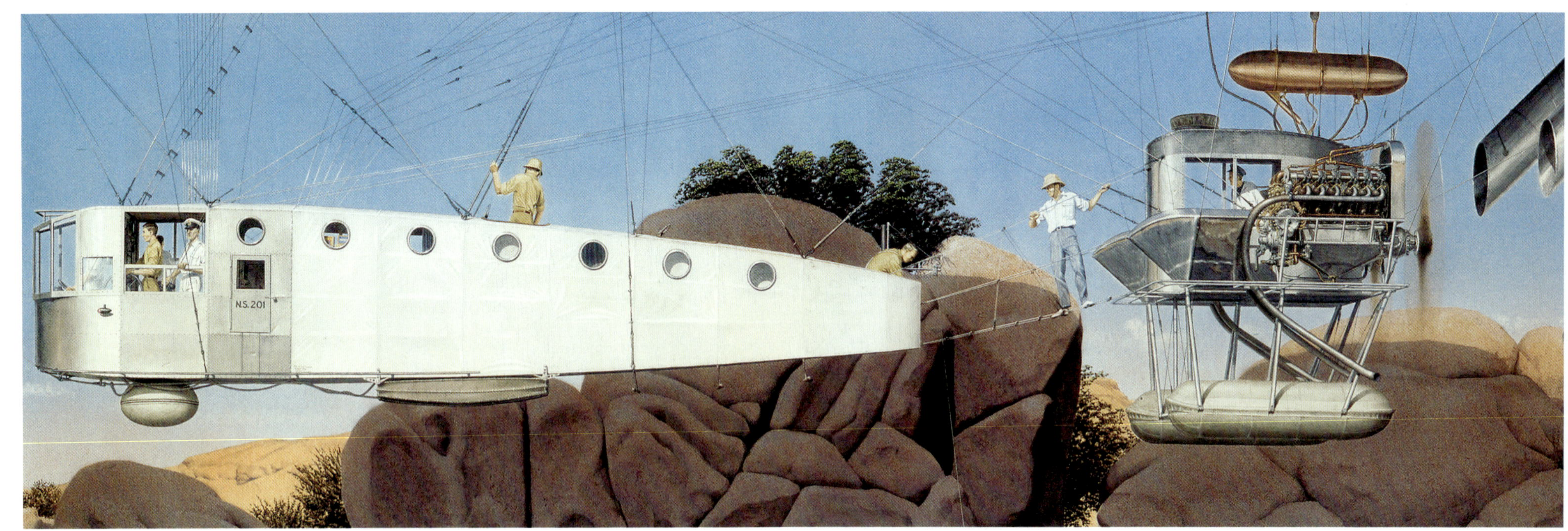

By "North Sea" up the Nile
Oils on Acrylics, 81 x 165 cm framed 1986

Exhibited: Royal West of England Academy, 1986
(Televised I.T.V. at opening. Critics pick of the paintings). (Notes p. 11)
Everard Read Gallery, Johannesburg, 1997

Published: Sunday Independent (RSA) – 20th July 1997

Built for the Admiralty during World War I, for anti submarine patrols over the North Sea, these were the largest blimps (non rigid "B type limps") ever flown. They carried a ten man crew in two watches for periods of anything up to four days without landing … hence my appropriation here.
Fiat engines made specifically for airships were used for a period but here I have reinstated the Rolls Royce Eagle VIIIs with features lifted from its derivative the Falcon engine (in case I am challenged). Both were precursors of the Rolls Royce Merlin engines that powered the Spitfires and Lancaster Bombers of WWII. The scoops behind the propellers are balonette intakes that inflate airbags within the canopy (overhead) to maintain its aerodynamic shape against seepage of the lifting gas. The figure on the wire walk is a portrait of the artist's grandfather in the fatigues of his RAF service in Mesopotamia in the early 1920s.

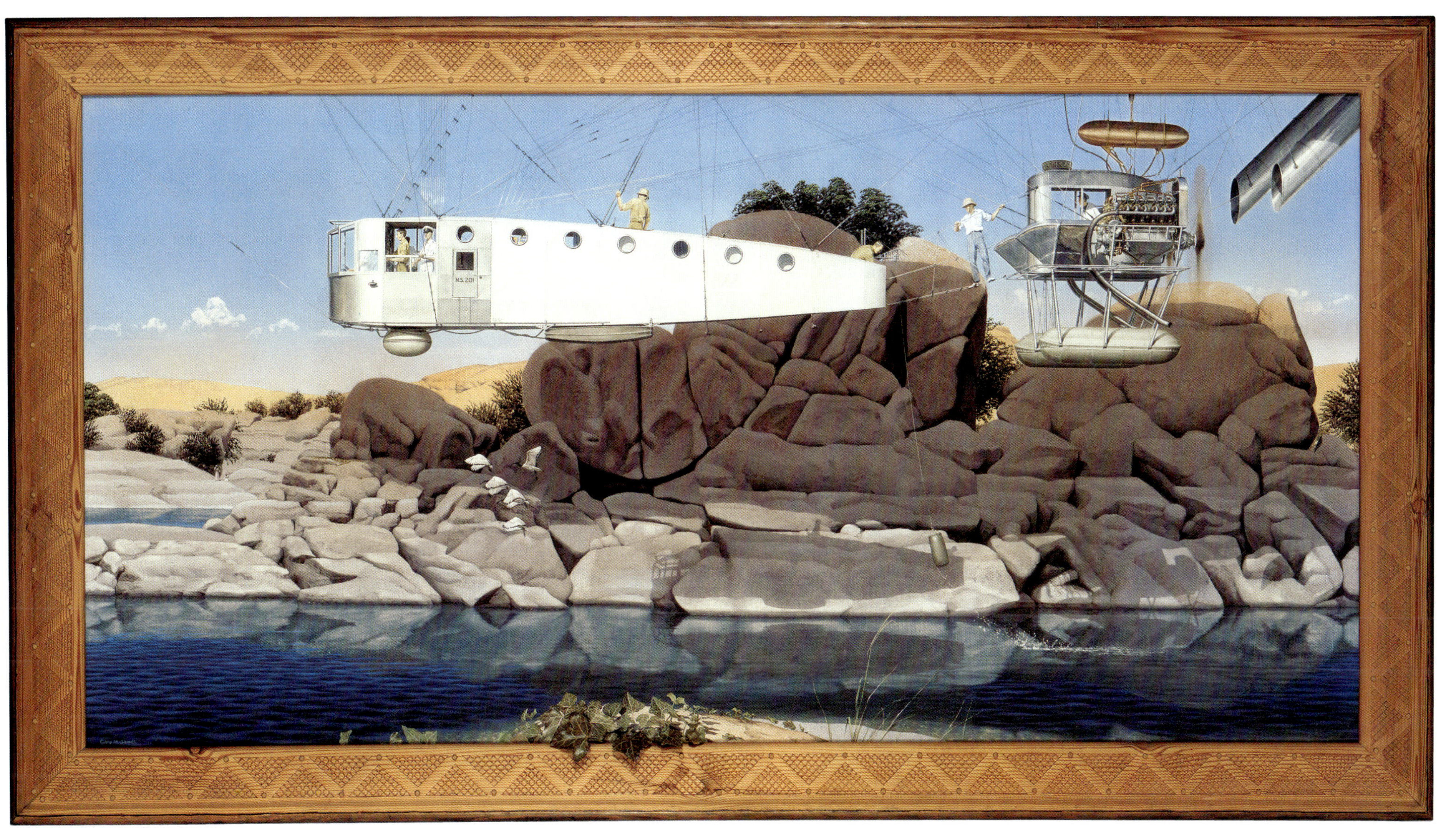

The three dimensional interfacing leaves on the frame above were made from aluminium and painted.

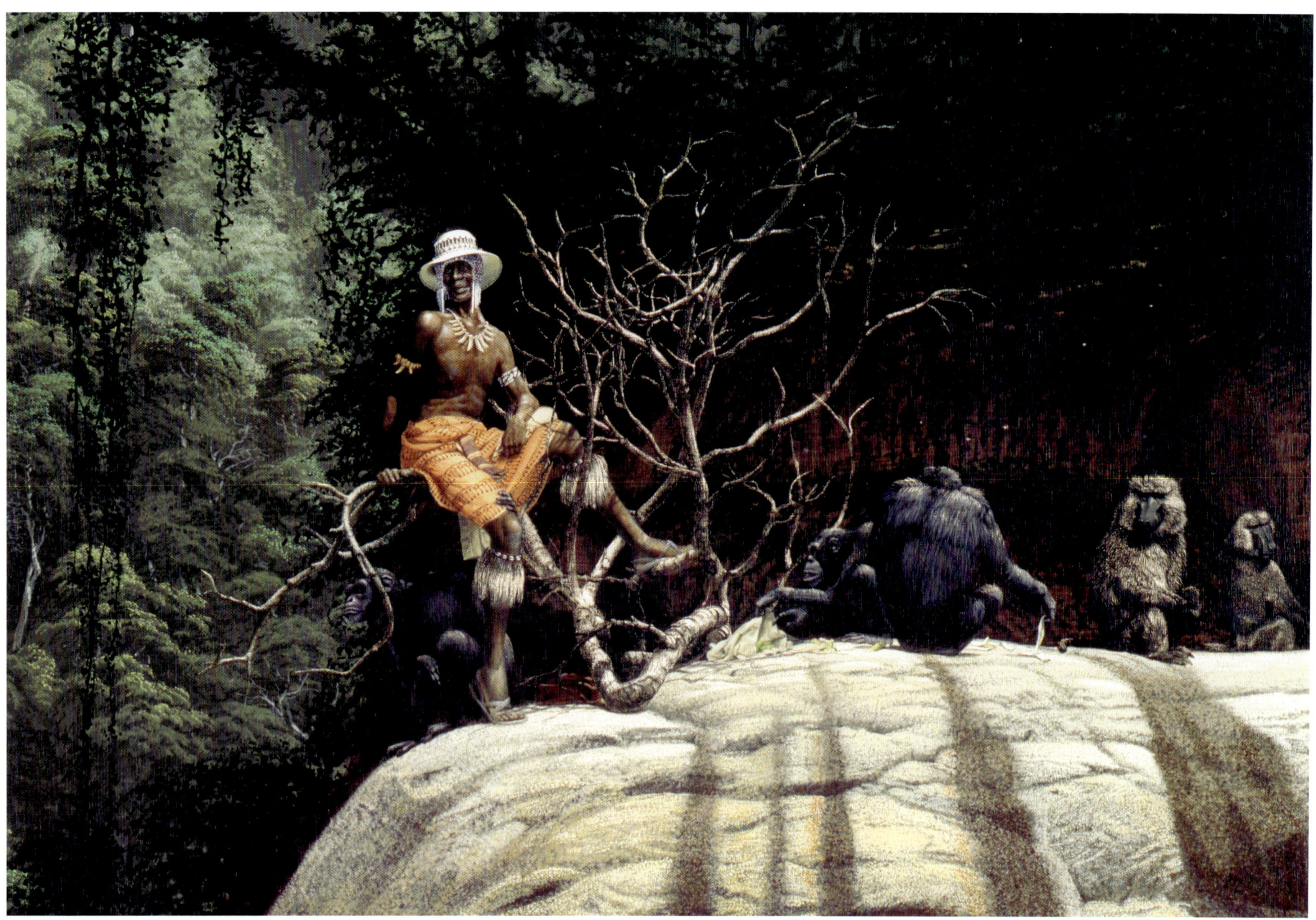

Awaiting the passing of the ants
Acrylic, 122 x 91.5 cm 1986 & 1988
Exhibited: Everard Read Gallery, Johannesburg, 1997

Assorted primates wisely yield the floor to siafu ants on the rampage. If, as rumoured, the gent in the fetching hat really is the "Keeper of the Graveyard of the Elephants" he is not letting on.

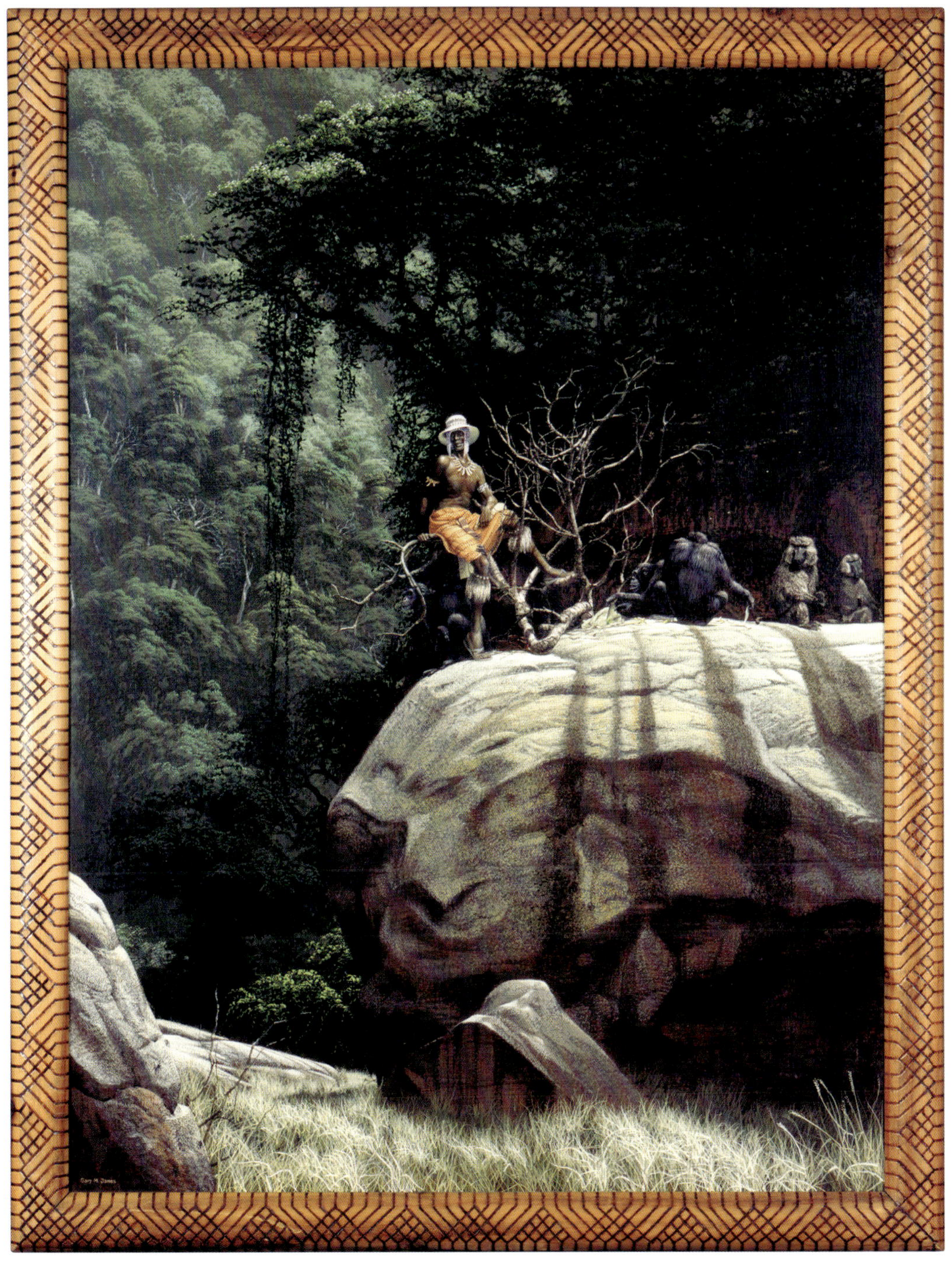

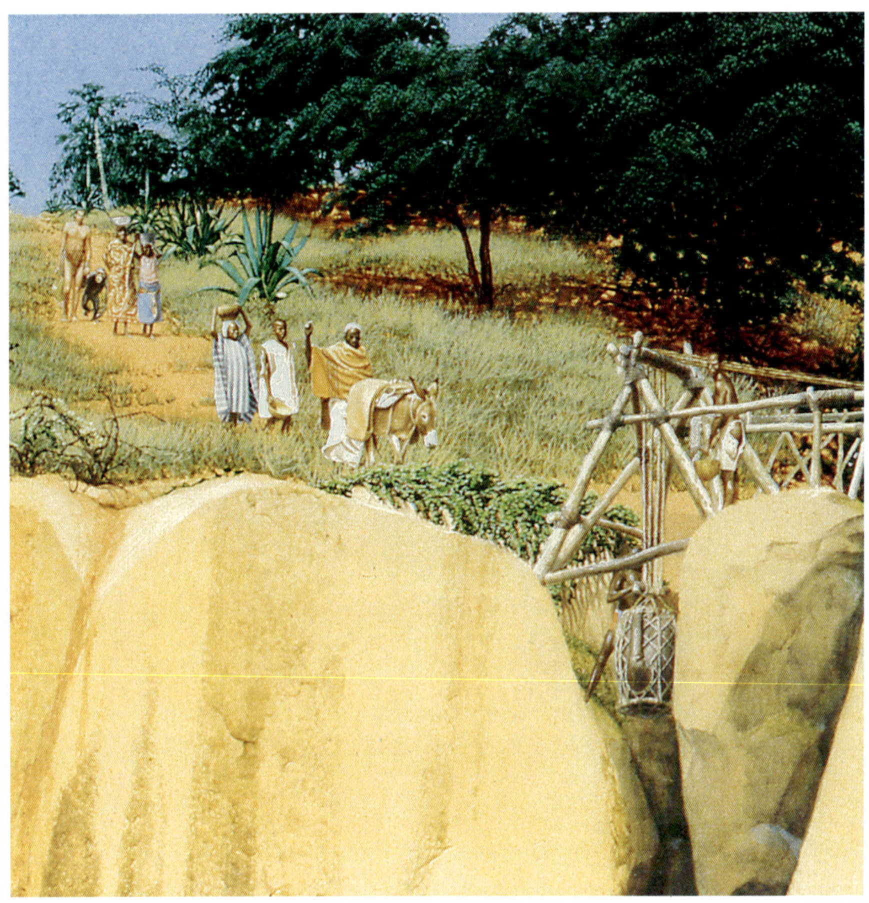

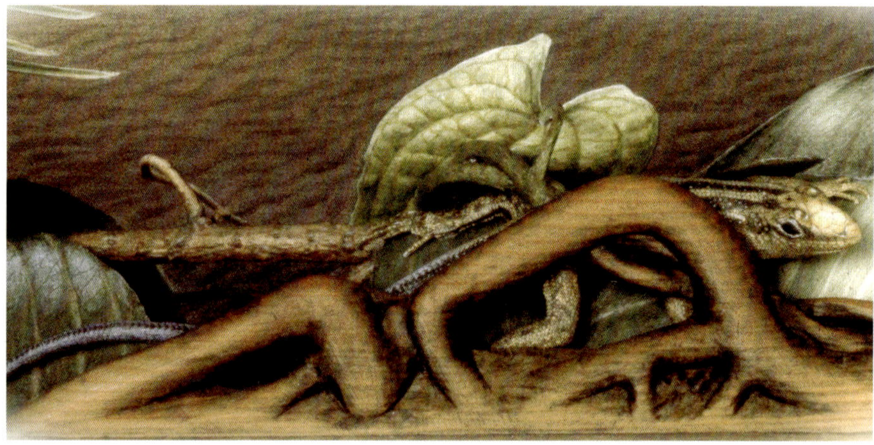

A Rainbow Skink (modelled)

Invited to their annual exhibition in the Westminster Gallery by the President of the Royal Society of Miniature Painters, Sculptors and Gravers, I was pressed to try my hand at the four inch by six inch format. I replied that in some respects 'River Market' was a miniature---a four foot by six foot miniature.

River Market

Acrylic & cedarwood, 124 x 185 cm framed, 1987/89

Exhibited: Royal West of England Academy, 1989
Royal Academy, 1990
Everard Read Gallery, Johannesburg, 1997

Published: RA Illustrated, 1990
Mitre (framing) Magazine, 1990
Reviewed in: The Daily Telegraph, 6th June 1990
The Times, 8th June 1990
Harpers & Queen, August 1990
Subsequently: Diversions magazine (R.S.A.), December 1997

A pan-African, trogladytic Liberty's Store stands at the junction of the Simahali po pote River and the Mto Ingine. Bas relief rock face carvings give an account of its wares. A basket lift powered by a water filled and wicker work reinforced counterweight serves upper levels, though Tarzan and Cheetah (top) need no such assistance.

Nearer to hand a rainbow skink emerges in 3D from the frame's interfacing undergrowth.

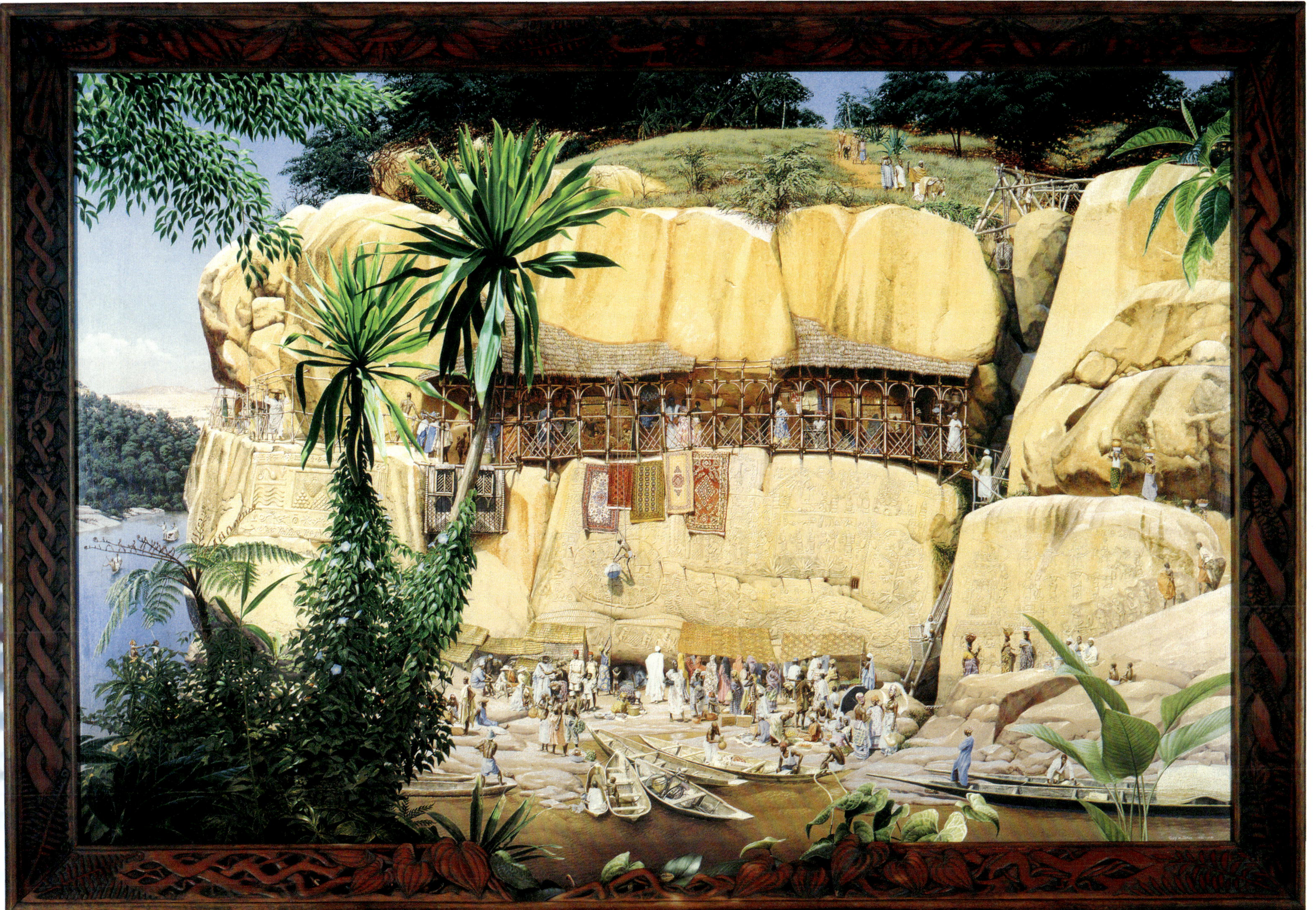

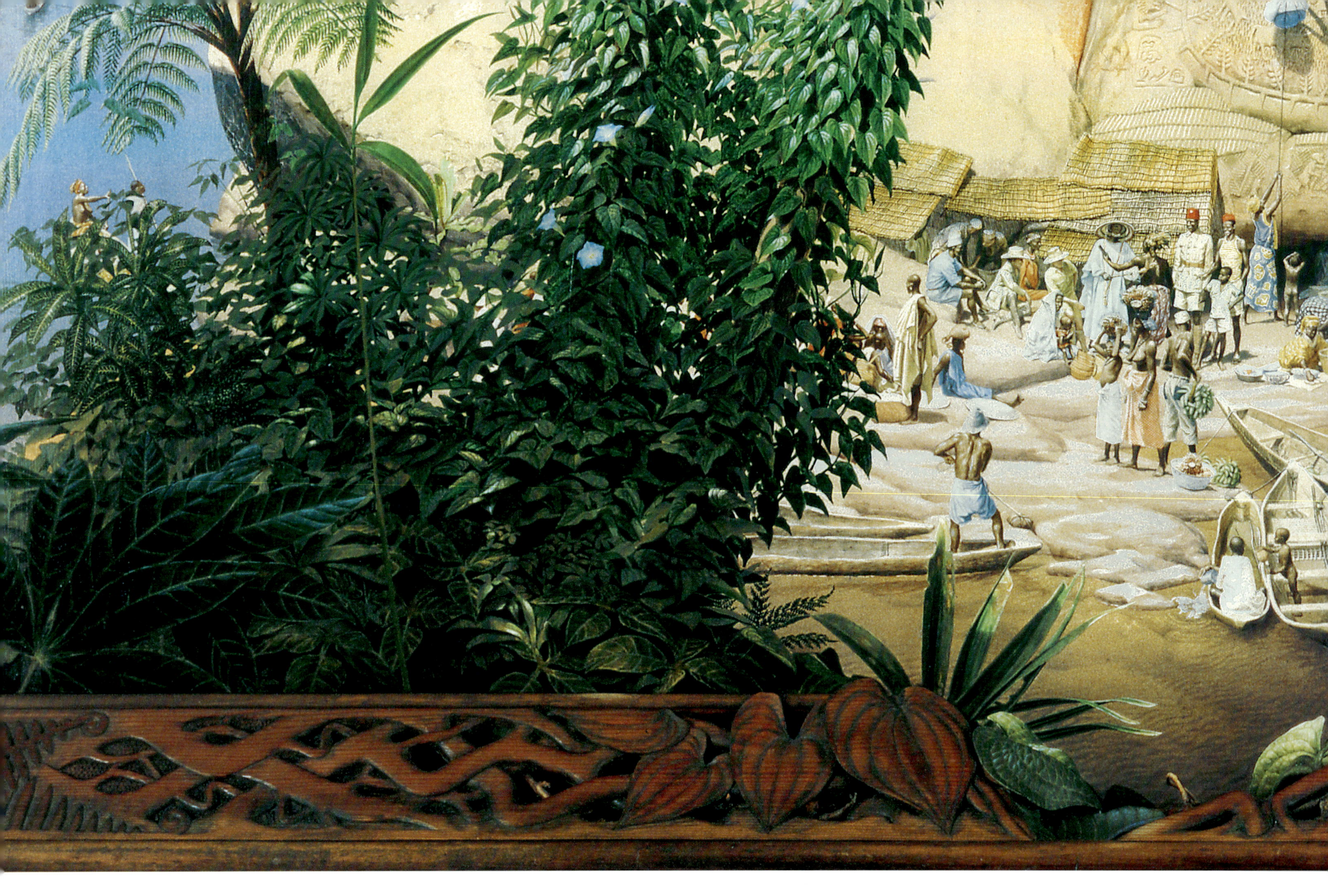

Market floor level The frame is pierced through to the undergrowth Ipomoea creeper climbs a dracaena steudneri tree The dimensions merge with leaves and twigs, part wood, part metal and part painted

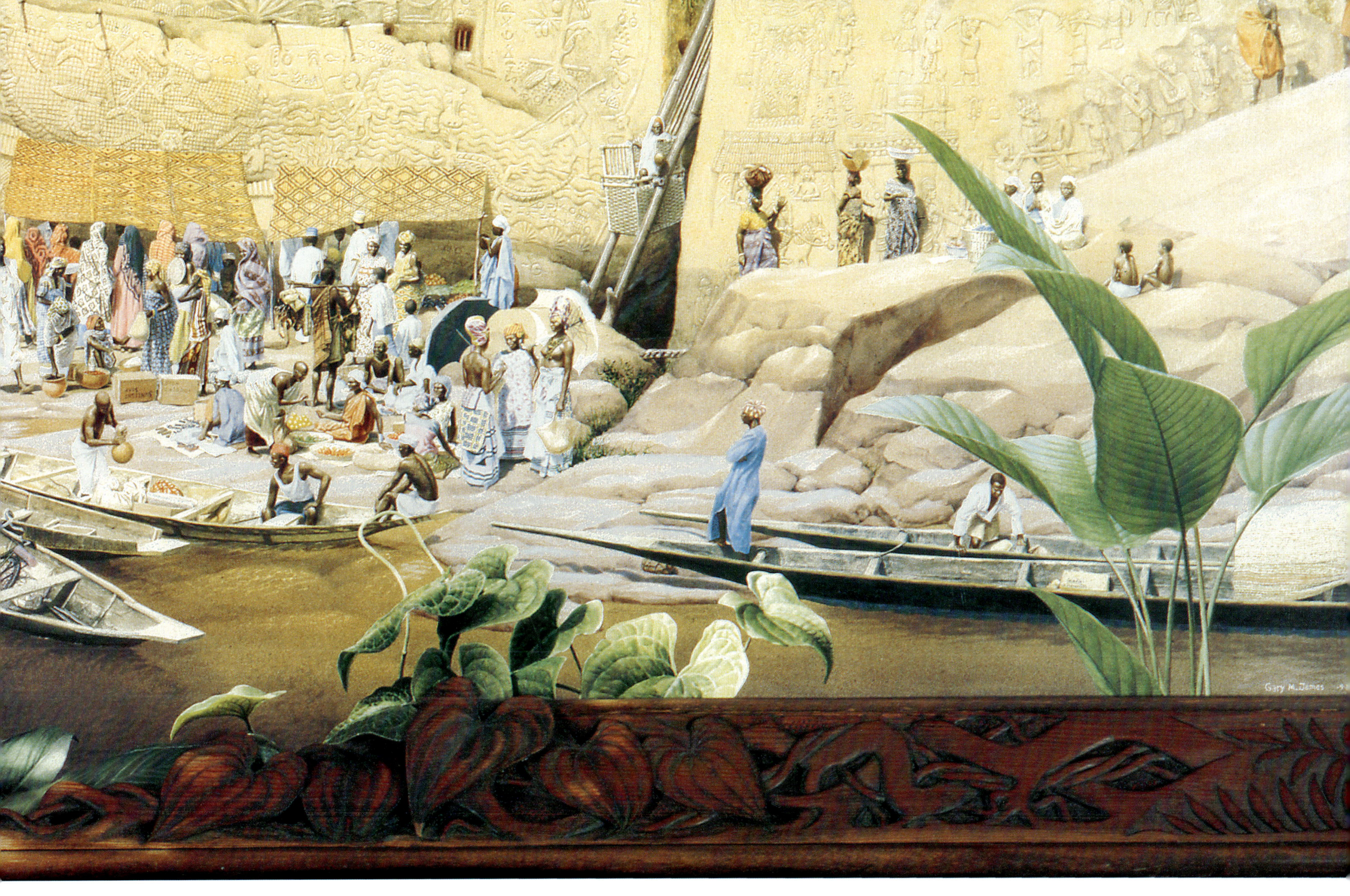

Someone has found a mouse in her mealie bag ...much to her companions' amusement.

Passengers ascend in the water powered 'Funicular' railway ....

.....whilst others make the ascent on foot.

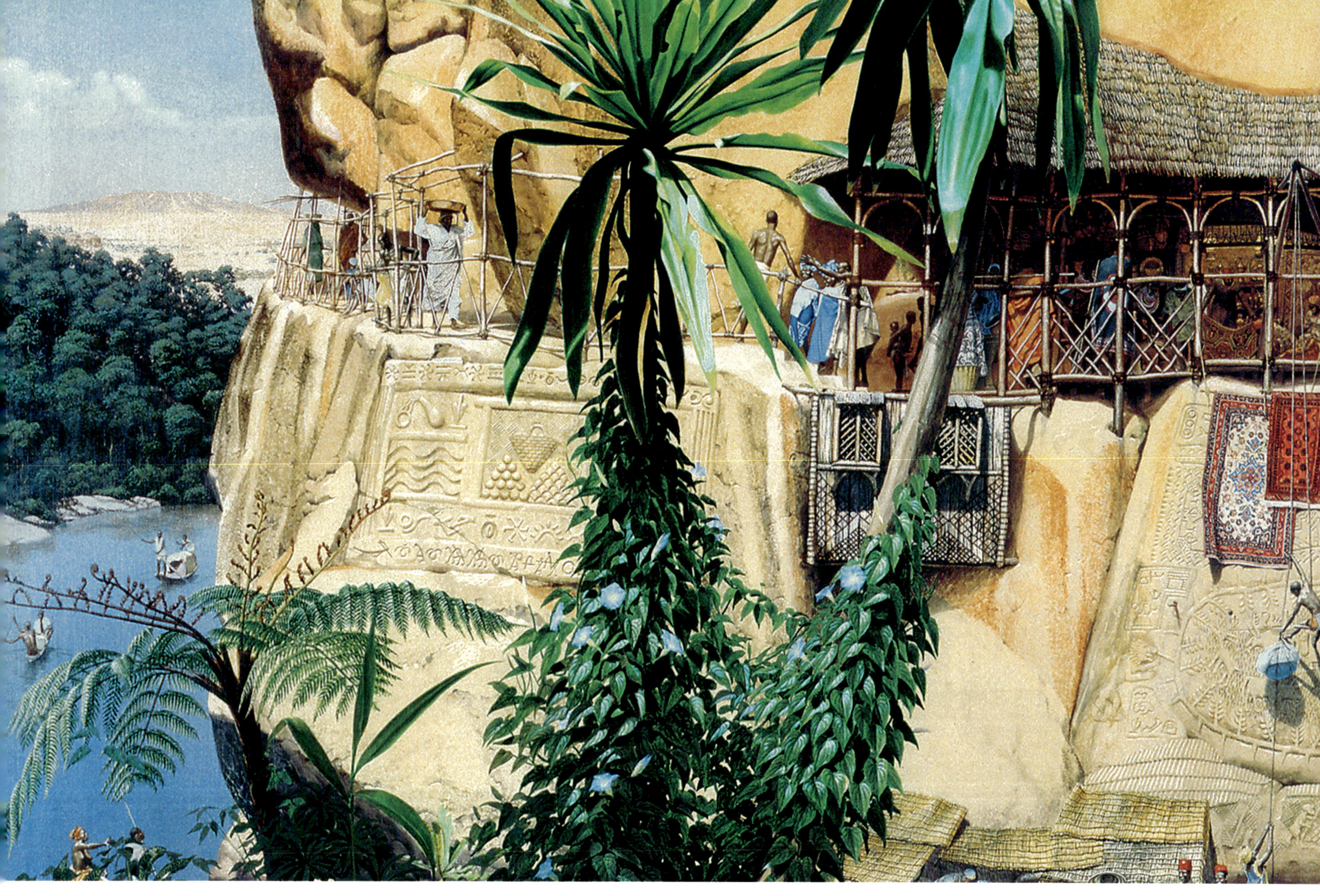

Gallery level

Bas relief pictogram says "Welcome to River Market"

A little mild flirtation

Bucket conveniences

Pots, pans & wire

Metalwork & carpet emporium in the chamber behind

La

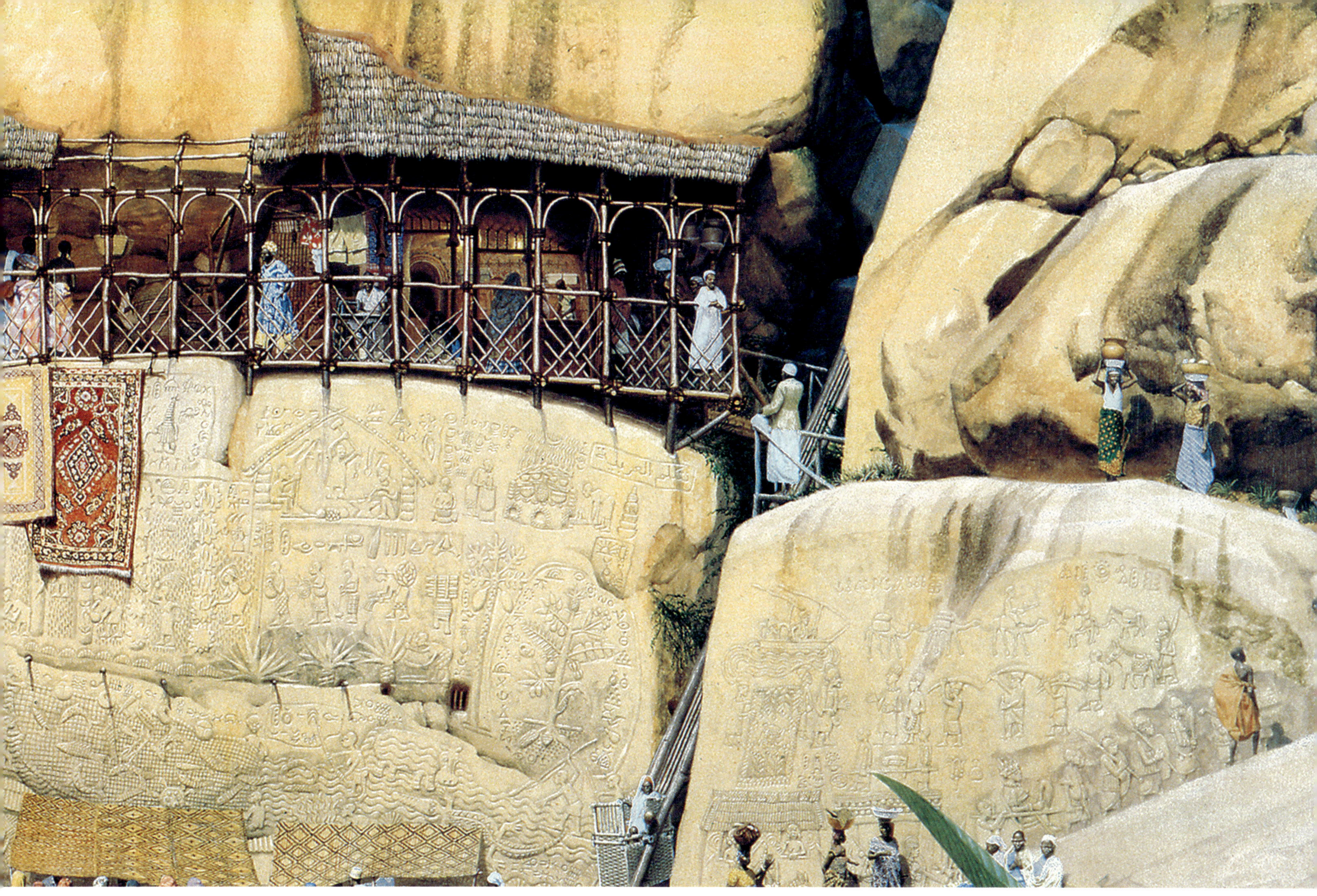

Basket ware

Entrance to "medicine" chamber

Haberdashery chamber

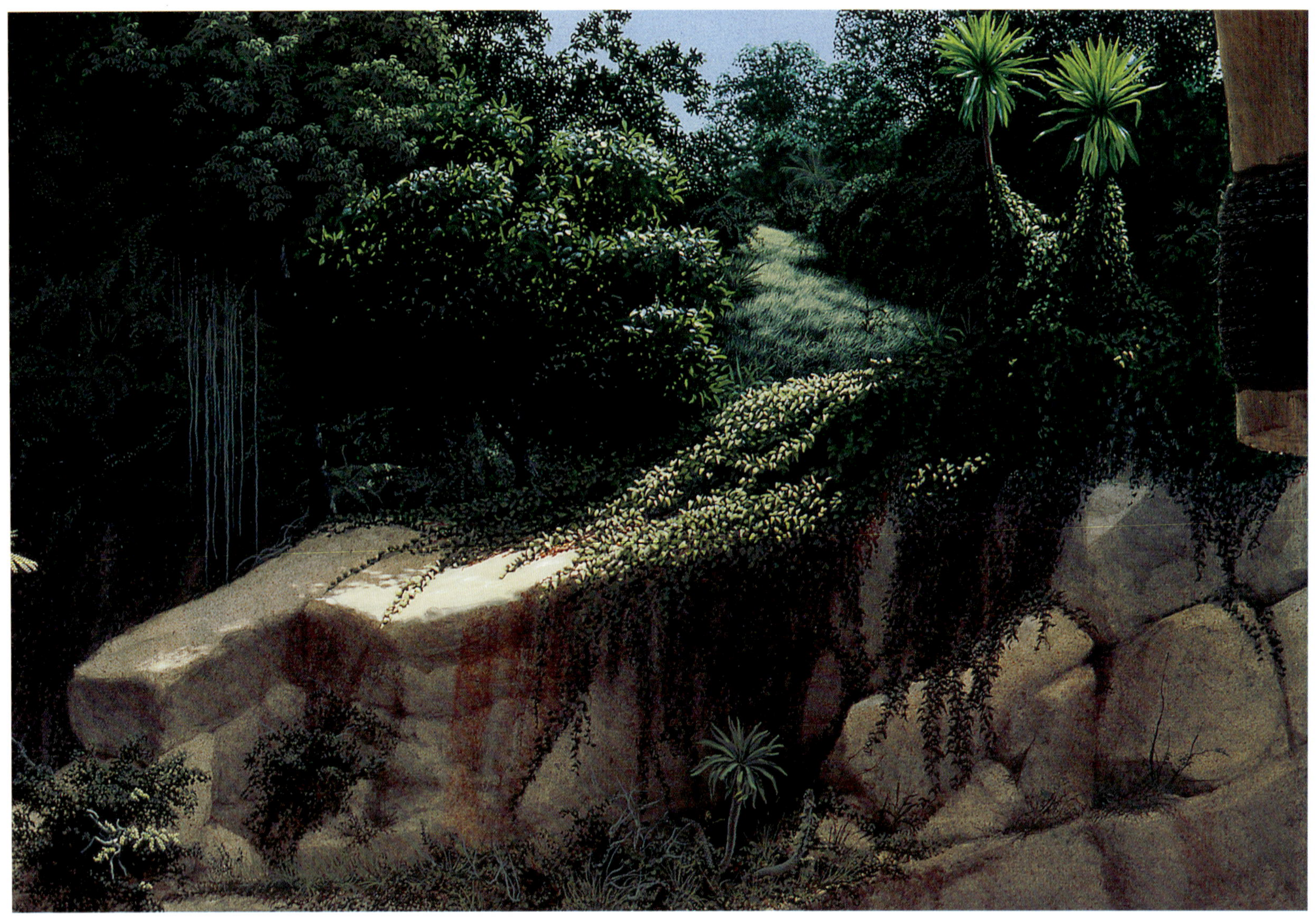

View from the Gallery (River Market 2)
Acrylic, cedar and pine wood, 122 x 183 cm 1991/92
Exhibited: Everard Read Gallery, Johannesburg, 1997

The view point for River Market 1 is up behind the dracaena plant, top right. In contrast to the market bank all is quiet opposite. As in Arnold Böcklin's famous paintings "The Isle of the Dead" (1880+) there are catacombs up in these cliffs (P 85), and the vertical cleft marks the entry to a pathway up to them.

A strange incident occurred on one occasion when pall bearers stumbled at the top of the slope and dropped their load...which slipped over the edge. A pirogue coming in to moor below was struck amidships by the airborne Dear Departed and sank. Was it pure coincidence that it carried the in-laws of the deceased, with whom it was said he had long been at odds?

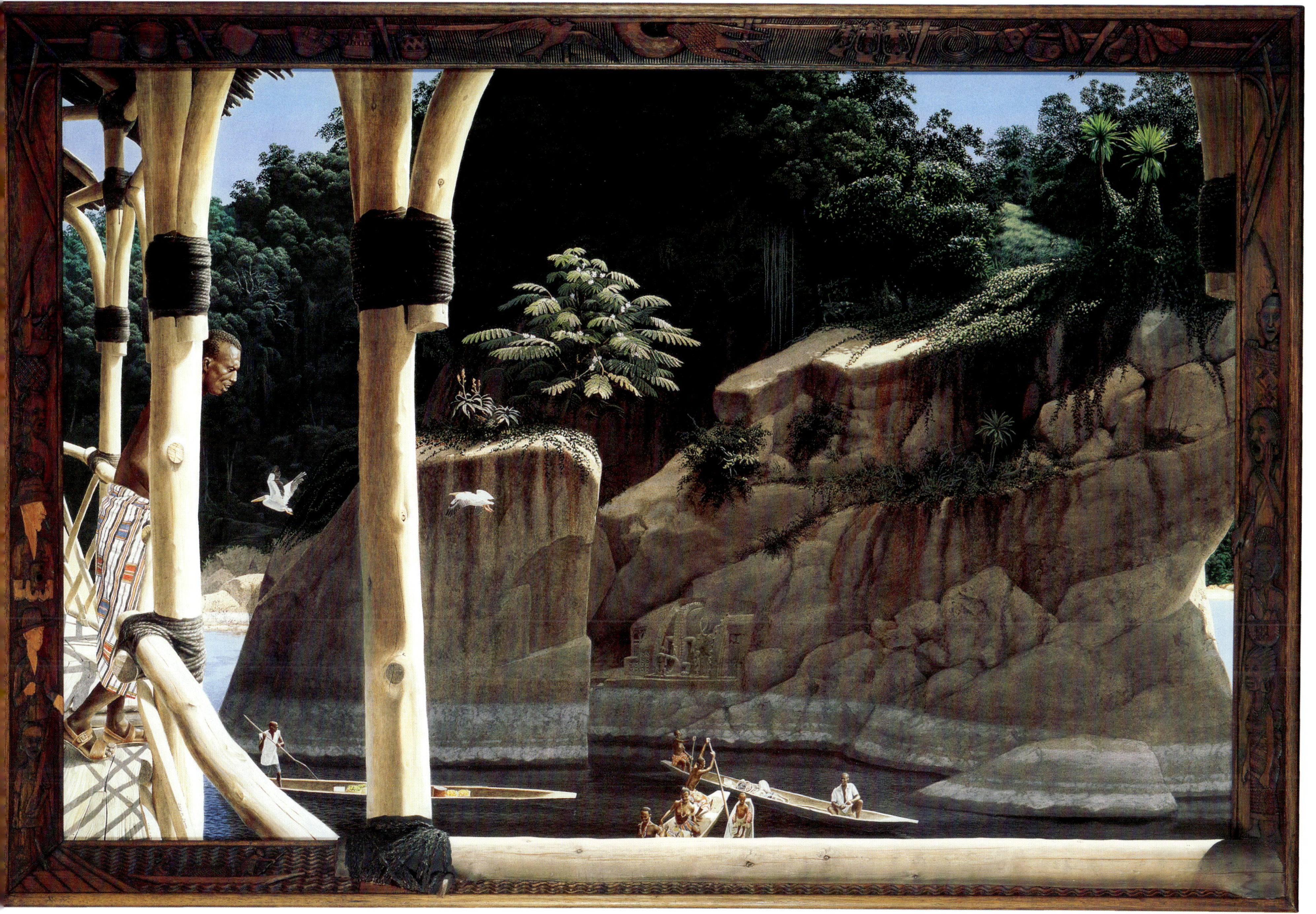

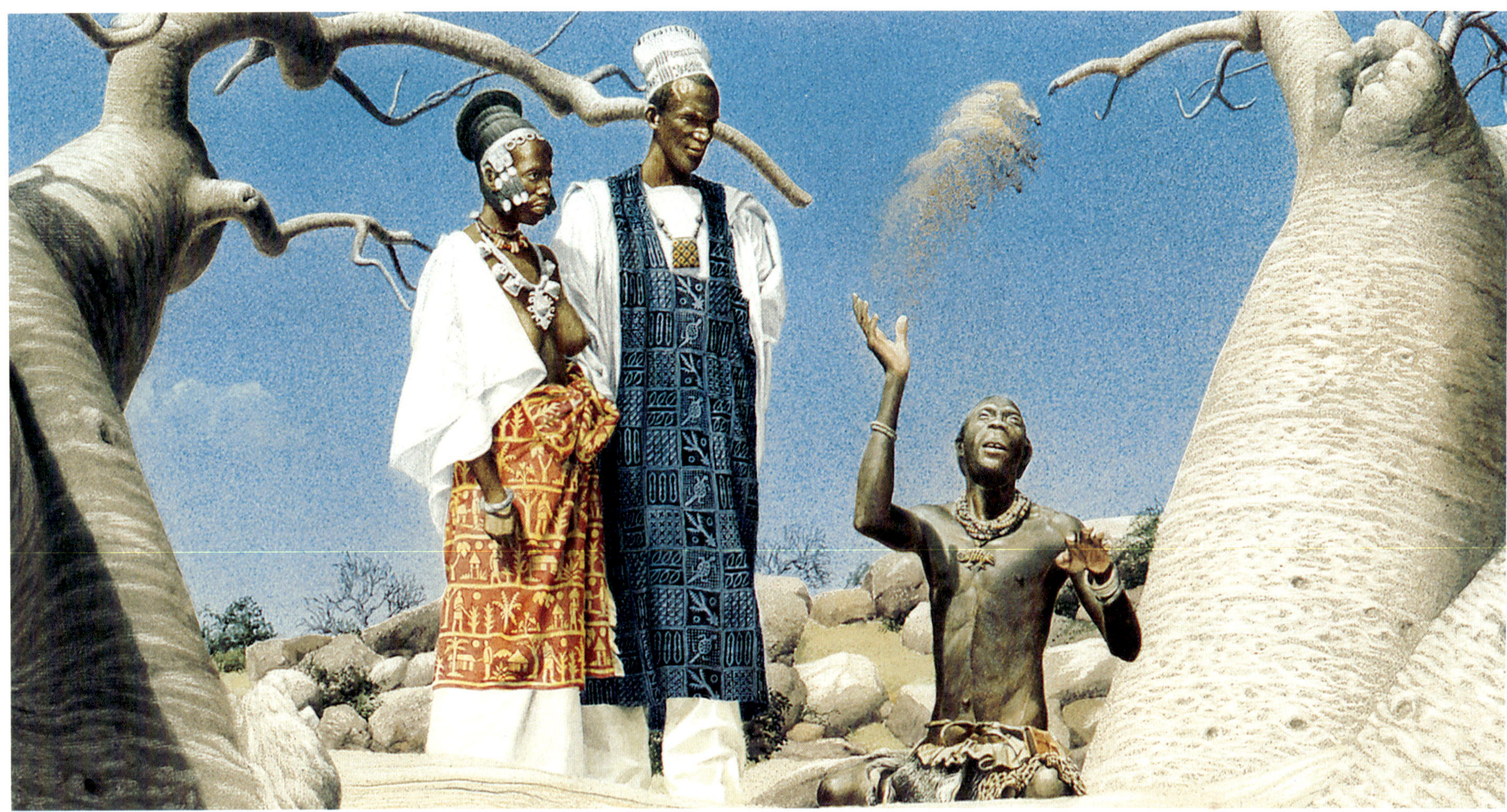

Forecast

Acrylic, 91.5 x 122 cm, 1989/90

Exhibited: Royal Academy Summer Exhibition, 1991
Barber Surgeons' Hall (as 'A consultation') 1993
Everard Read Gallery, Johannesburg, 1997

Published: RA Illustrated, 1991

Newly-weds consult a famous soothsayer …

Mwaguzi*	One son and five daughters.
Client	One son! Are you sure Mzee?*
Mwaguzi	The bones say so Mwanangu.*
Client	Cast them again.
Mwaguzi	Once cast they cannot be cast again Mwanangu … and the baobab you are in is propitious as you know.
Client	How if I was to go to the Mwaguzi at Mafuta?
Mwaguzi	You are welcome to seek a second opinion of course. But the baobab has spoken … and a beer hall mwaguzi will foresee as many sons as beers that you buy him. Rejoice in your one good son Mwanangu – and the profit that five good daughters will bring.
Client	And the profit from my oil palms?
Mwaguzi(Casts again)	Ah, that is good too and should bring you five good sons in law.
Client	Well that is something.
Mwaguzi	Would it please you to cast the bones for your driver?
Client	No. He already has three sons.

*Mwaguzi – SoothsayerMzee – Old man (honorific).Mwanangu – My son.

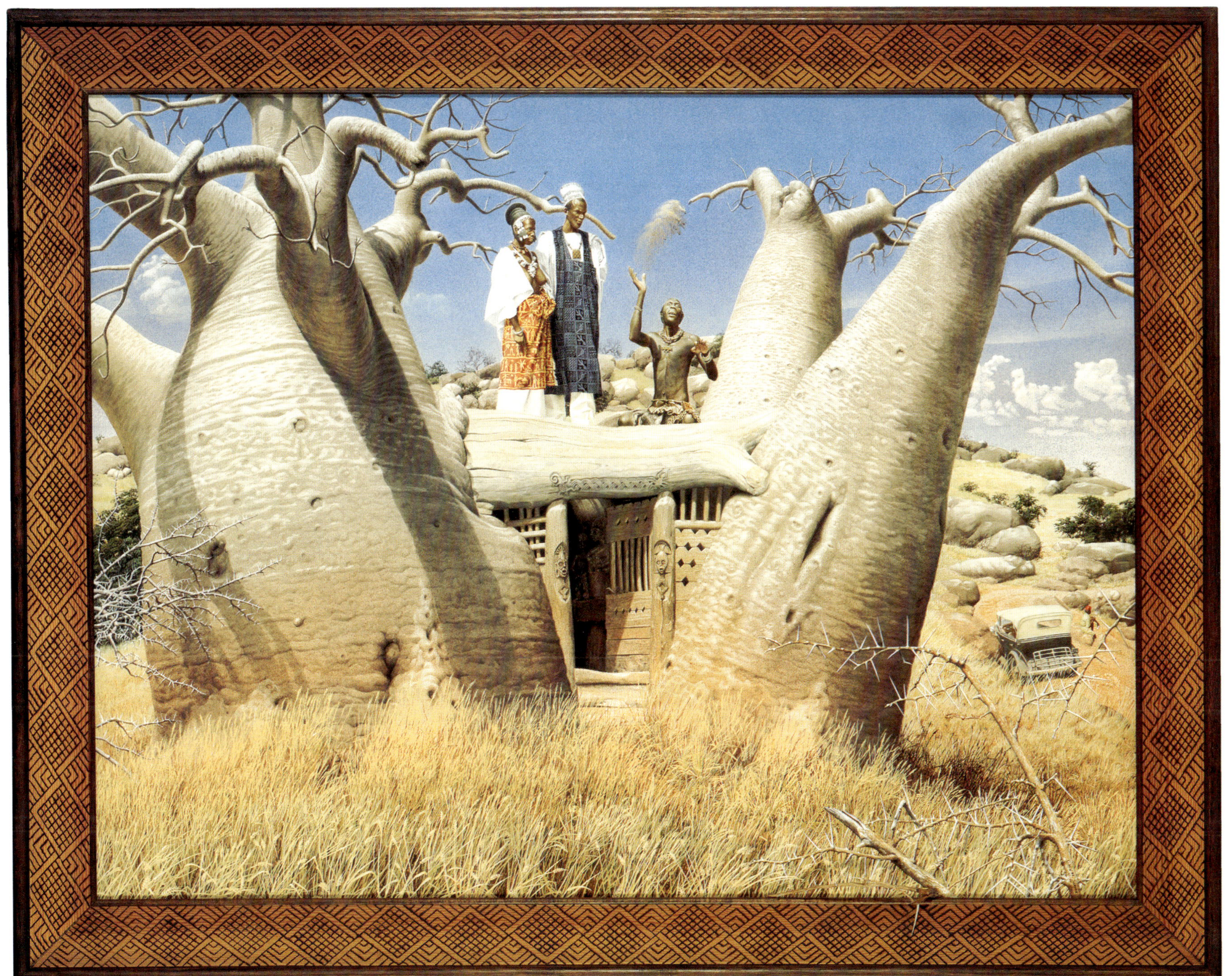

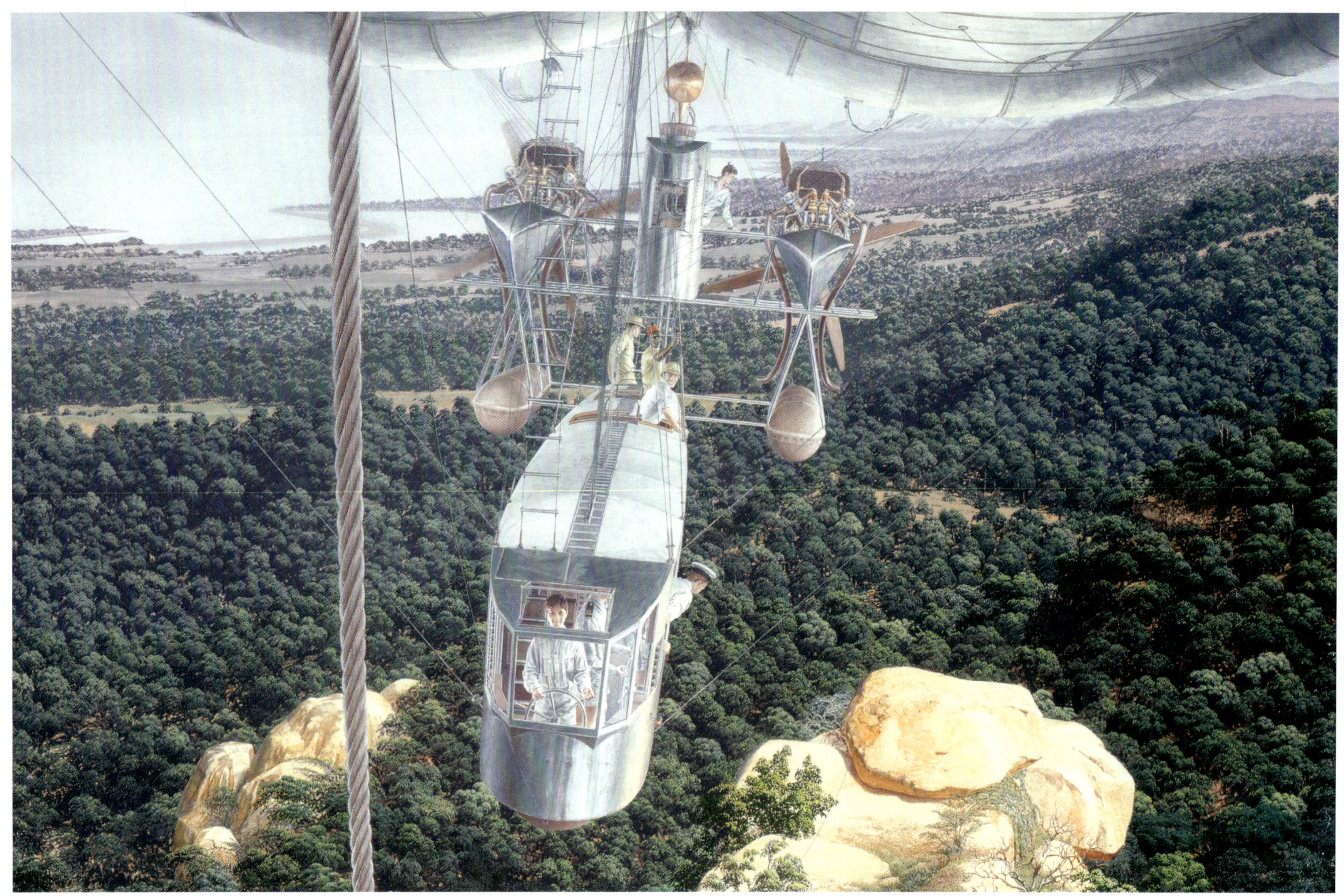

A view from the bosun's chair
Acrylic, 147 x 117 cm, 1994/95
Exhibited: Everard Read Gallery, Johannesburg, 1997
Published: The Star, newspaper, 21st July 1997

Blown off course by a tropical storm our "North Sea" airship makes an overnight mooring to an eroded volcanic core in place of a mooring mast. The anchor man bravely rides the bosun's chair down the cable to secure the grappling anchor.

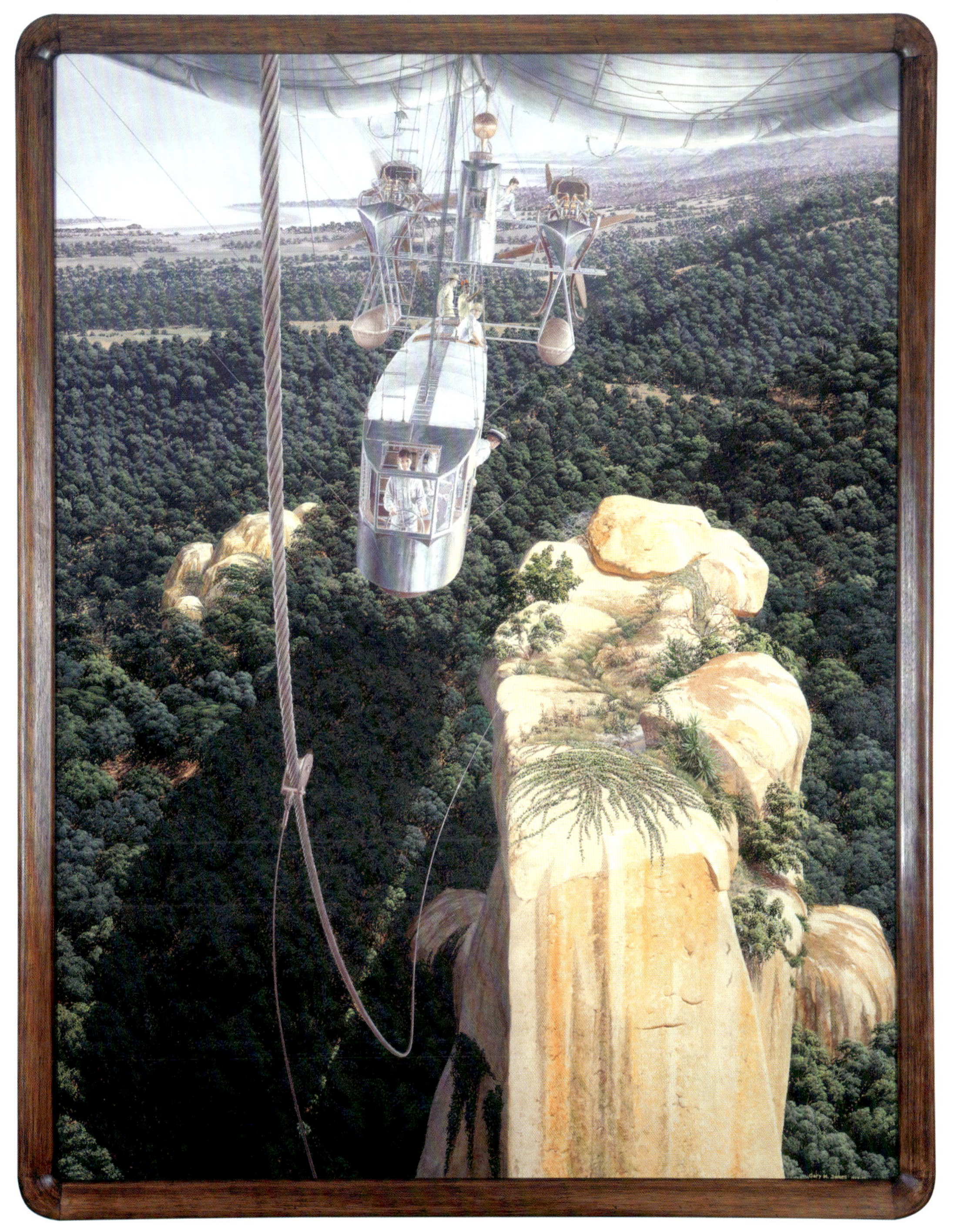

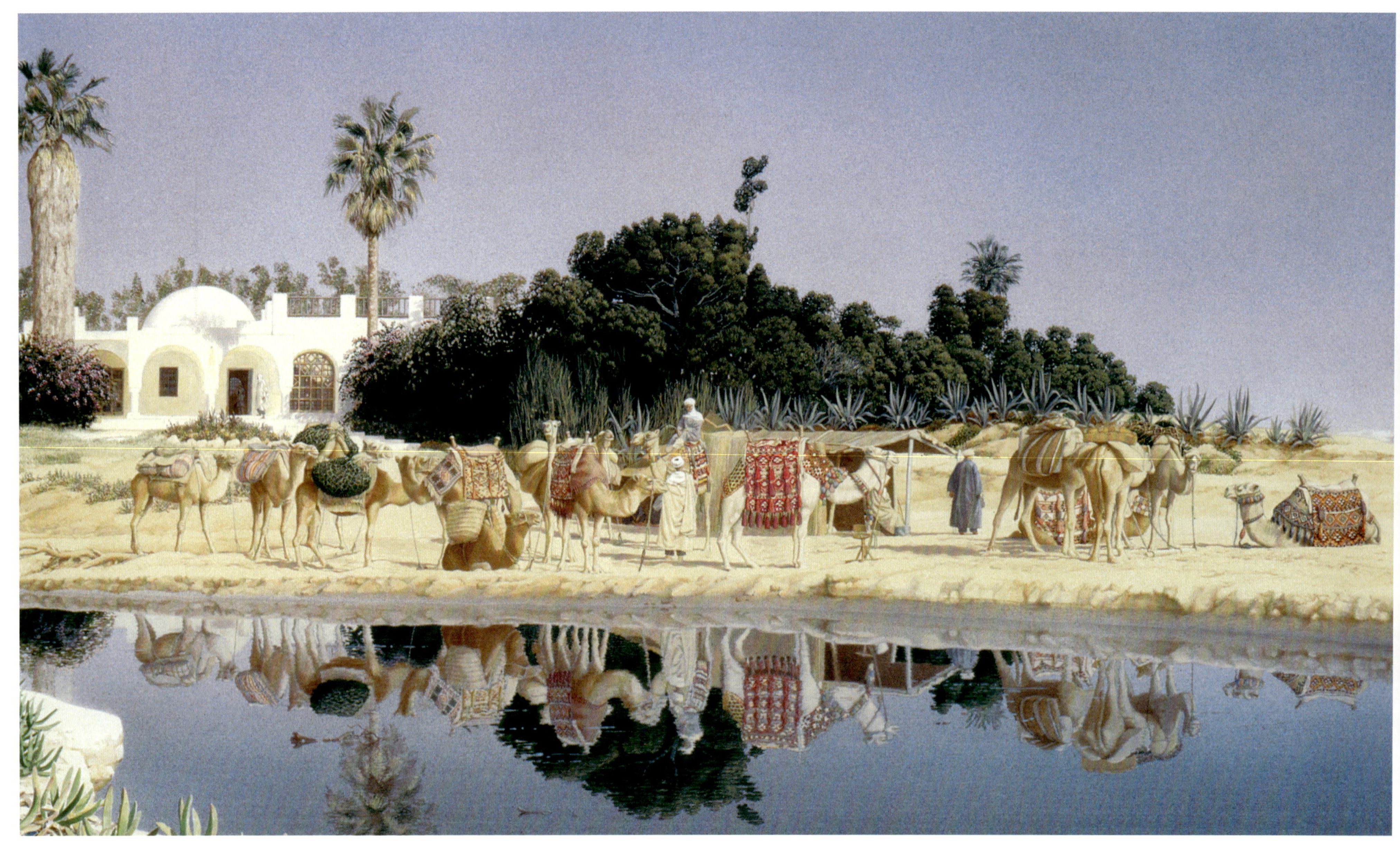

Morning Start
Acrylic, 61 x 122 cm, 1995
Exhibited: Everard Read Gallery, Johannesburg, 1997

The camp stirs preparing for a caravan into the interior. Arrangements are being made with guests of honour in the villa behind.
Variations on a scene in Tunisia.

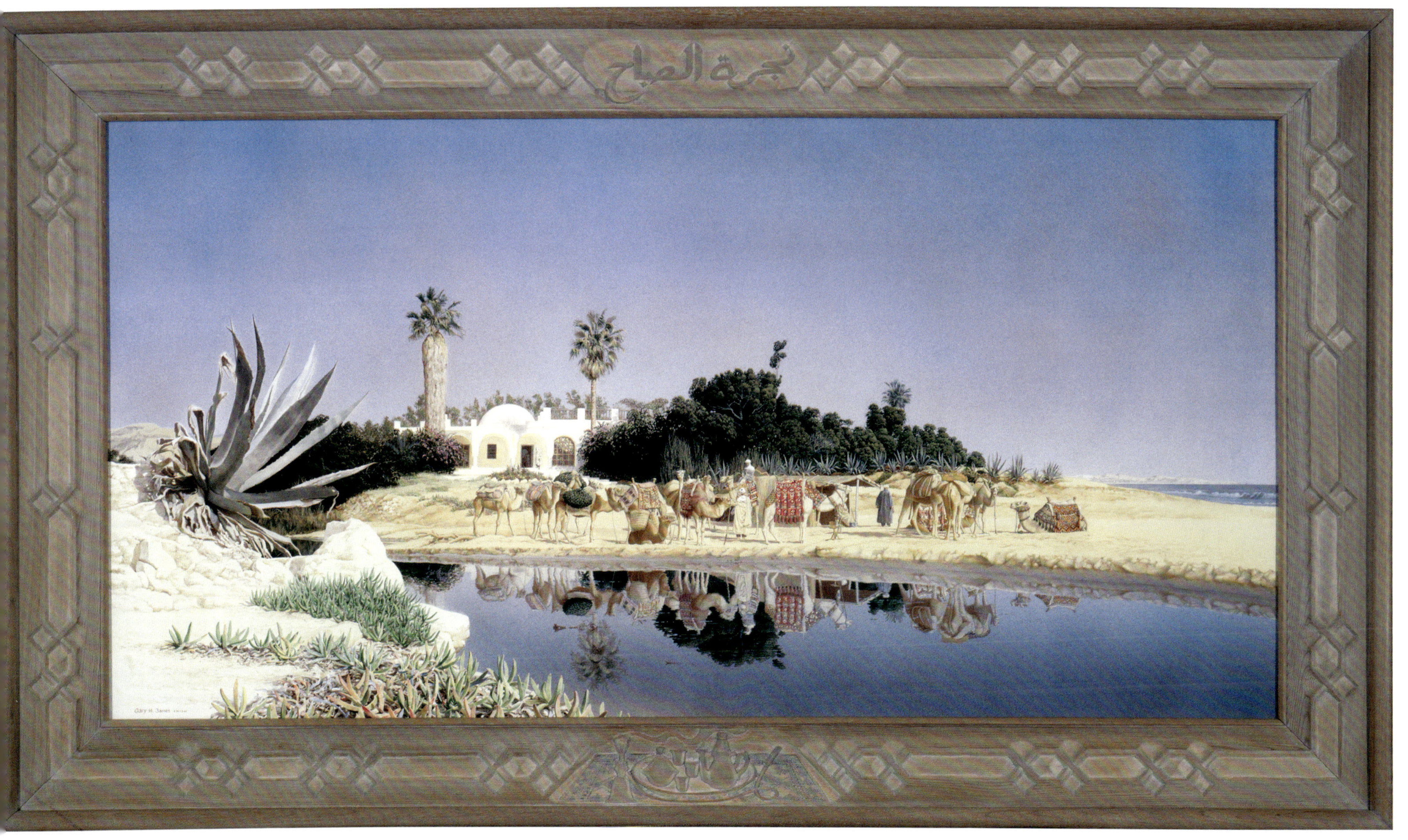

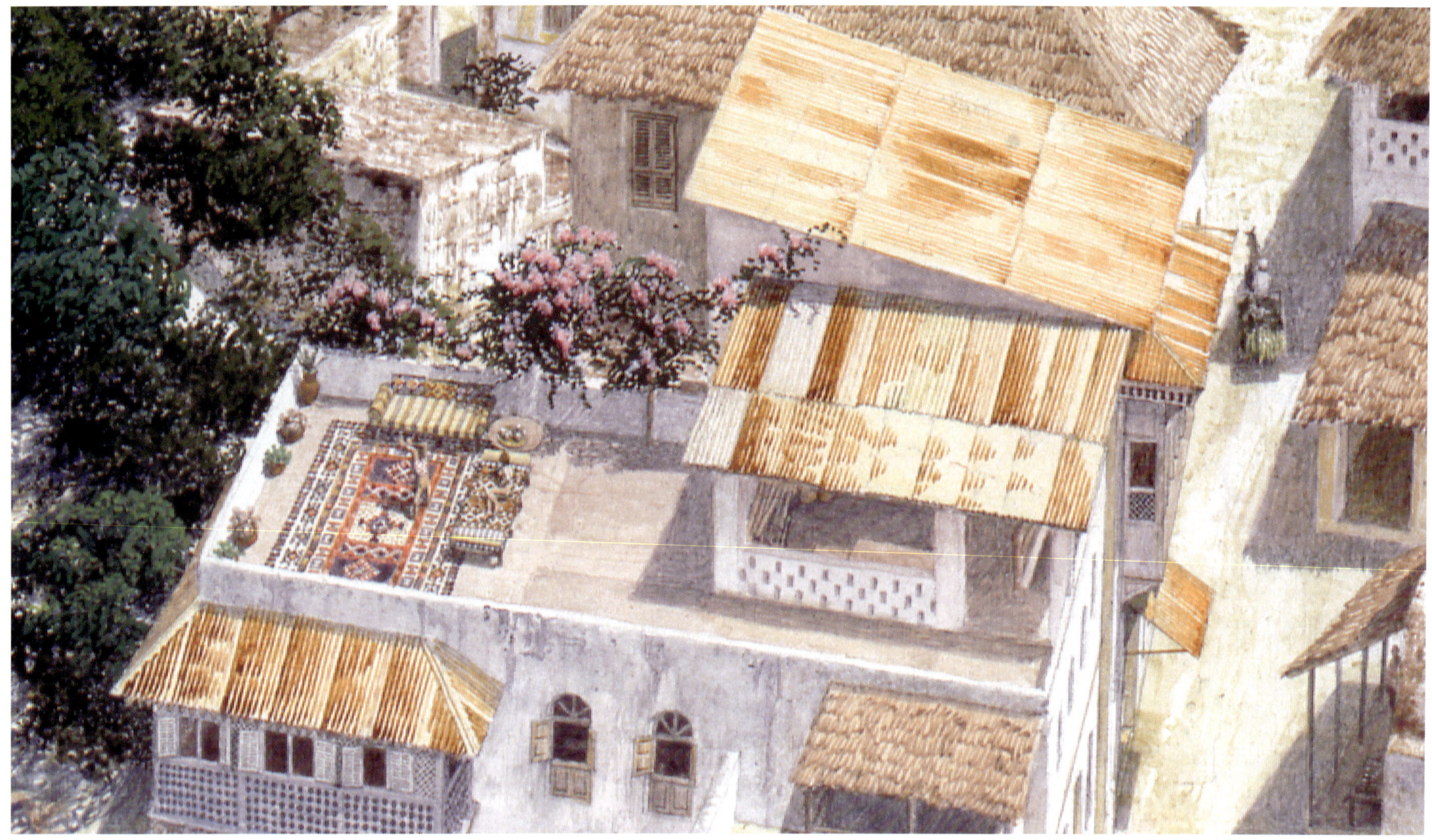

Coasting

Acrylic, 127 x 137 cm, 1998/99

Exhibited: Everard Read Gallery, Johannesburg, 1999

To conserve fuel and cool engines our "North Sea" drifts in a gentle off shore breeze. A course adjustment sees us passing slowly over a small fortified island settlement. A break in the reef allows access to a small harbour with dhows and fishing boats.

The populace below are just beginning to notice the large alien shape coming their way – and thankfully have no fire-arms to hand.

A young man on a carpeted roof terrace impressing his enamorata on an ottoman by doing a handstand, spots us from his inverted position and falls over. Following his gaze the young lady's scream can be heard from up here.

(the strange fence protruding into the lower channel is a fish trap).

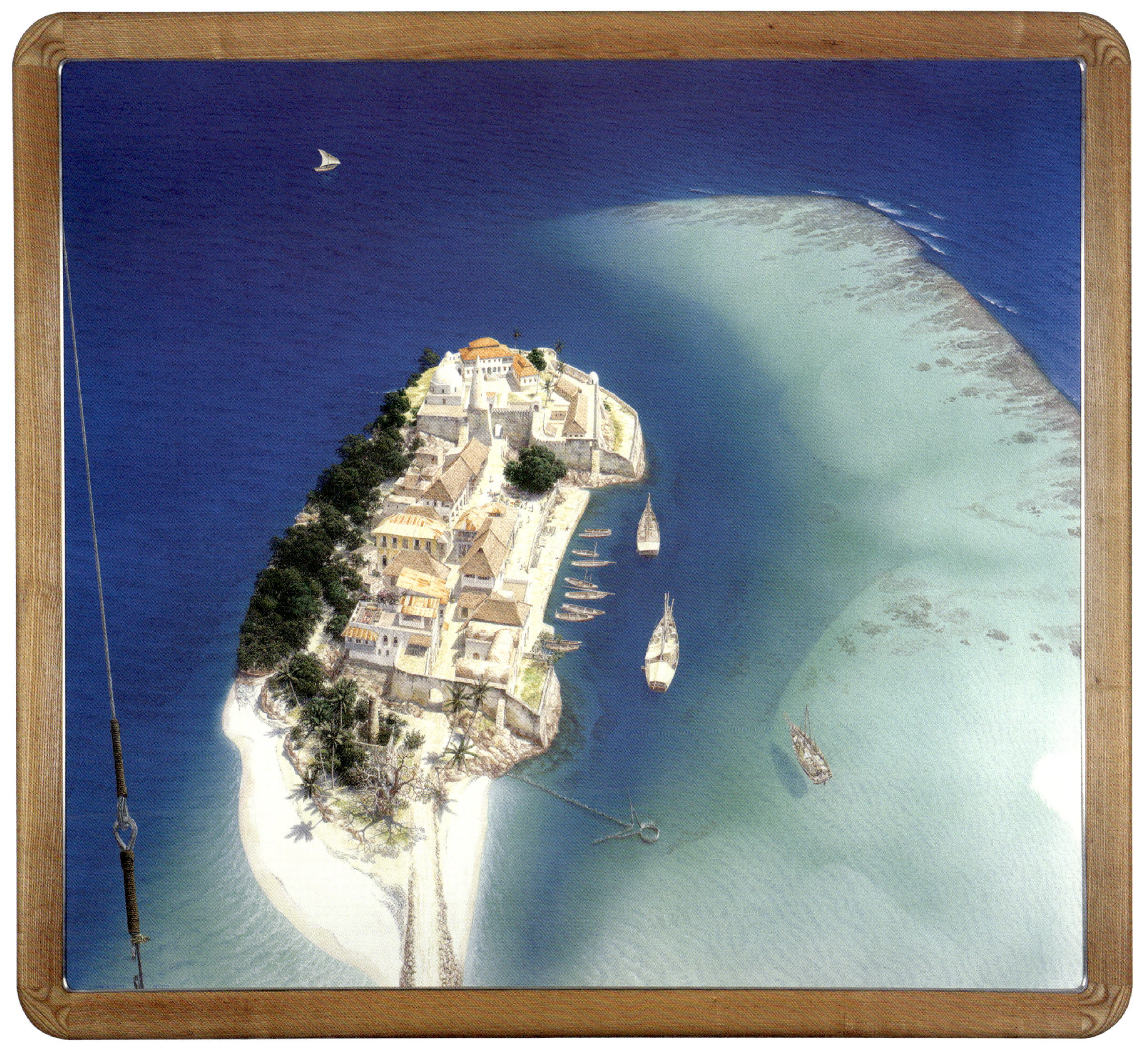

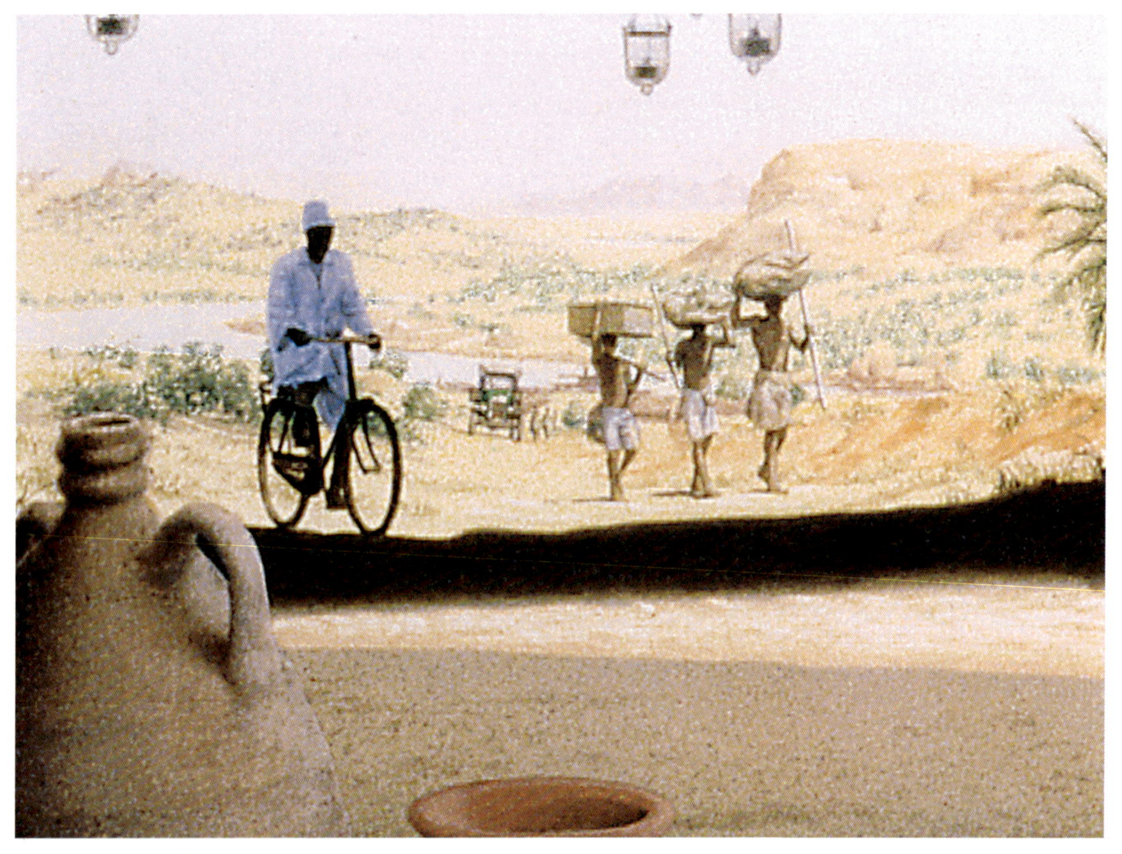

Soko la Pango
Acrylic & mixed media, 127 x 203 x 15 cm framed
1998 & 2000/01. Frame contains "glazed" interfacing cabinets.
Exhibited: Art London Fair, Chelsea, 2001
Everard Read Gallery, Johannesburg, 2001

The Simahali po pote River winds its way between cliffs that in places are riven by old water courses. Here these see service as a subterranean souk. The town above, Soko la Pango, or Cave Market, is divided in two by a deep gulley, or nullah that has become the main thoroughfare.

Commerce is conducted by river and by camel caravan from far and wide and Aladdin's cave could not compare with this for sights, sounds and smells. The many lamps using scented oils make the latter quite heady. And no prizes for spotting the visitor from "Casablanca" up in the "Star Chamber". (Thus named for its ceiling pattern).

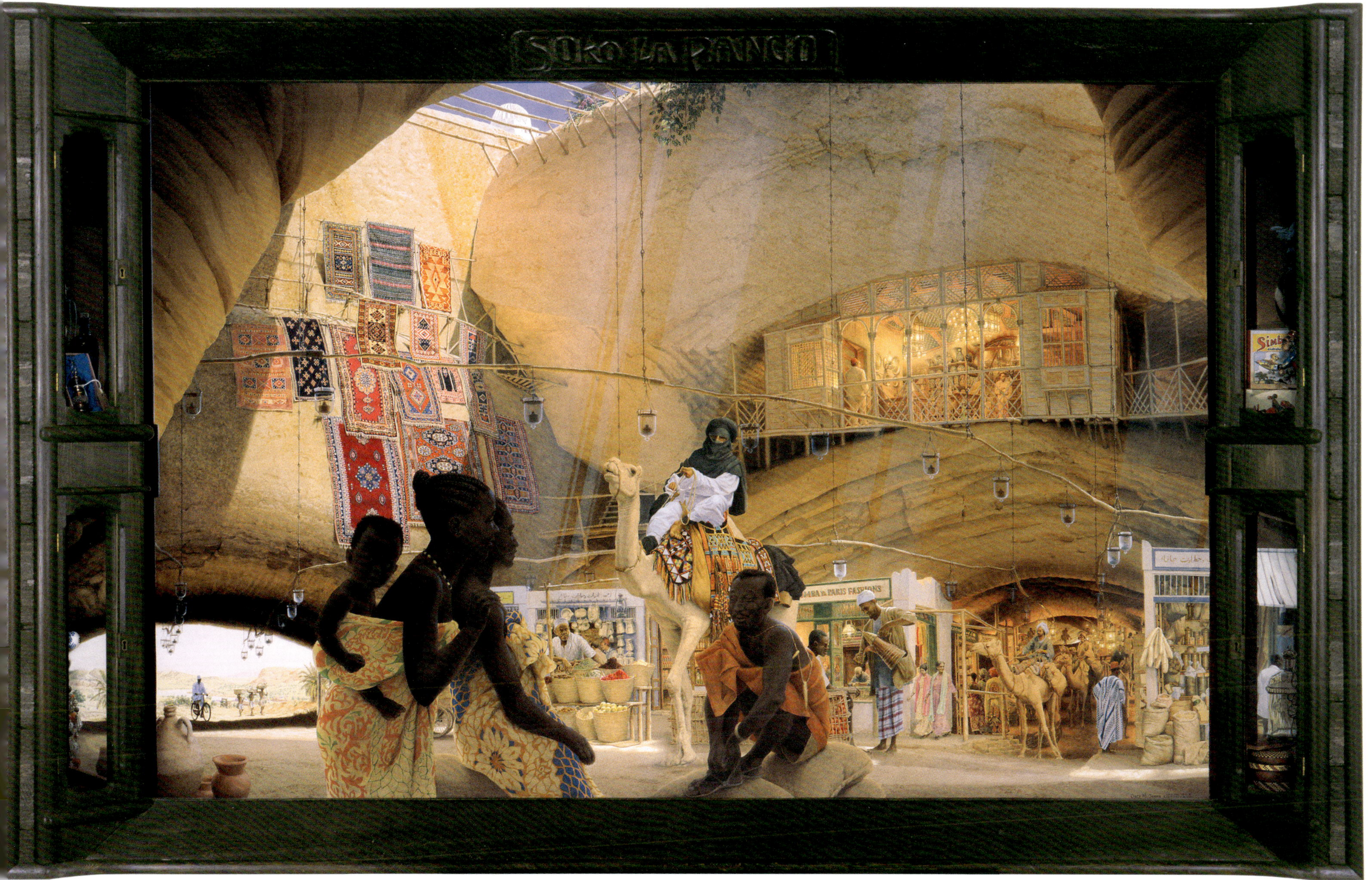
SOKO LA PANGO
PARIS FASHIONS

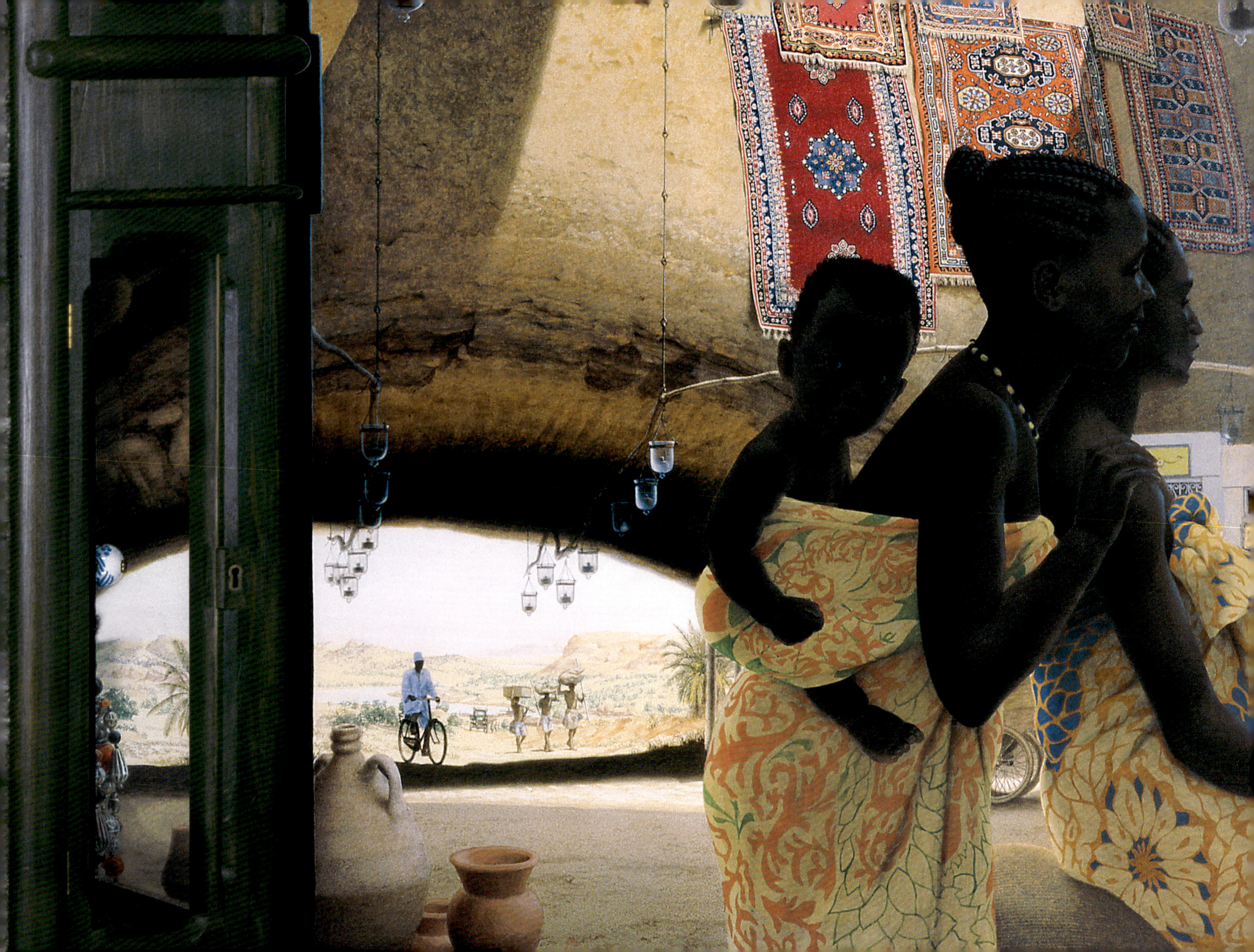

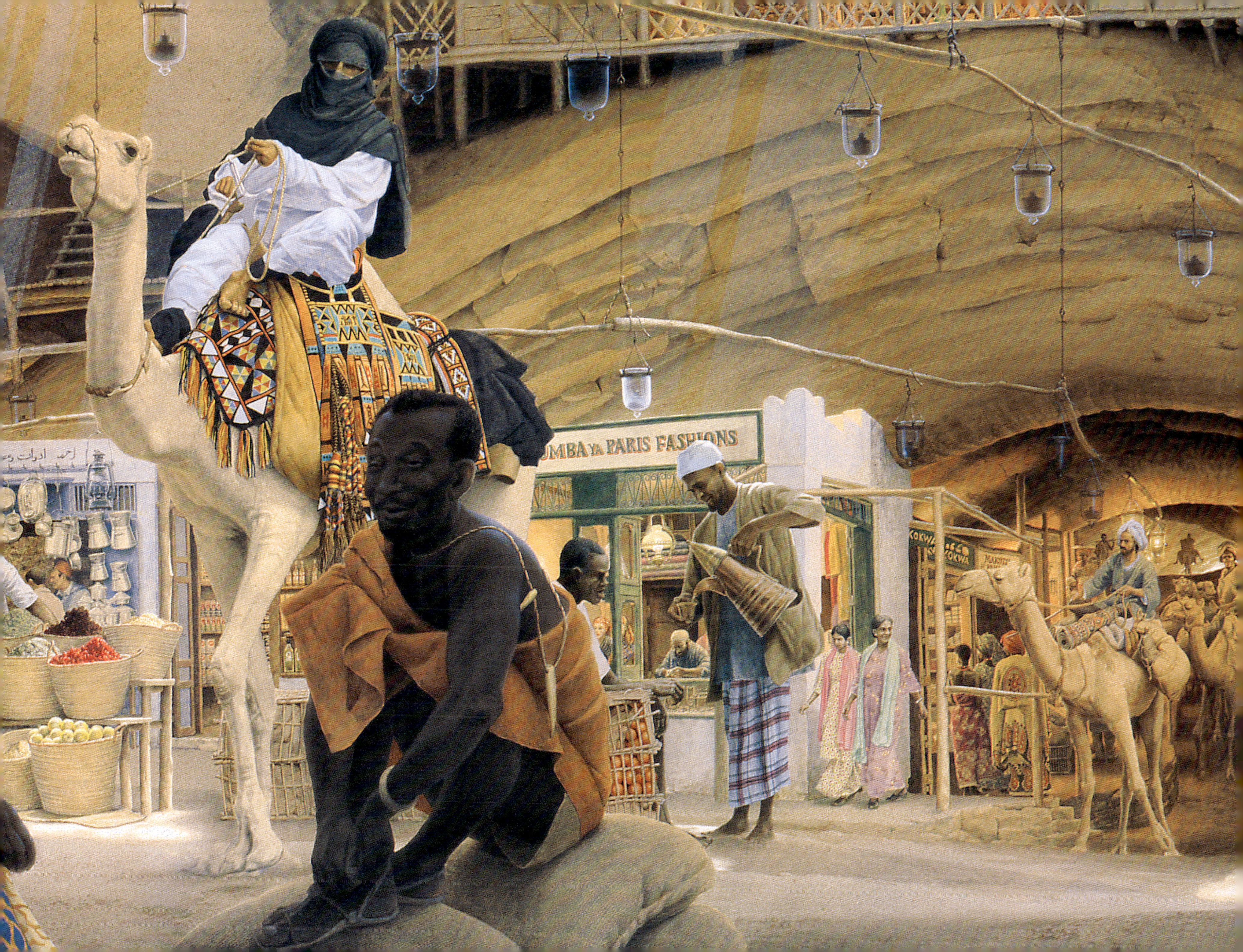
UMBA YA PARIS FASHIONS
KOKWA

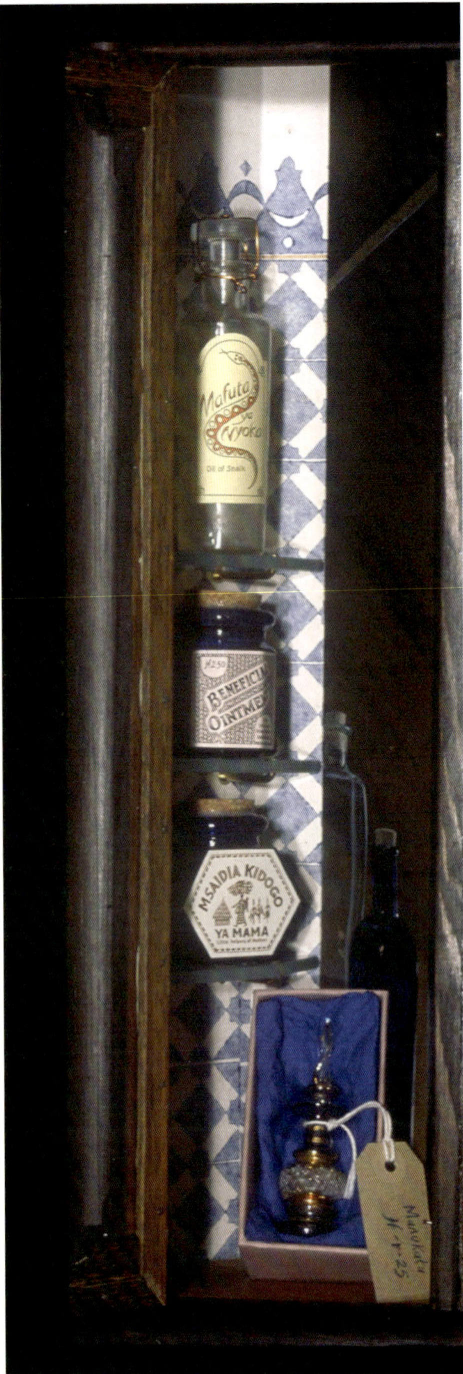

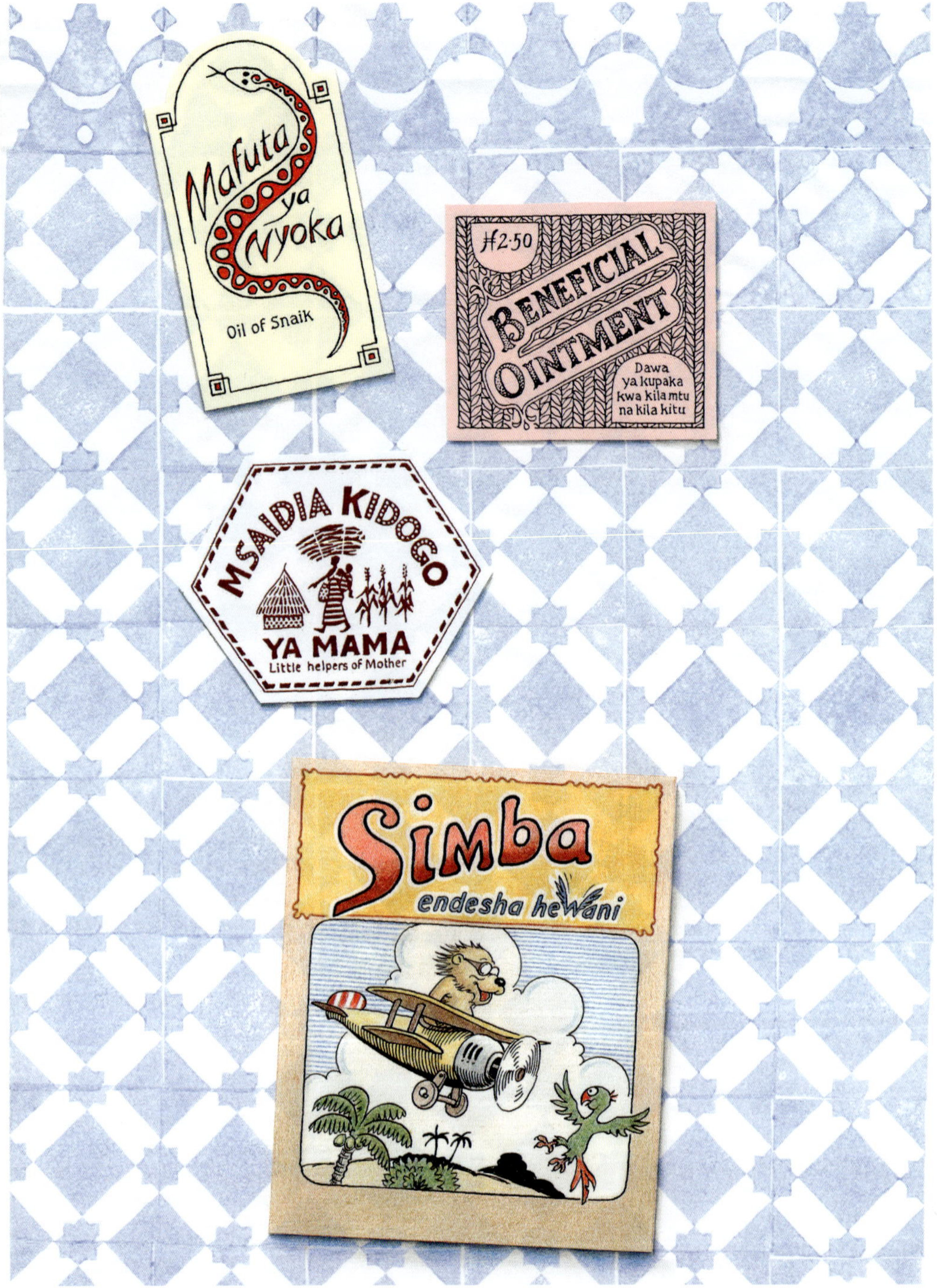

Mafuta ya Nyoka

Oil of Snaik

H2·50

BENEFICIAL OINTMENT

Dawa ya kupaka kwa kila mtu na kila kitu

MSAIDIA KIDOGO YA MAMA

Little helpers of Mother

Simba

endesha hewani

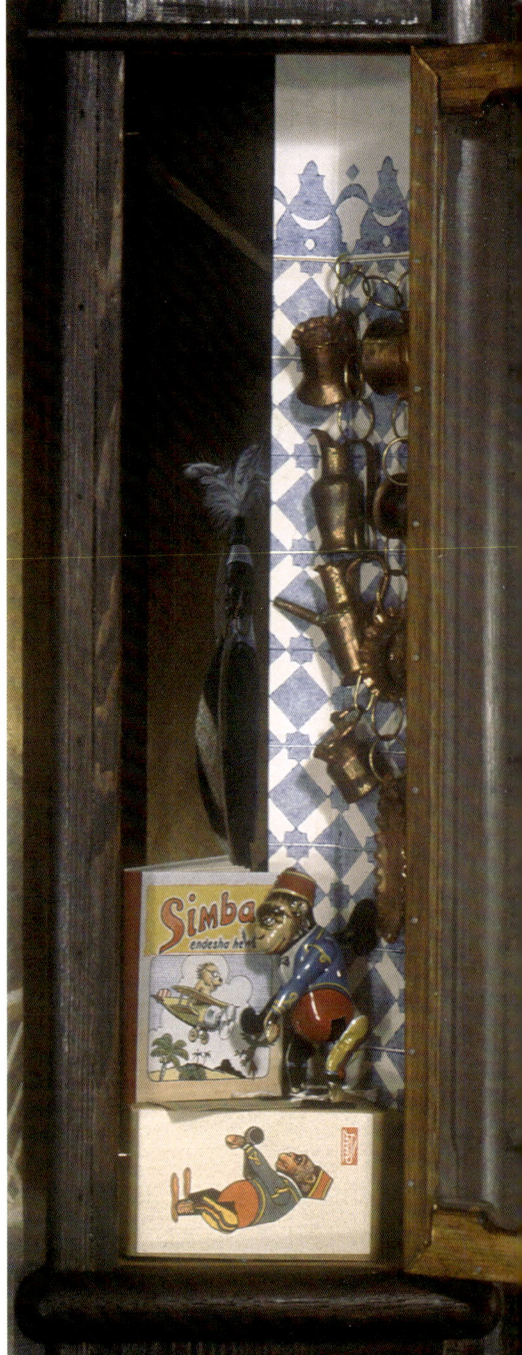

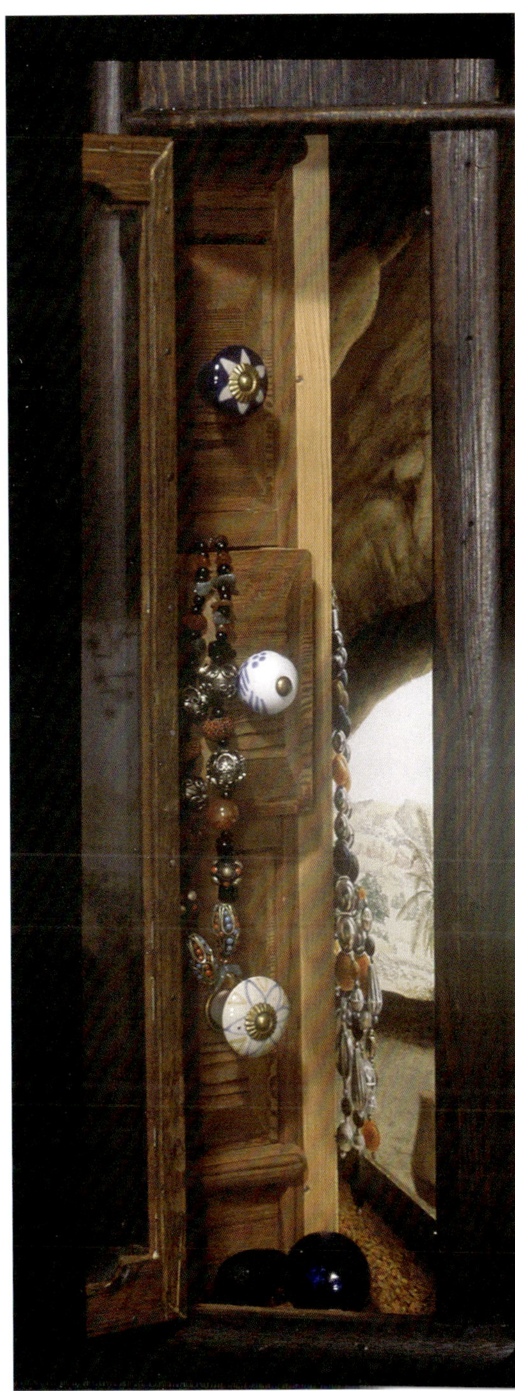

CONTENTS OF THE 'GLAZED' CABINETS

The cabinets bracket our view. The photographs were taken before the doors were 'locked'.

TOP CABINETS
(left hand page)

Far left
MEDICINES
"Mafuta ya Nyoka"(snake oil)

"Beneficial Ointment" –
Q – Beneficial for what?
A – What have you got?

"Msaidia Kidogo ya Mama"
(Mother's little helpers)

Bottle of perfume
(from Assuan. Full at closure)

All 3D

Right (on left hand page)
TOYS
Miniature brass & copper pots and pans.

Carved warrior (2D)

Clockwork tin plate toy monkey

A tiny book for tots, "Lion goes flying"
Quote:
"Aark" squawks Perkins the parrot. "Lions isn't for flying!"

BOTTOM CABINETS
(this page)

Left
JEWELLERY
(contents of drawers 'unknown')

Necklaces
(from India. 2D & 3D)

Perfume bottle
with bulb sprayer

Right
TRINKETS
(contents of drawers 'unknown')

Ornamental scent bottle with silver filigree.
(Afganistan? 2D)

Tin, clad in ornamental woven leather.
(West Africa – carved and painted wood.
3D & 2D)

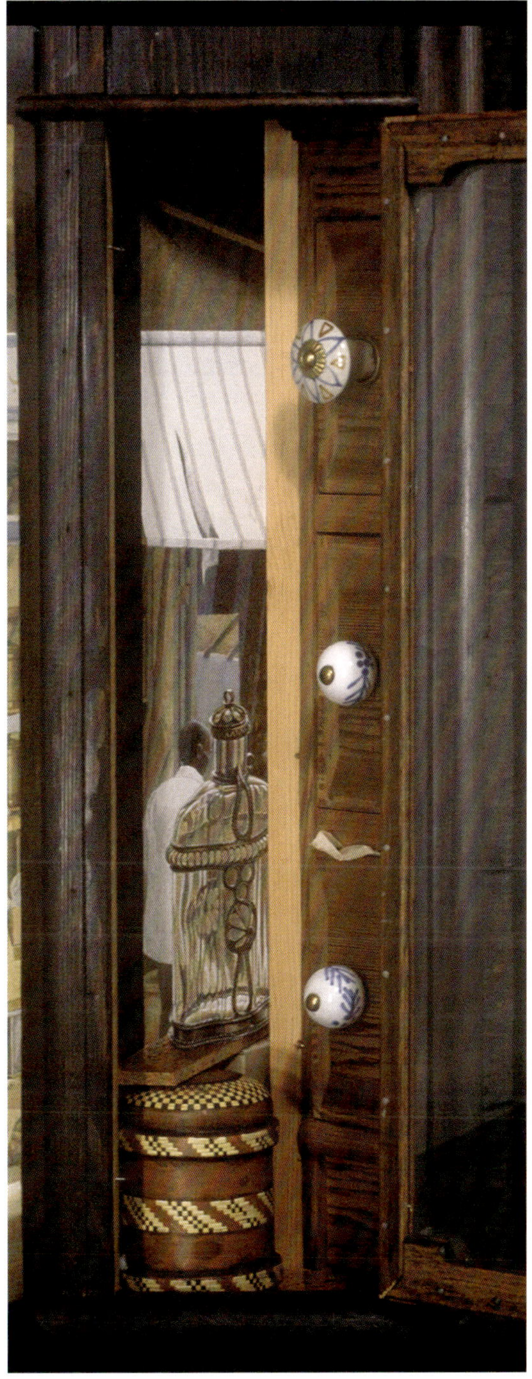

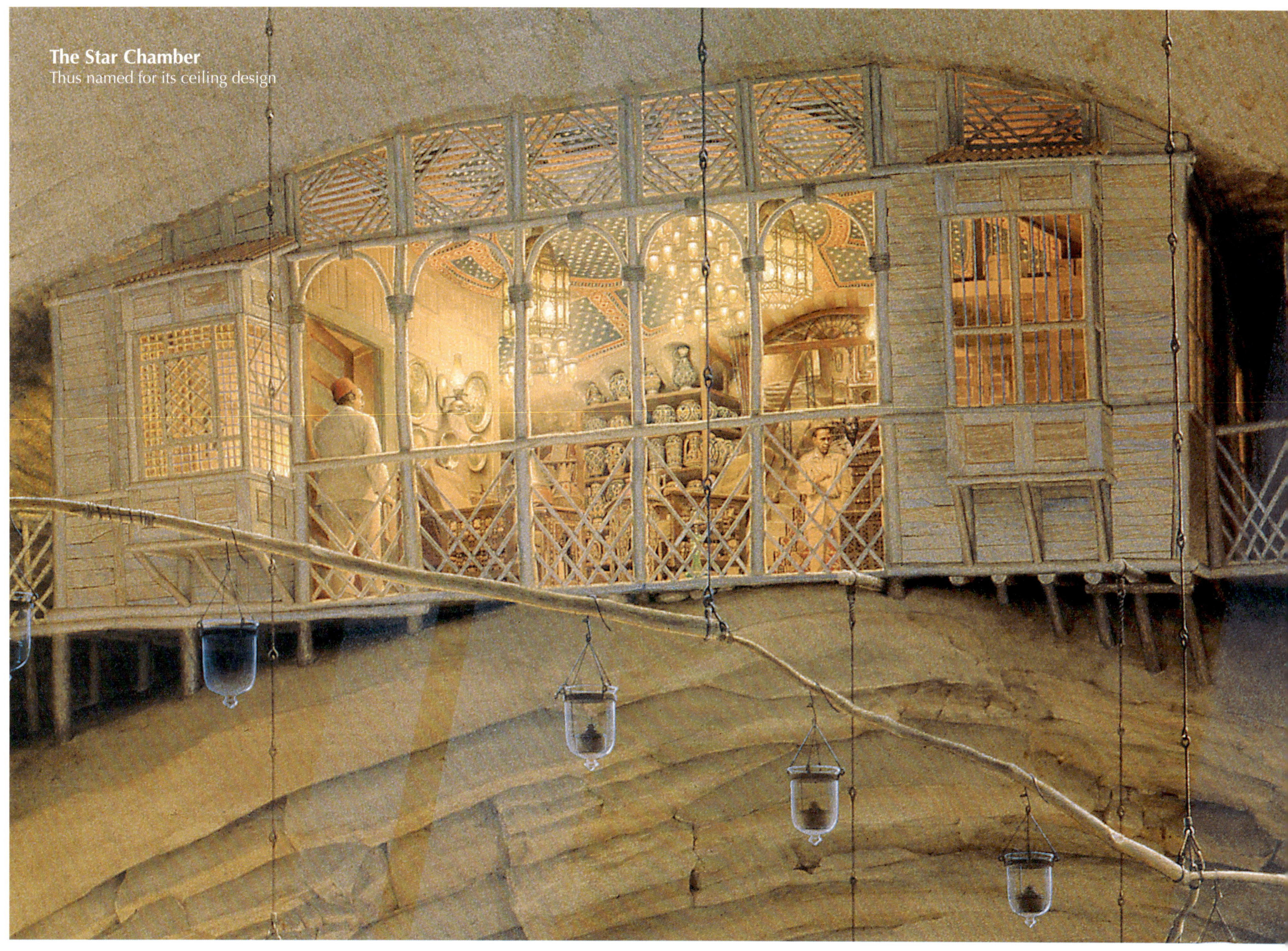

The Star Chamber
Thus named for its ceiling design

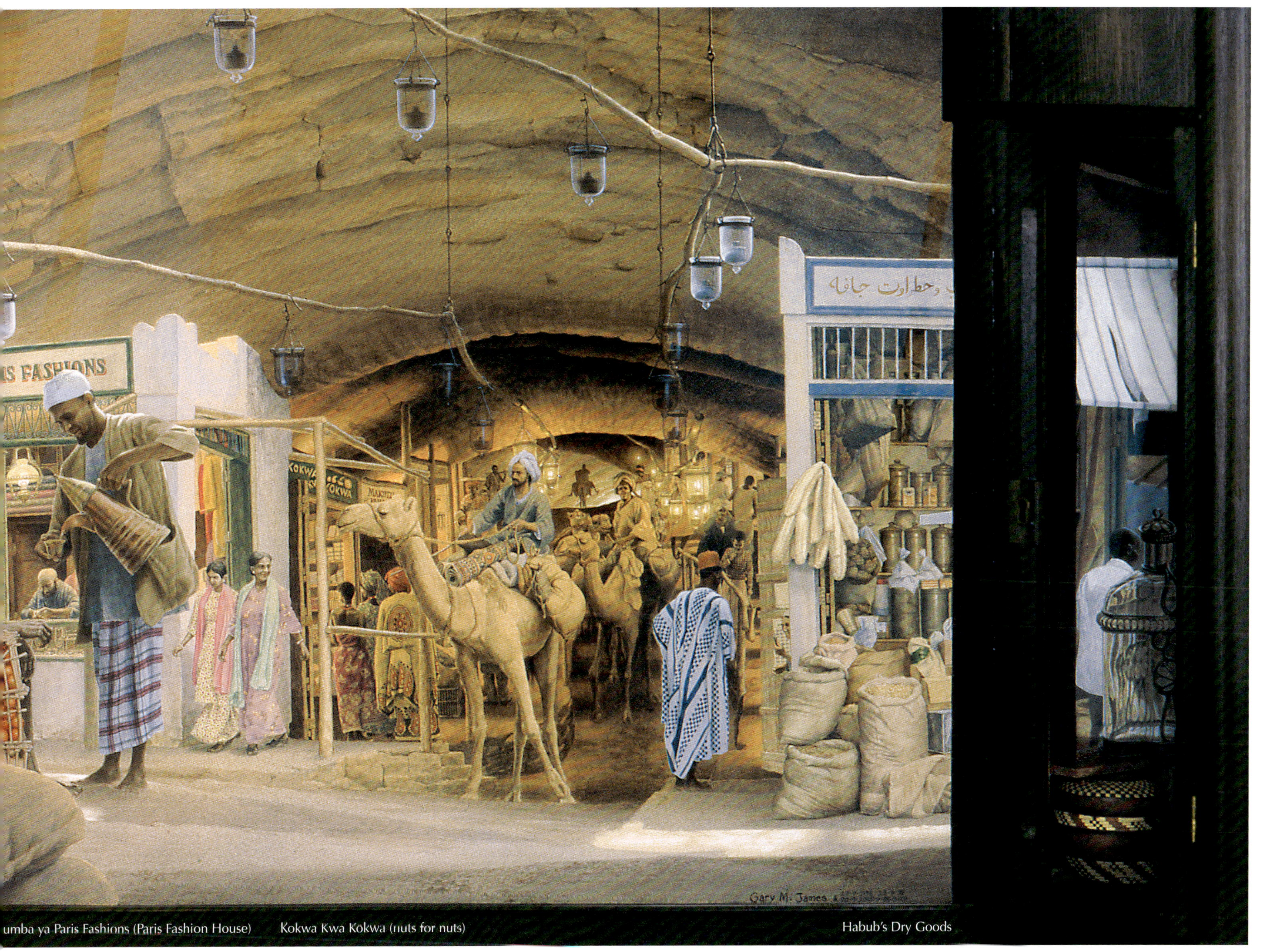

umba ya Paris Fashions (Paris Fashion House) Kokwa Kwa Kokwa (nuts for nuts) Habub's Dry Goods

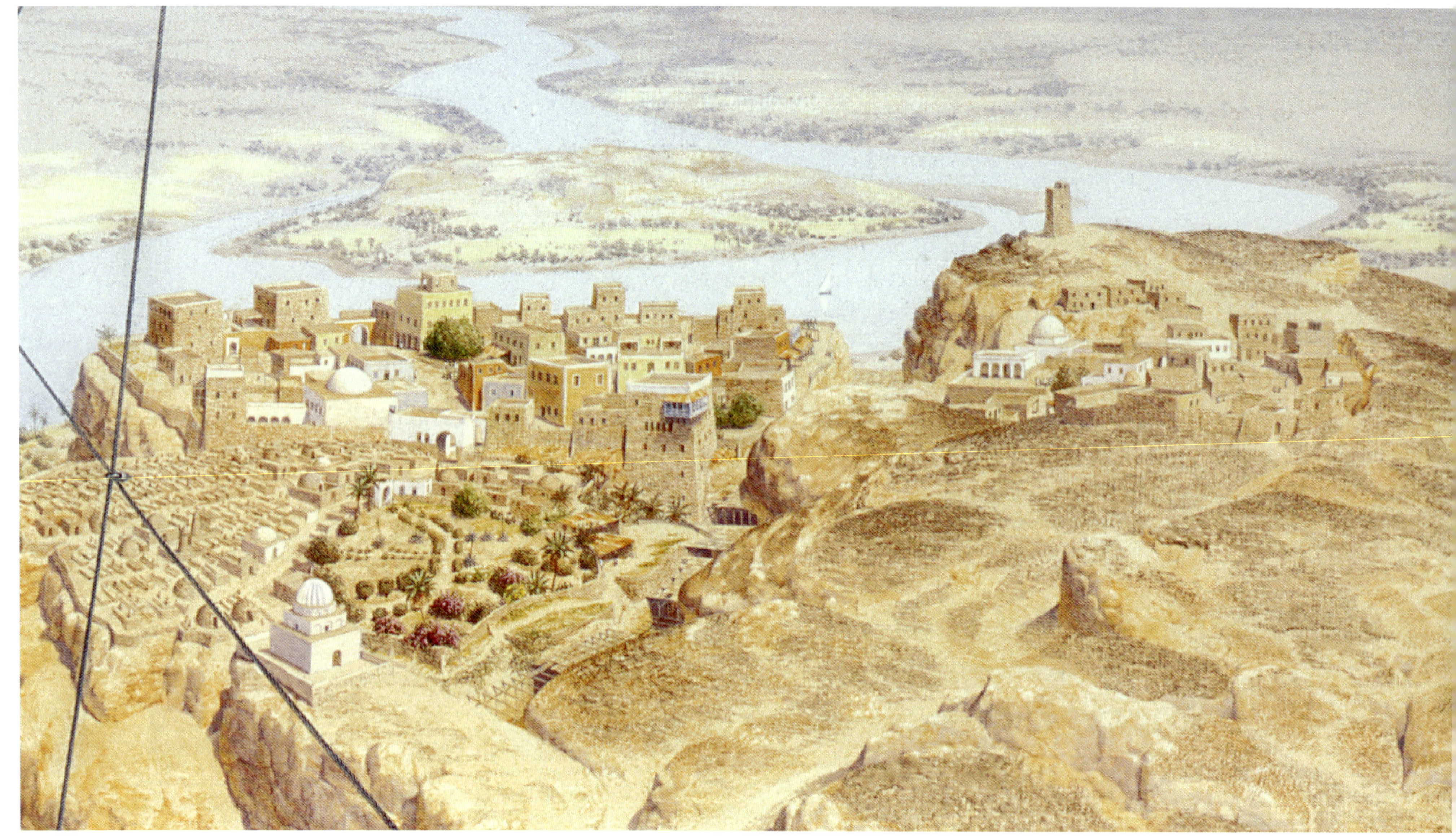

Following the Simahali po pote

(Soko la Pango beneath)

Acrylic, 101.5 x 152.5 cm, 2001/02

Exhibited: Everard Read Gallery, Johannesburg, 2002

Cockpit crew: The artist's older son Patrick (Patch) fore, younger son Alex aft.

Our "North Sea" approaches Soko la Pango with engines turned off, silently, upwind so as not to provoke a rush to arms and to allow friendly vocal overtures. From here one can even hear a shepherd's smoker's cough.

Engines will be restarted to come about once beyond the town and bags deployed for a water mooring by an island there. Best to allow delegations by boat rather than face a concerted rush.

(Note to go with detail). There is a side spur off the main nullah, below the central tower with the blue painted mashraffiyya balcony. Opposite this, set into the cliff face is a rather novel establishment – The Café Souk, that features in the next painting.

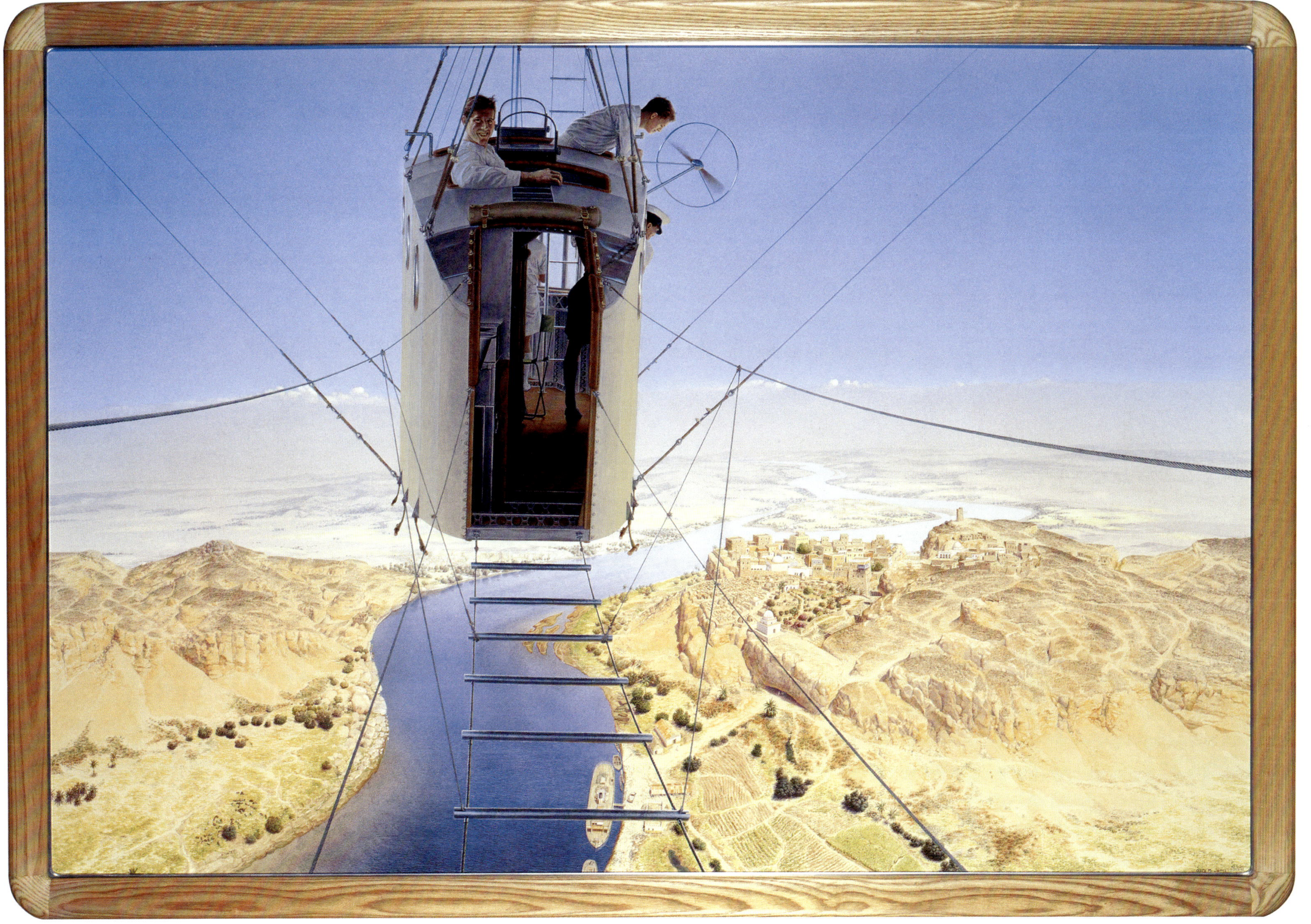

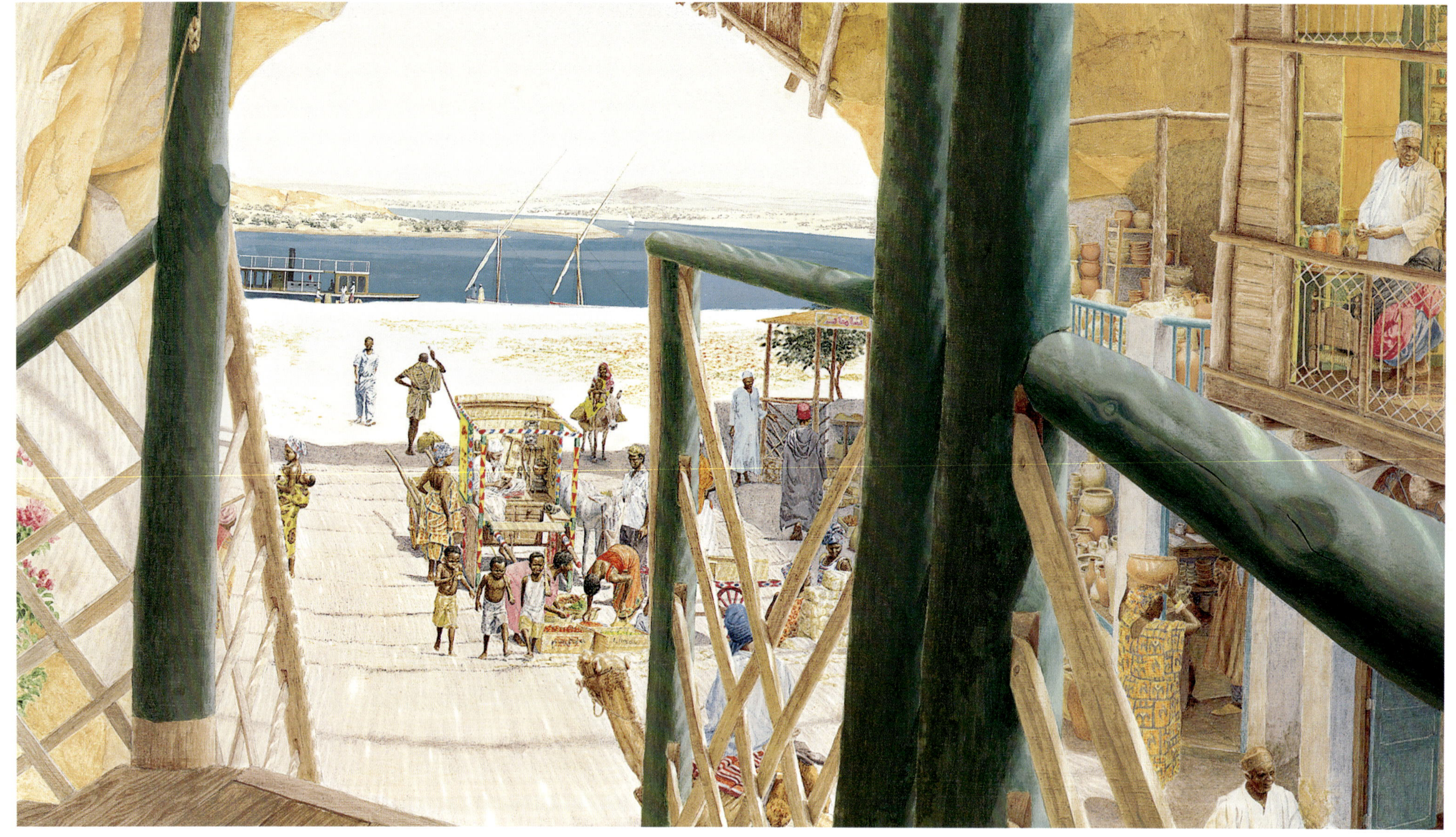

At the Café Souk

Acrylic, cedar & pinewood, 124.5 x 185.5 x 12.5 cm framed. 2003/04
Exhibited: Everard Read Gallery, Johannesburg, 2004

And here it is. Welcome to the Café Souk. It's a bit of a climb up the rickety staircase beneath the papyrus stem sun screens but the Turkish coffee and the sweet meats are highly recommended.

A local and a visiting Tuareg exchange comments regarding the antics of a strange group in the far pavilion (who would be no strangers to enthusiasts of Hollywood comedies of the 1930s and '40s.

But here comes a crewman in blue overalls approaching the Bab al Sud, or South Gate, to conduct us to the river boat "Le Douanier Rousseau", seen moored at the river bank beyond. River market is about two week's steaming up stream and unlike at the Café Souk wine or beer will be served with lunch after going about.

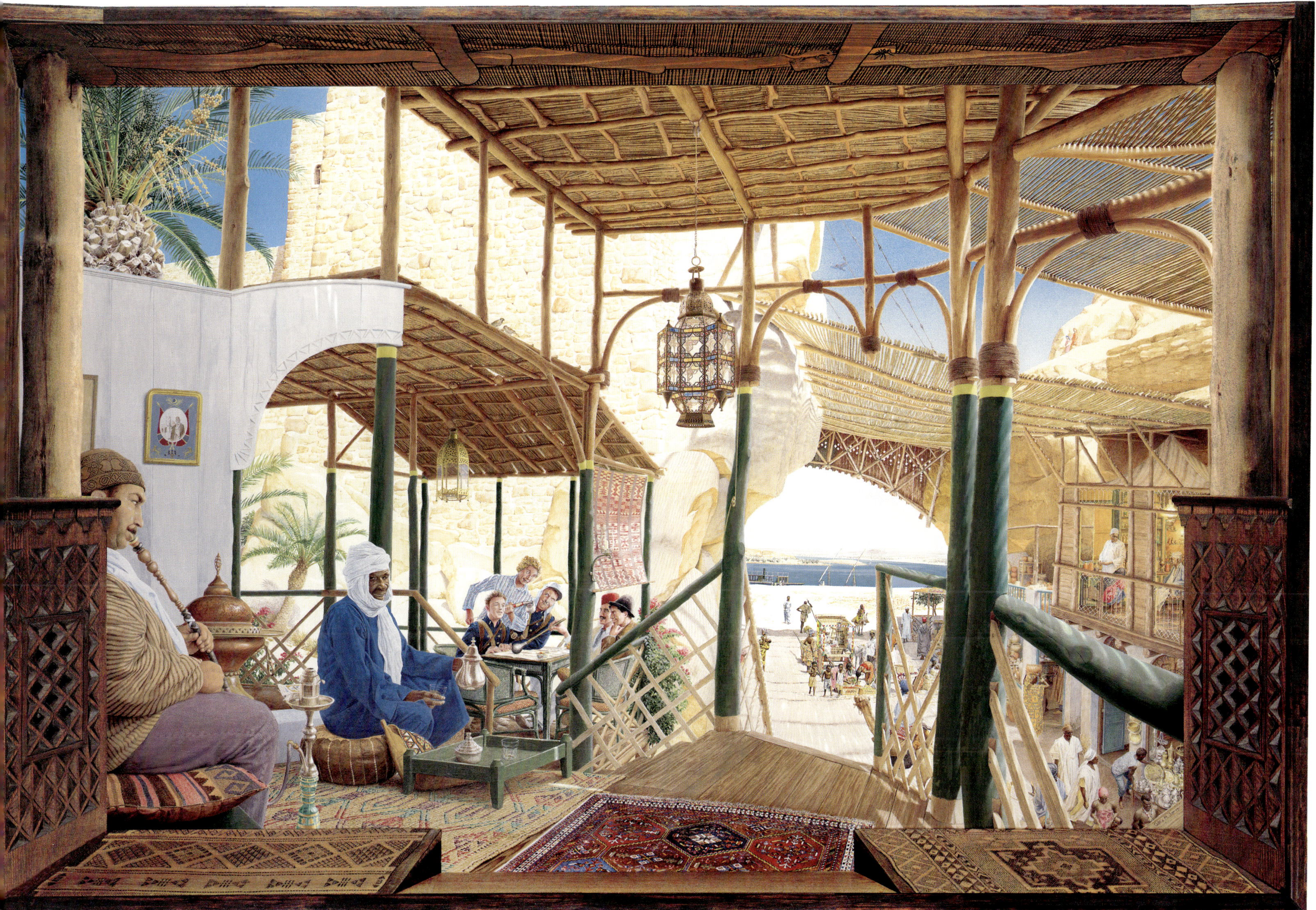

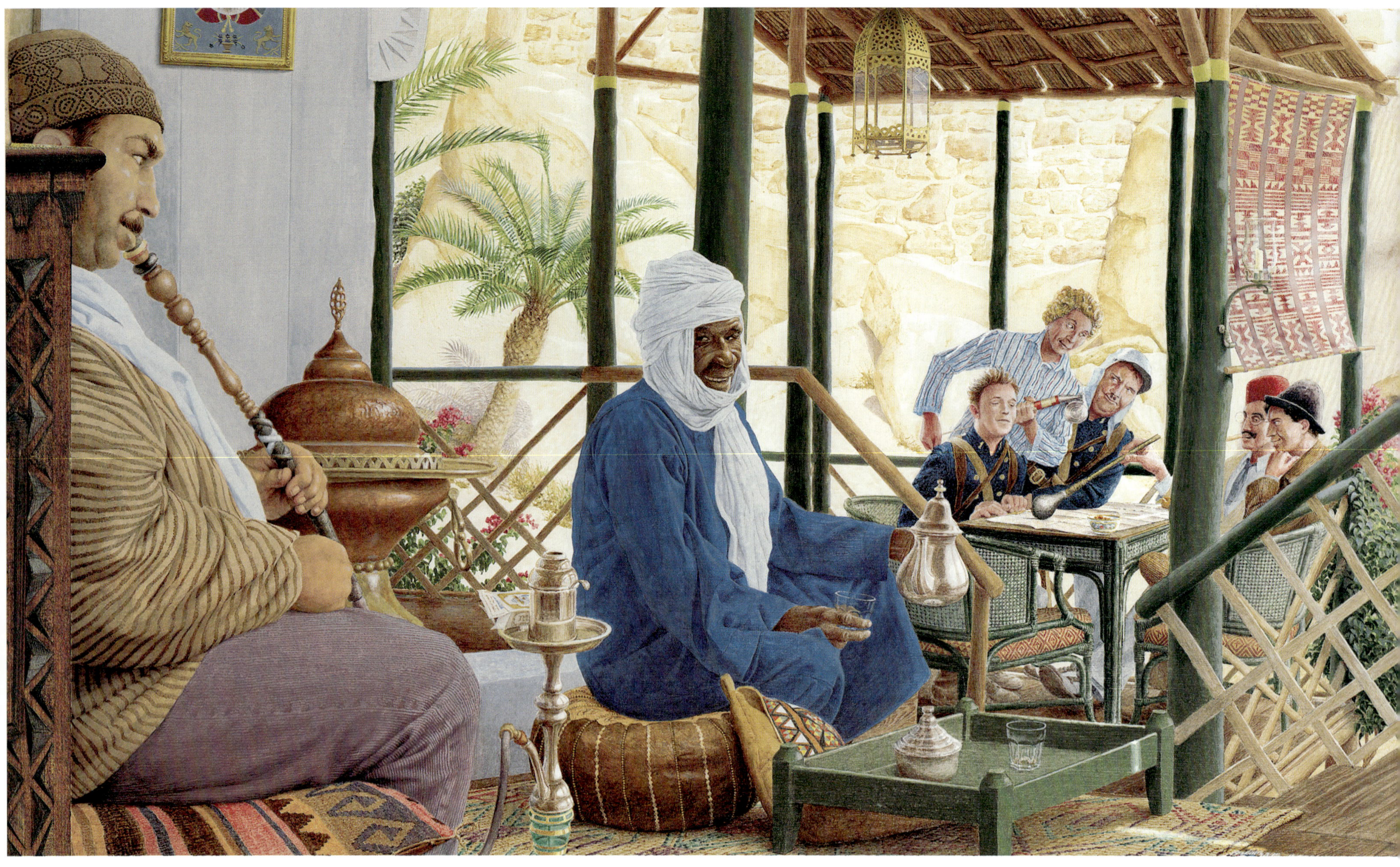

A shishah smoker exchanges banter with a tea drinking Tuareg regarding the strange antics of a group of strangers on the adjacent balcony.

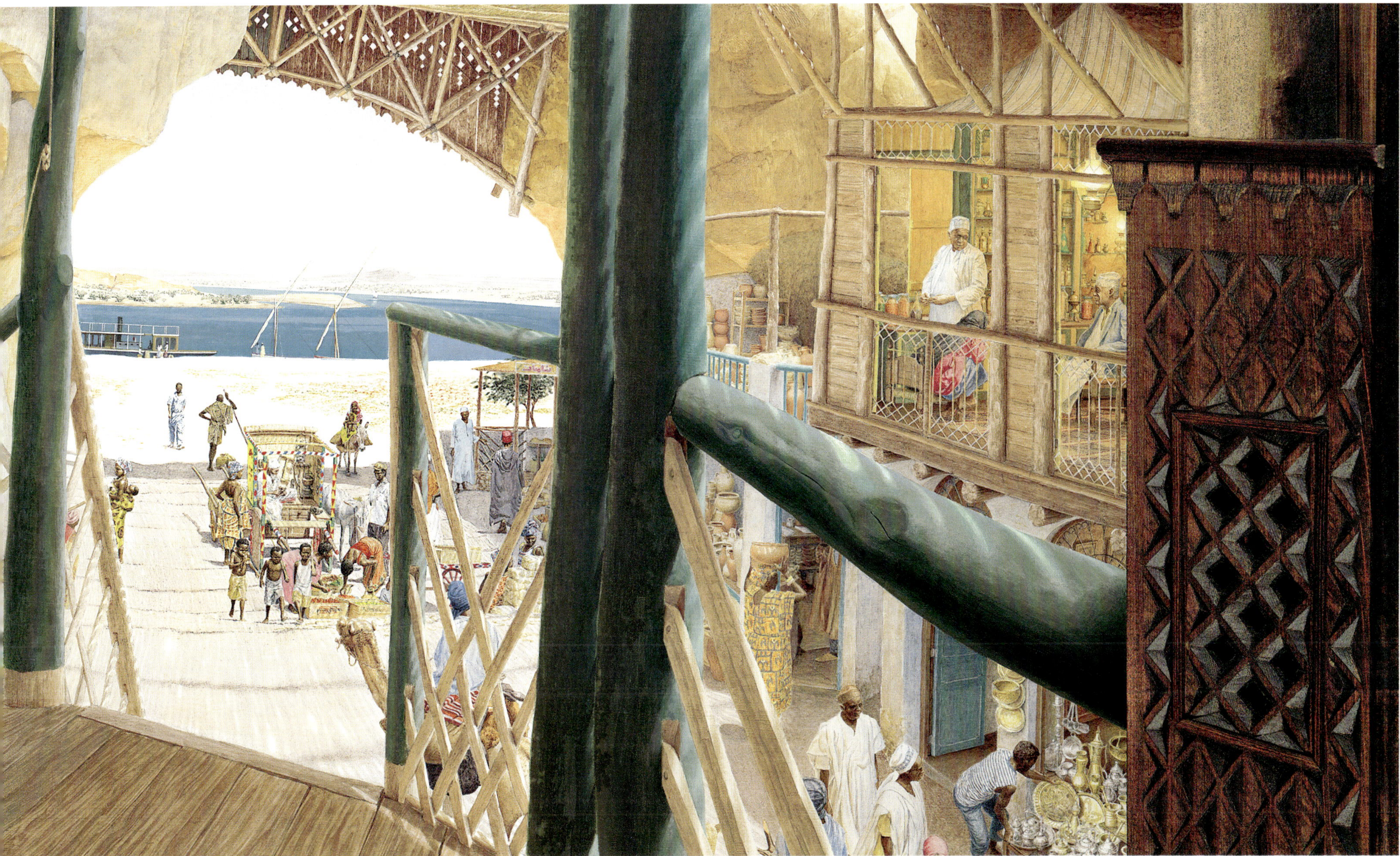

The Douanier Rousseau takes on stores

A peripatetic fundi (craftsman) makes repairs in his workshop cart

Three small boys think they're an army

An askari's guard post

A pot shop

Above – Customers sample the wares in an upstairs apothecary/perfumery.
Below – No need to call the askari – he is an employee straightening the metalwork display, not a shoplifter.

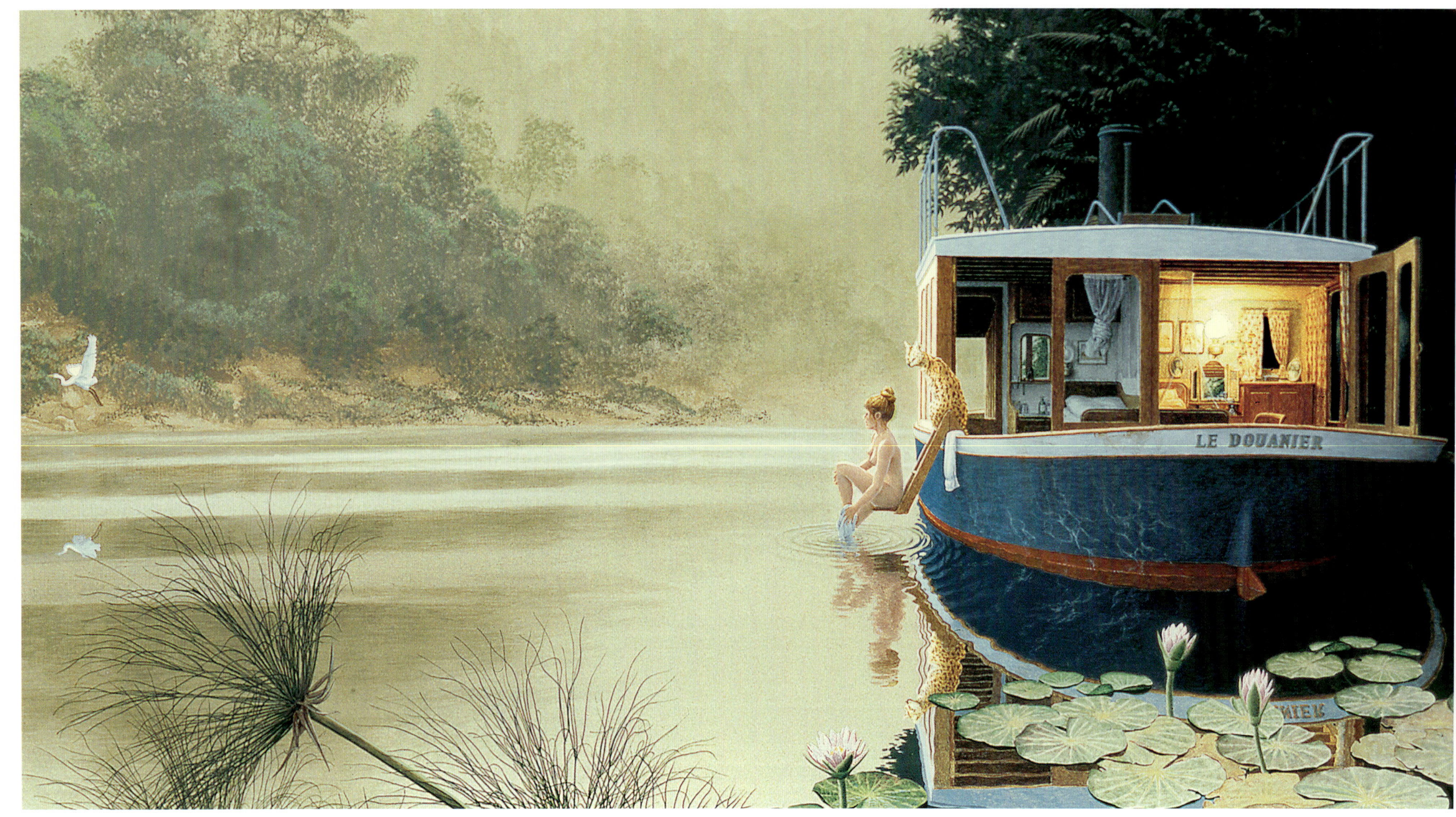

Dawn on Le Douanier ...
Acrylic & cedarwood, 91.5 x 152.5 cm 2002
Exhibited: Everard Read Gallery, Johannesburg, 2003

Artist's note:
"Le Douanier Rousseau" is named in honour of Henri Rousseau, naïve genius painter of tropical jungles in 1900s Paris. Friend to the more famous modernists who nicknamed him "Le Douanier", he had the advantage of never having been nearer to a tropical jungle than the Jardin des Plantes in Paris.

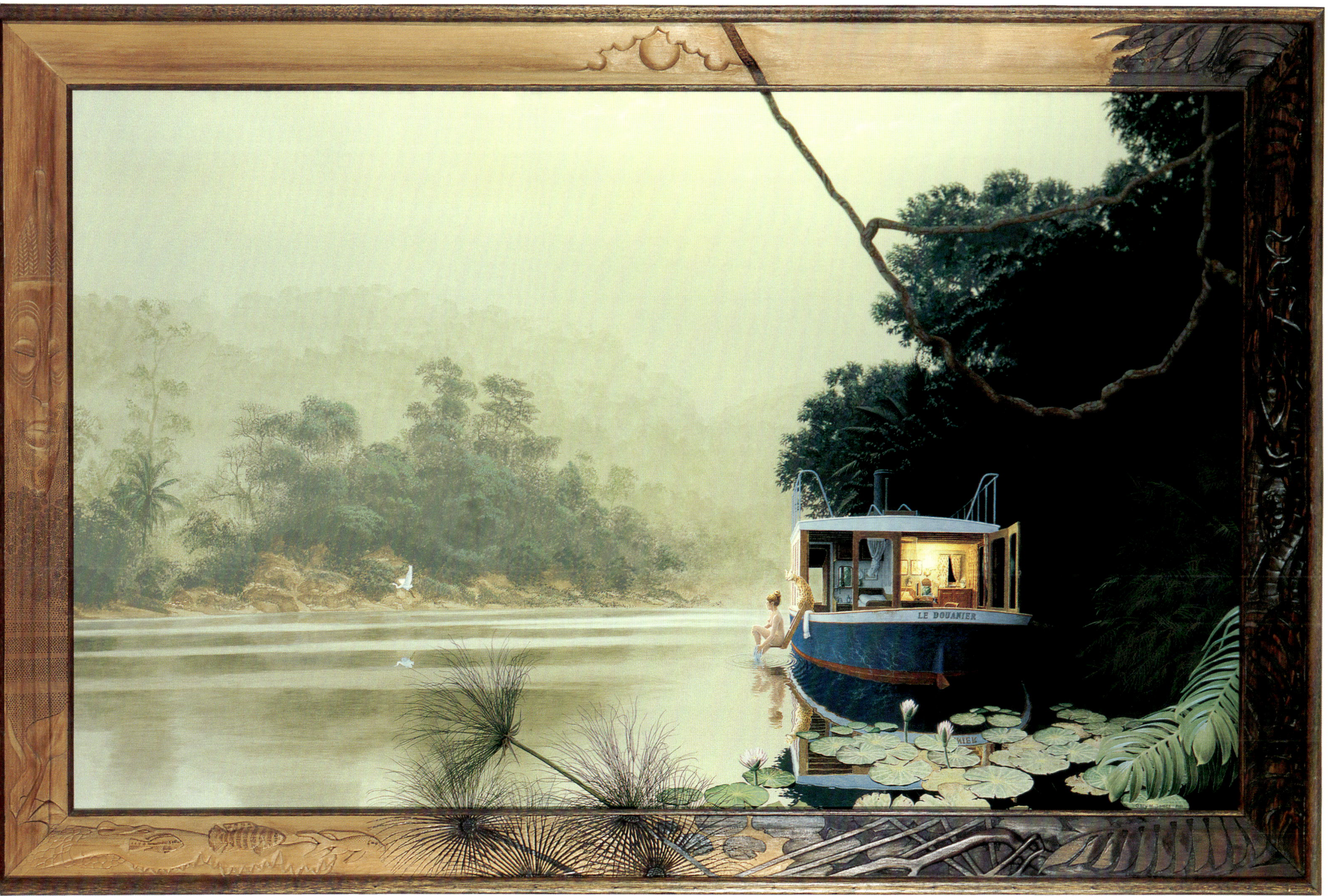
LE DOUANIER

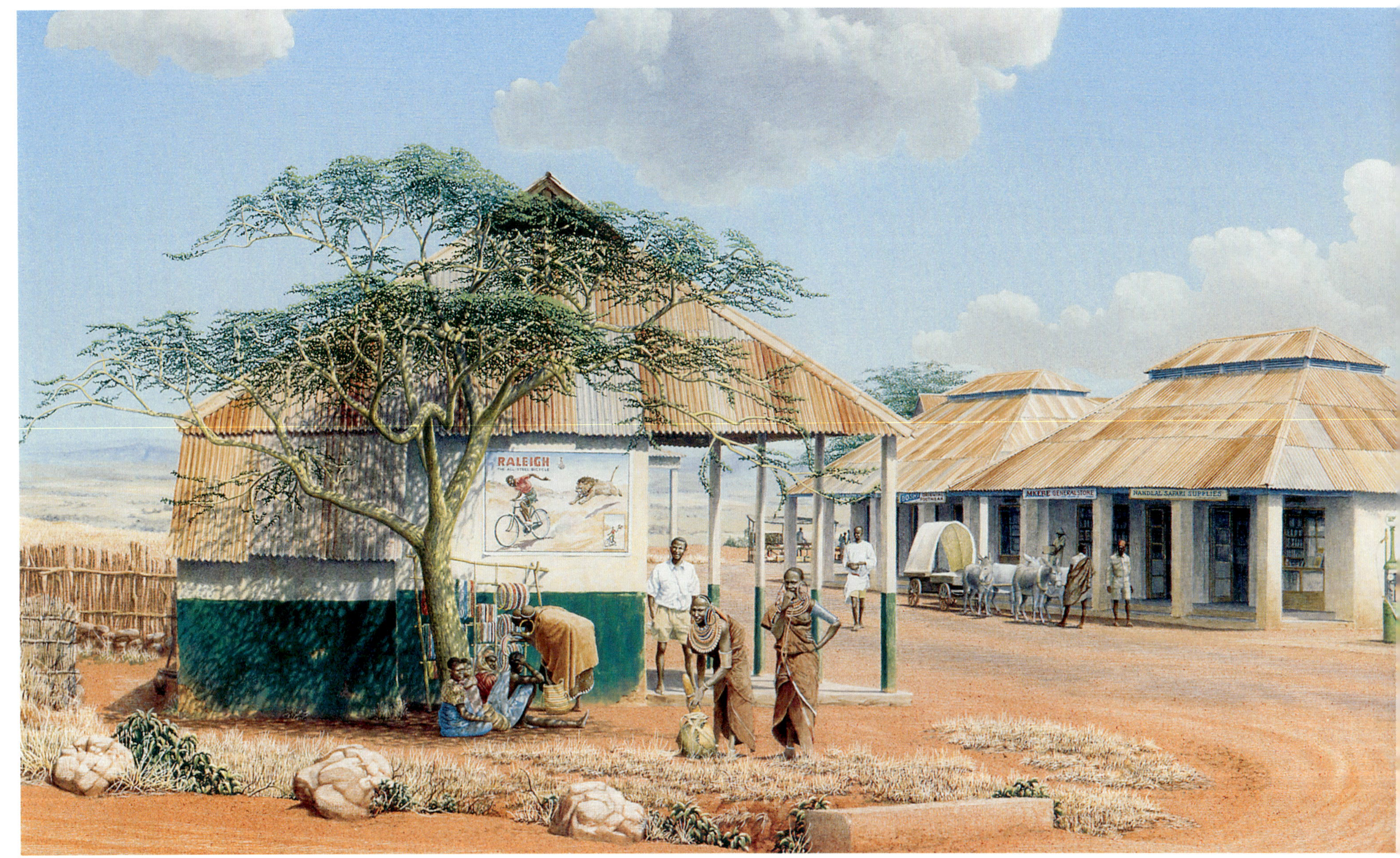

The Cowboys come to town
Acrylic & cedarwood, 93.5 x 139 cm framed, 2004/05
Exhibited: Everard Read Gallery, Johannesburg, 2005

A cattle ranching settler gives a lift into the local township to a party of his Masai neighbours. With them he has come to a certain rapprochement whereby they assist with his herding in exchange for a certain number "going missing". Also, cross breeding his Herefords with the Masais' Zebu bulls gives a better yield and more resistance to pests like the tsetse fly.

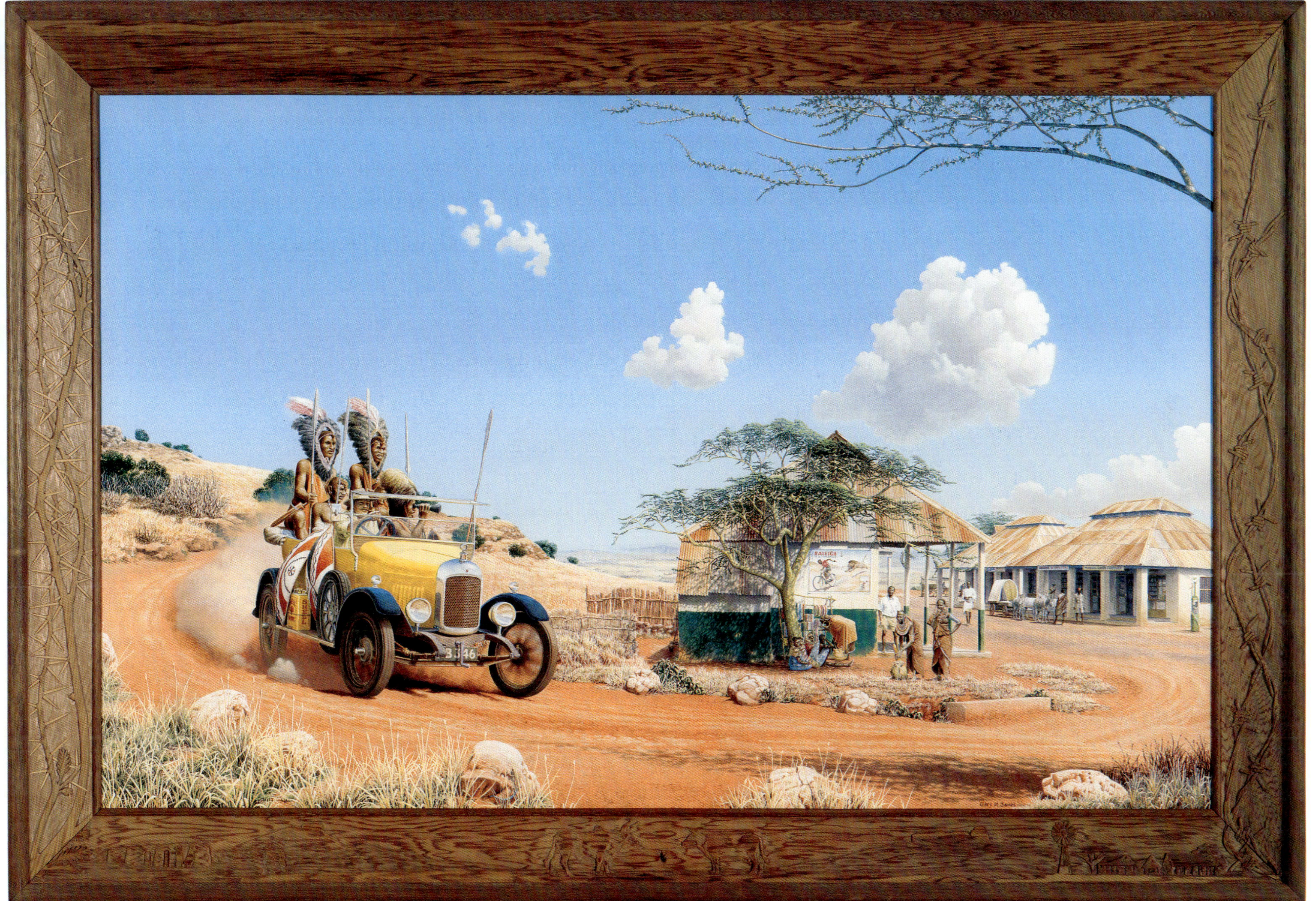
RALEIGH

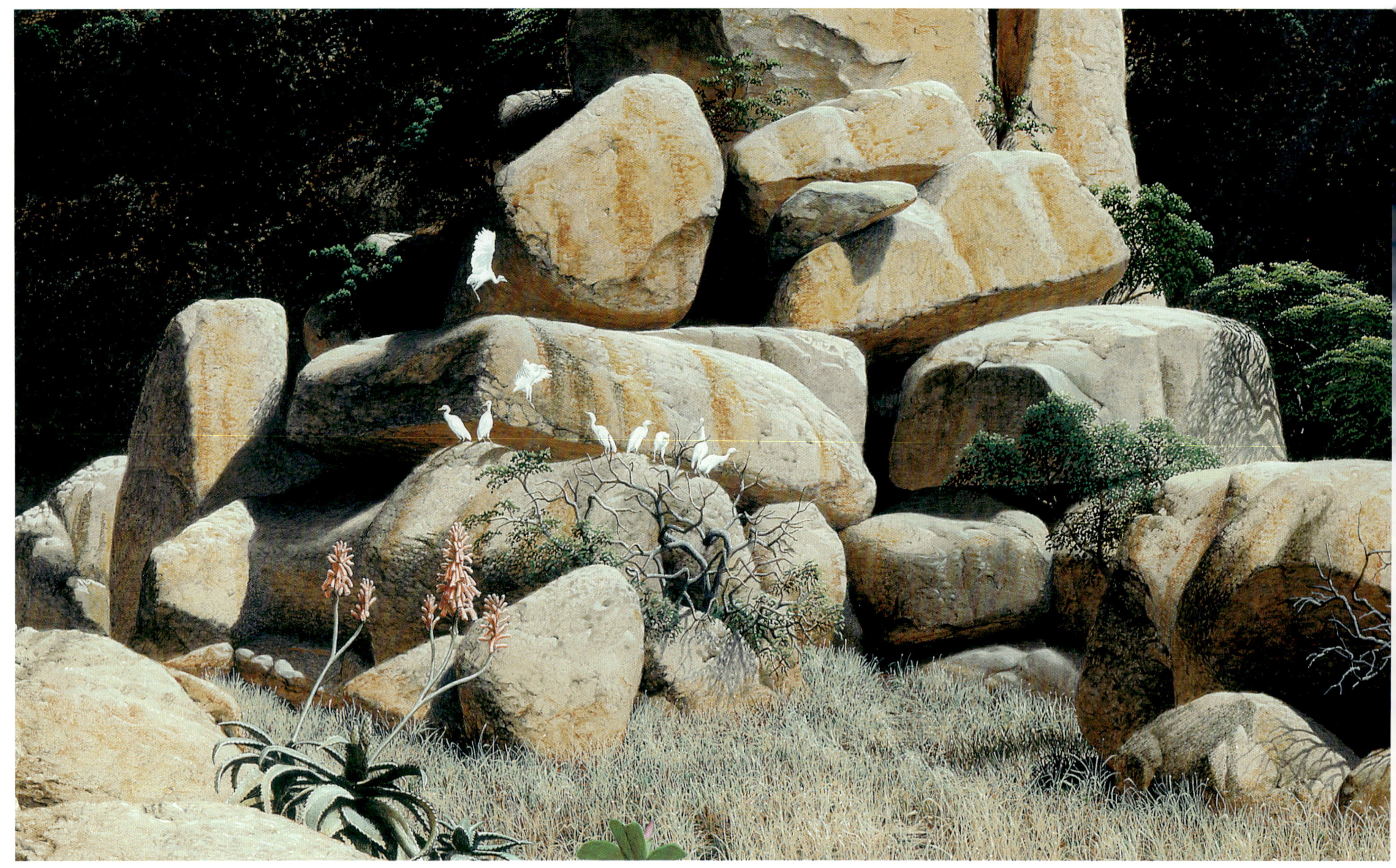

Ivory Tower
Acrylic & cedarwood, 93 x 138 cm framed, 2005/06
Exhibited: Everard Read Gallery, Johannesburg, 2008

An eroded volcanic core makes a modest cenotaph to all those elephants fallen to the hunters' guns. If the egrets congregating on their petrified host's back expect insects to be stirred up by elephantine feet presently, there are none....feet that is.

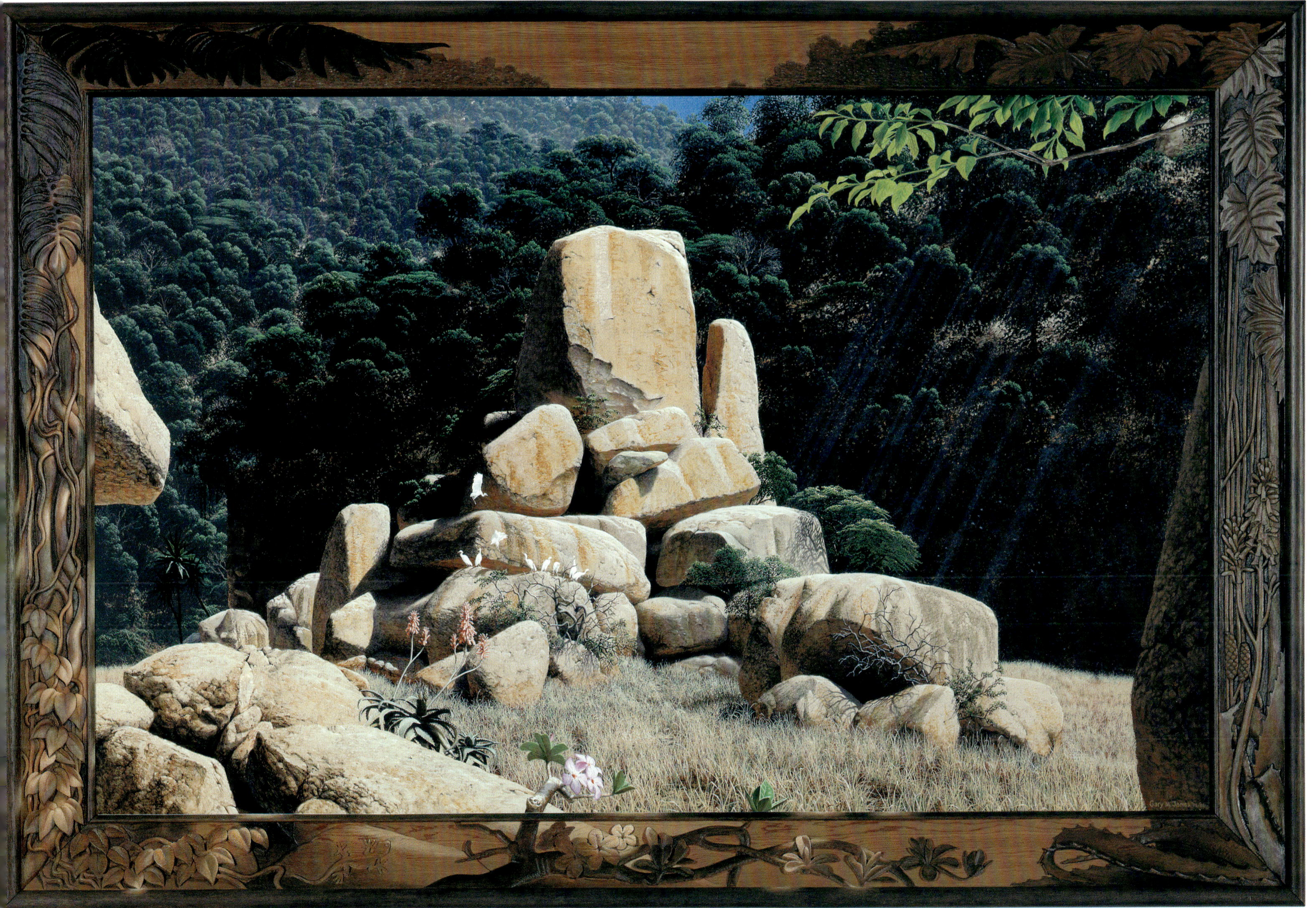

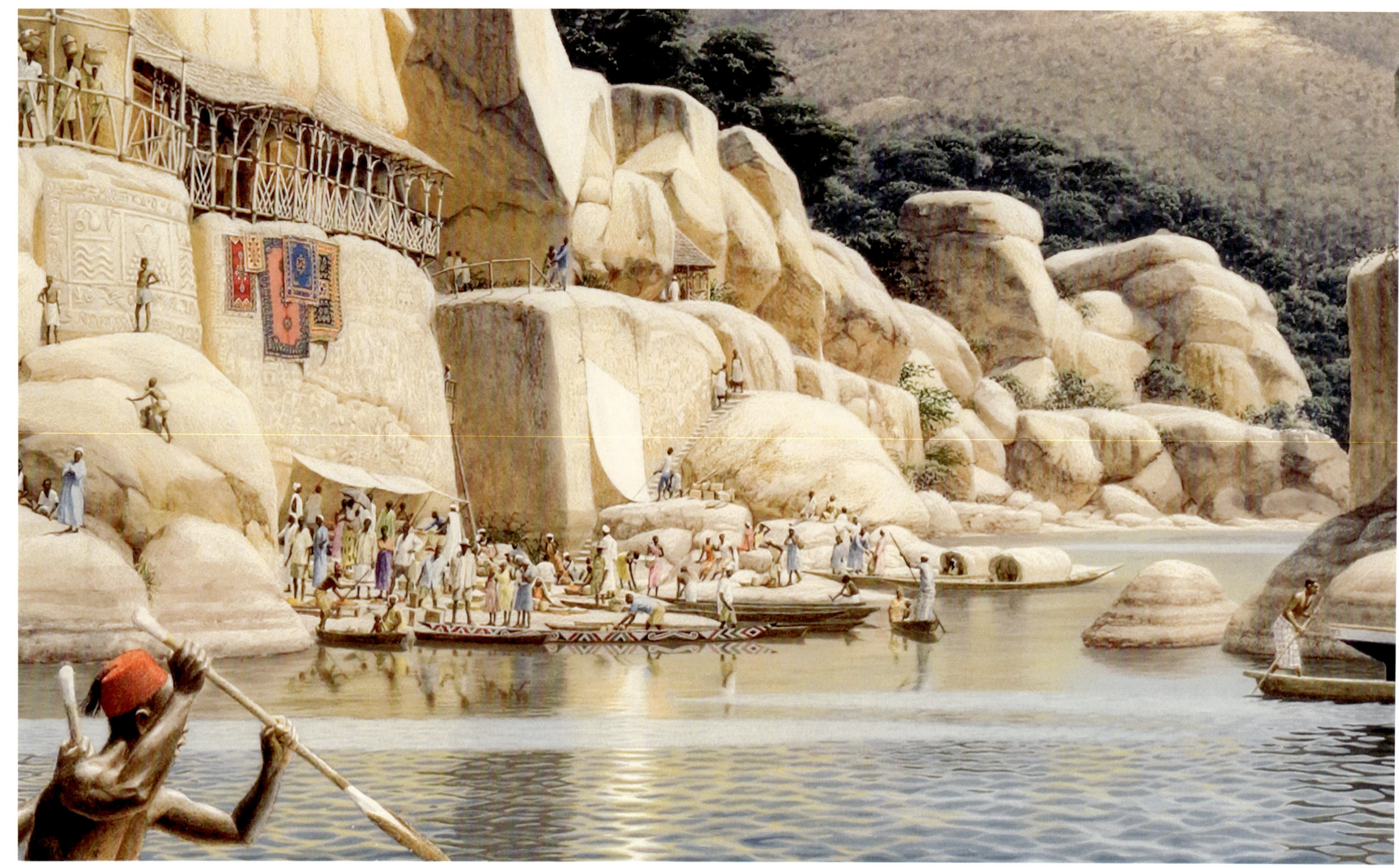

Return to River Market (RM 3)
Acrylic & cedarwood, 127 x 218 cm framed, 2006/07
Exhibited: Everard Read Gallery, Johannesburg, 2008

The chief of the region that contains Soko ya Mto, or River Market, meets a chum from his old English college days and his wife, recently arrived on the Douanier Rousseau. En route to view the ruins of an old Swahili trading/slaving entrepôt on the "chief's royal barge", he points out a rock on a bend in the river where he once speared a Nile Perch the size of a man. "A very small man" says his daughter mischievously indicating a tiddler.

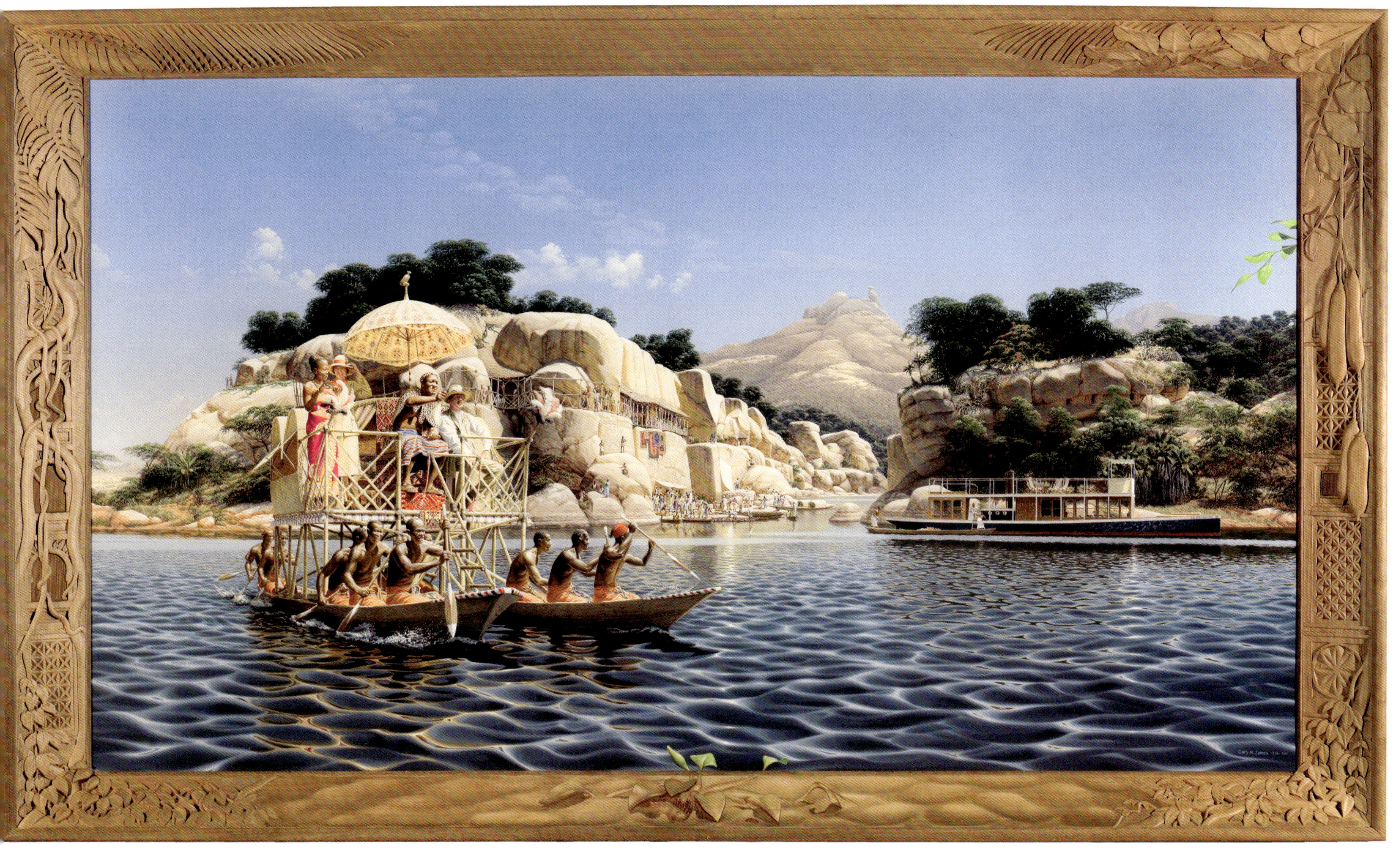

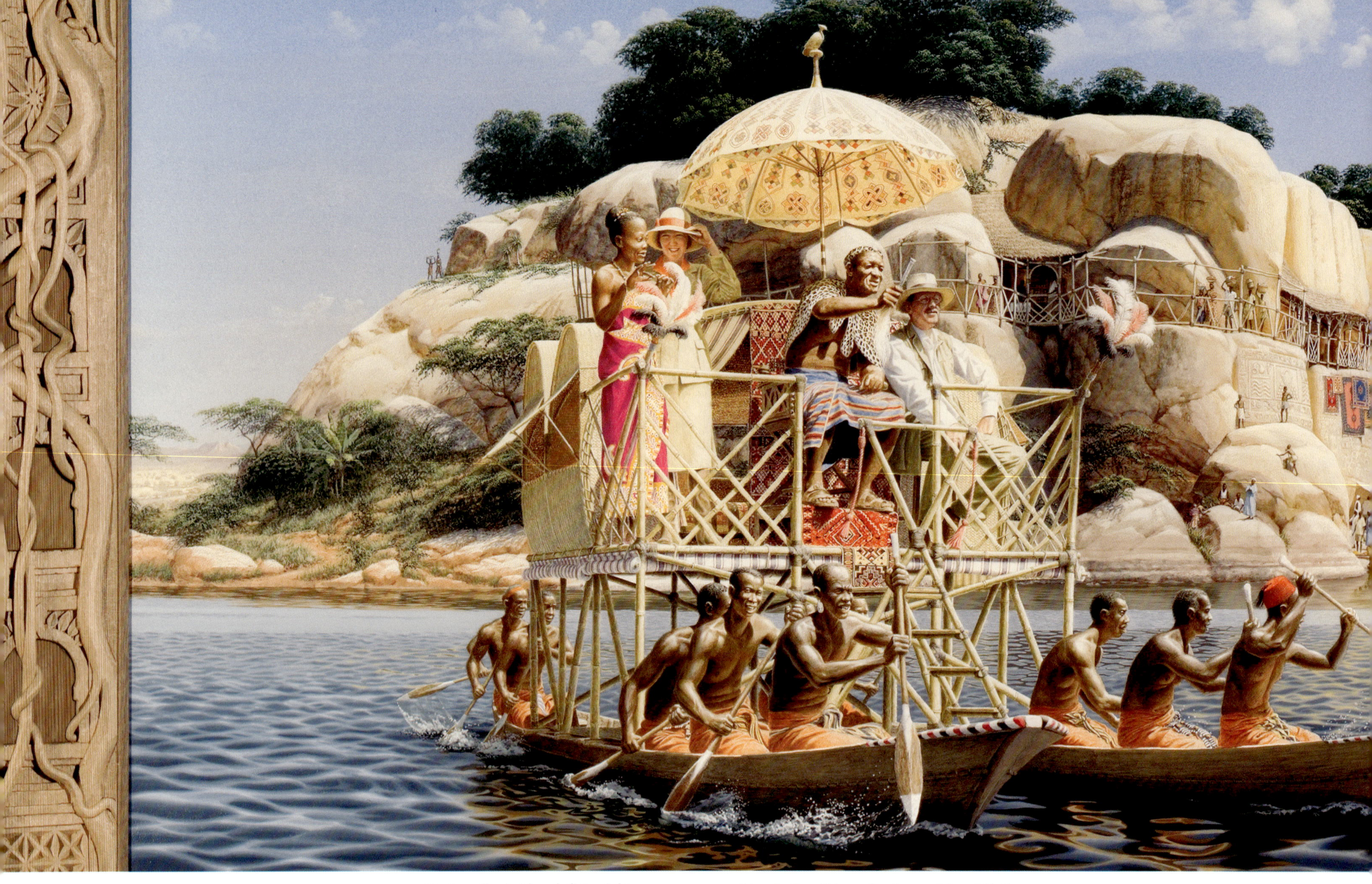

Cast on the bridge, left to right:

Mmabathu, P.A. at the Everard Read Gallery
who tragically died, just as the painting was completed
Paulette, the artist's wife
"Mac", Caretaker at the ERG and himself of chieftain's stock
The artist, sans beard

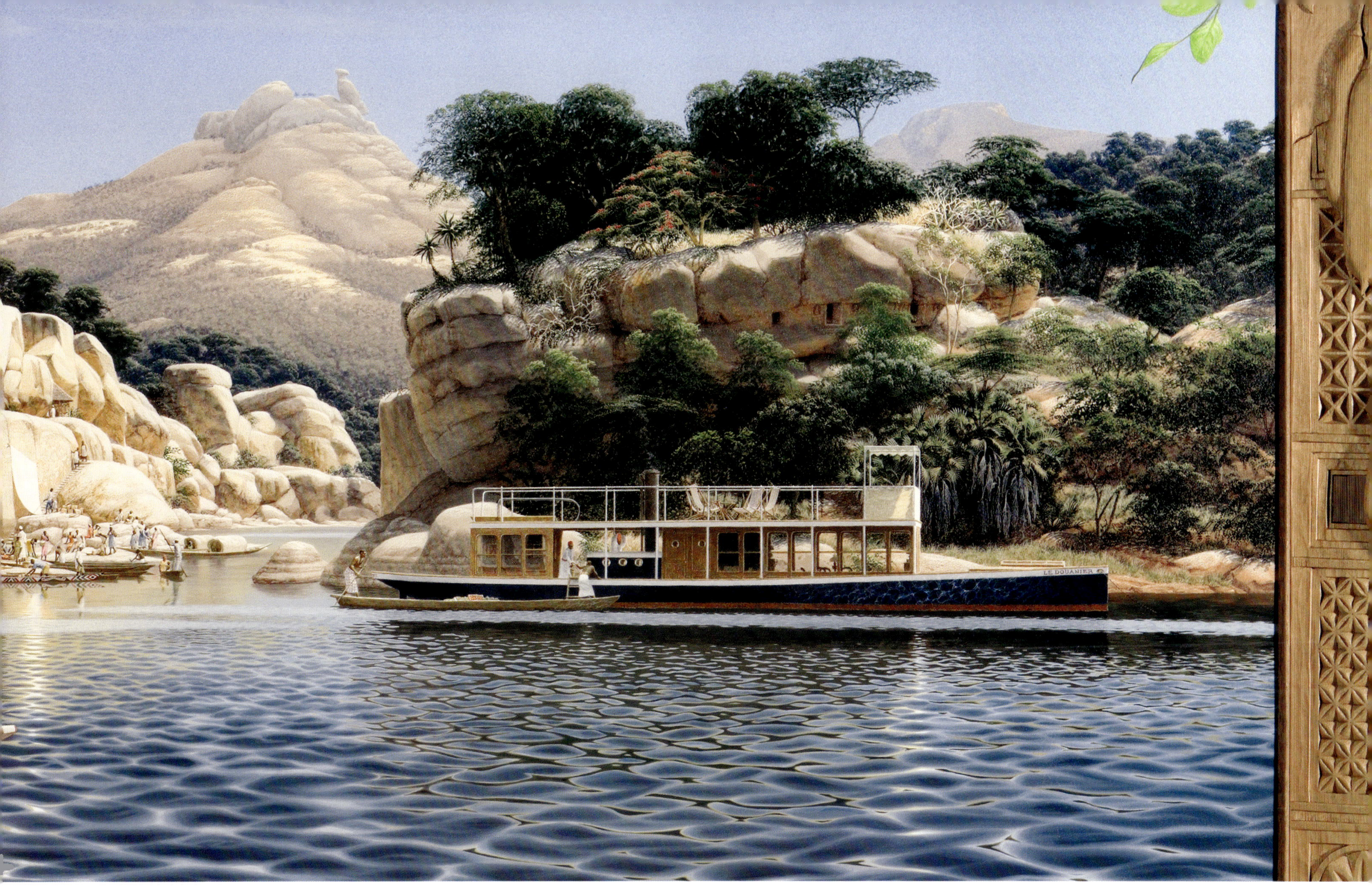

The Mawe Ndege "Bird Rock"

"Le Douanier Rousseau" moored beneath the entrances to catacombs on the 'The Isle of the Dead' (technically only an island in periods of flood).

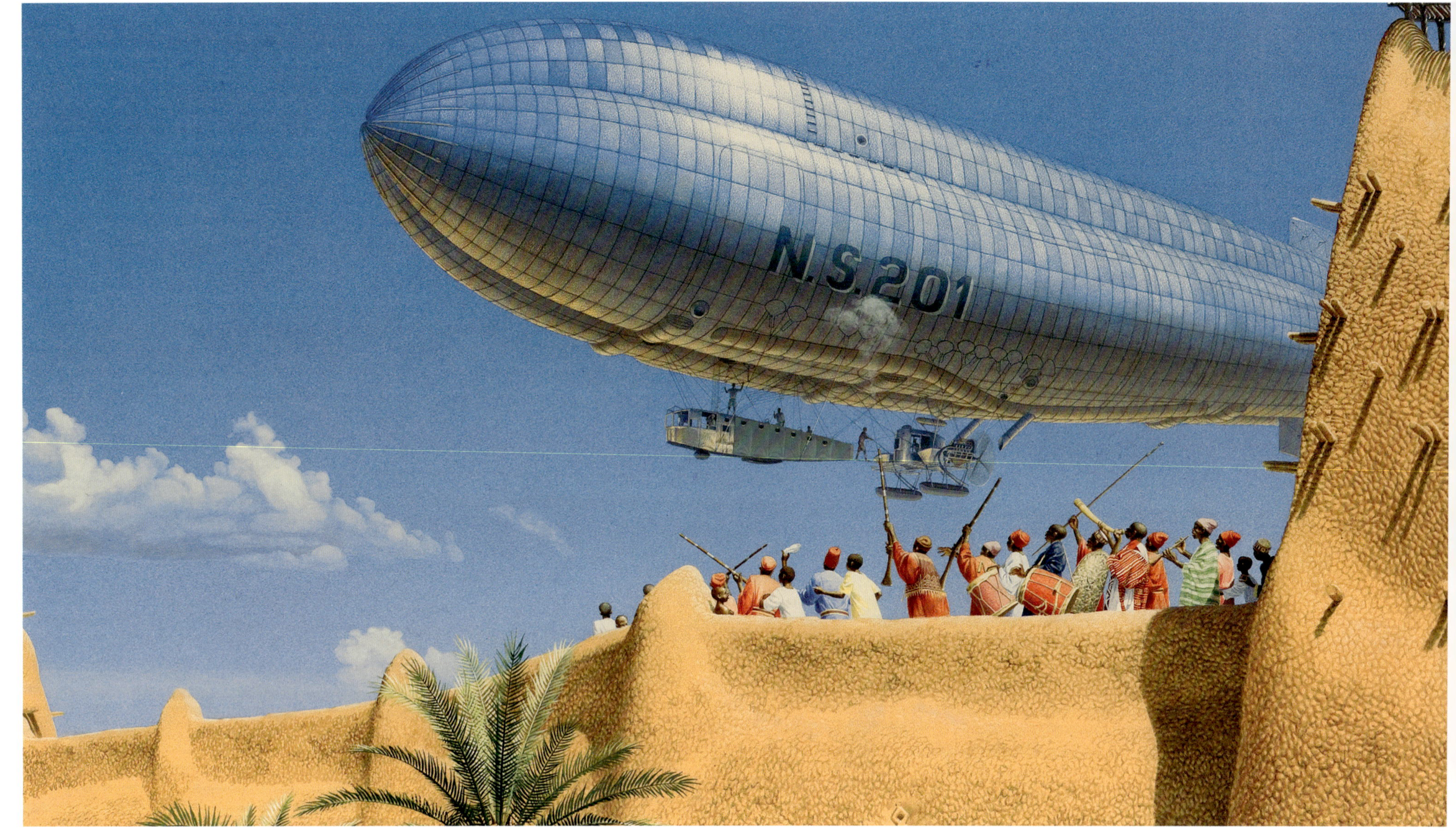

"... followed clamorously along the town walls .."
Acrylic & cedarwood, 95 x 155 cm framed, 2007
Exhibited: Everard Read Gallery, Johannesburg, 2008

Stopping over at a mud walled township in order to service the engines after a sand storm, our North Sea's departure causes almost as much excitement as its arrival "out of the blue".

Having to conserve fuel there could be no joy rides given – just a few guests on board at a time. There is one passenger now though – Addash, the chief's son, who means to cut a dash by arriving out of the sky at Zawaleh, where he has business with the family of his betrothed. They are likely to be less than impressed when he touches them for a camel for the return journey – and no, he couldn't take one on board with him.
A scratch band of horns, trumpets, drums and muzzle – loaders sees the take-off followed clamorously along the town walls, waving until out of sight.

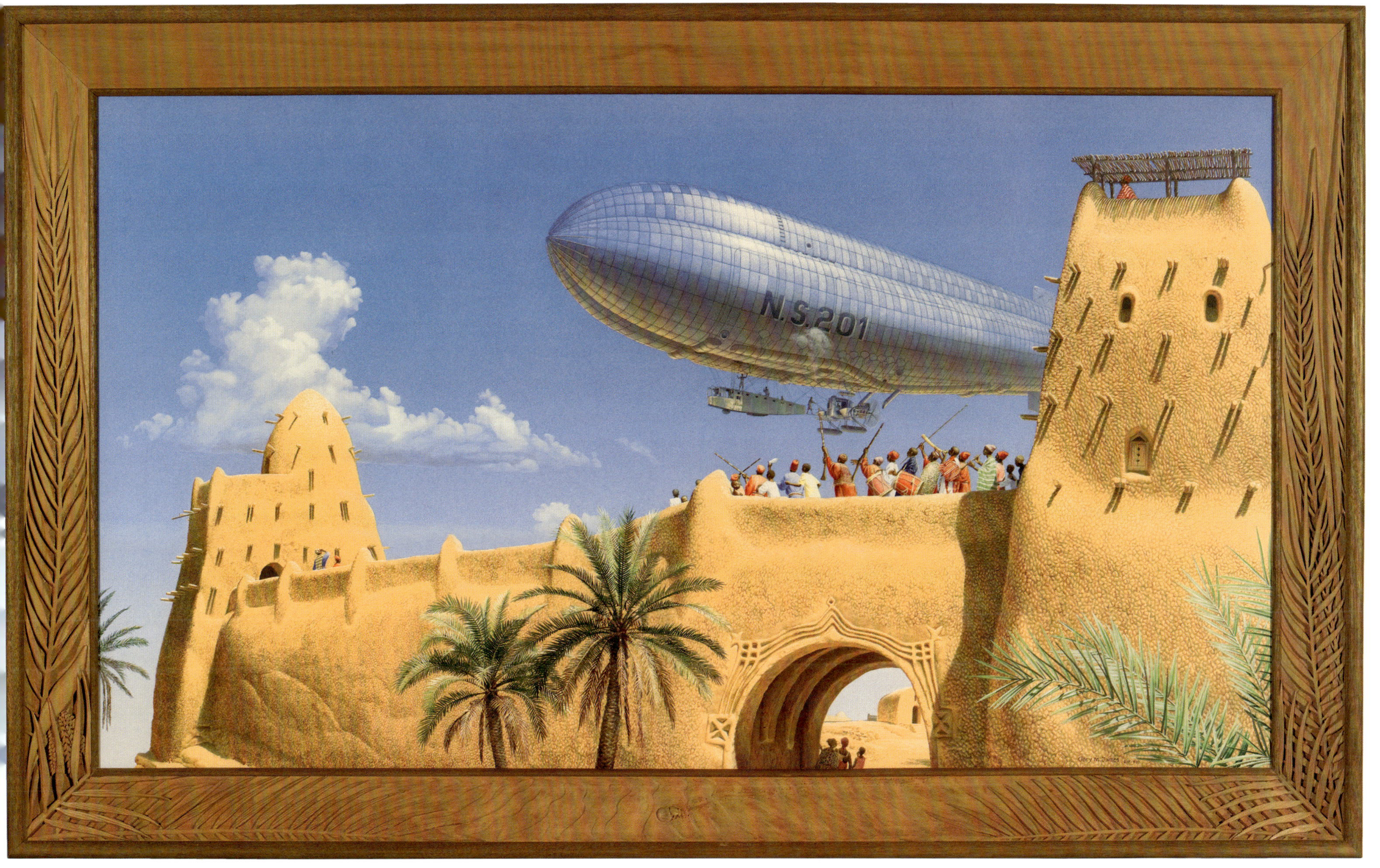
N.S.201

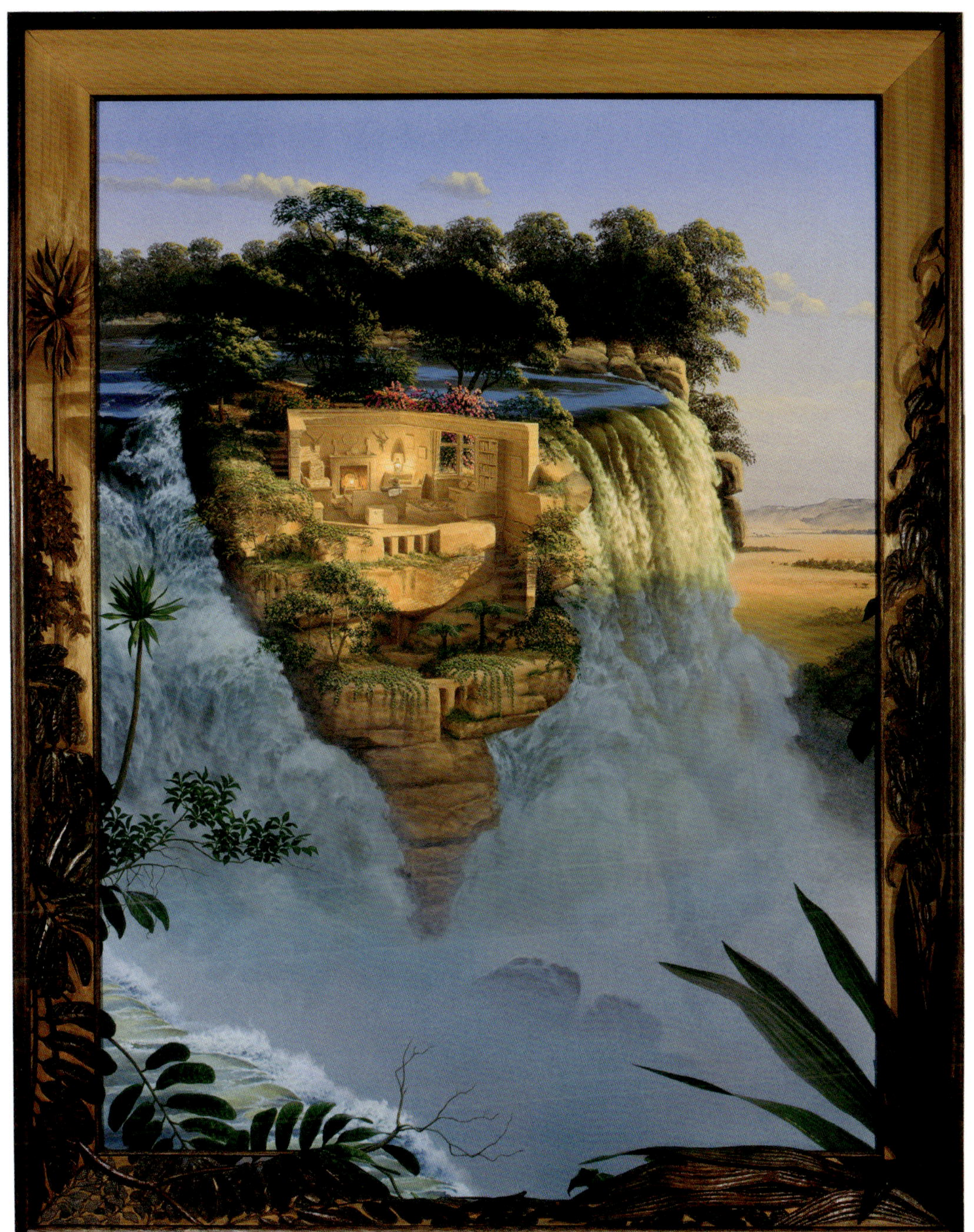

Thunder House
Acrylic & cedarwood,
140 x 110 cm framed, 2007/08
Exhibited: Everard Read Gallery, Johannesburg, 2008

All is stone in this stage set open to the sky – the three-piece suite, the cushions, the books on the shelves and the tessellated coloured stone carpets.

Even the wireless is stone, snatches from old favourites that it might otherwise have relayed chiselled above the picture rail thus;
"Oh, give me a home, where the buffalo roam", and
"So no matter where I roam, I'll stay right here".
And all around the river of time thunders past this requiem to the brief colonial period.

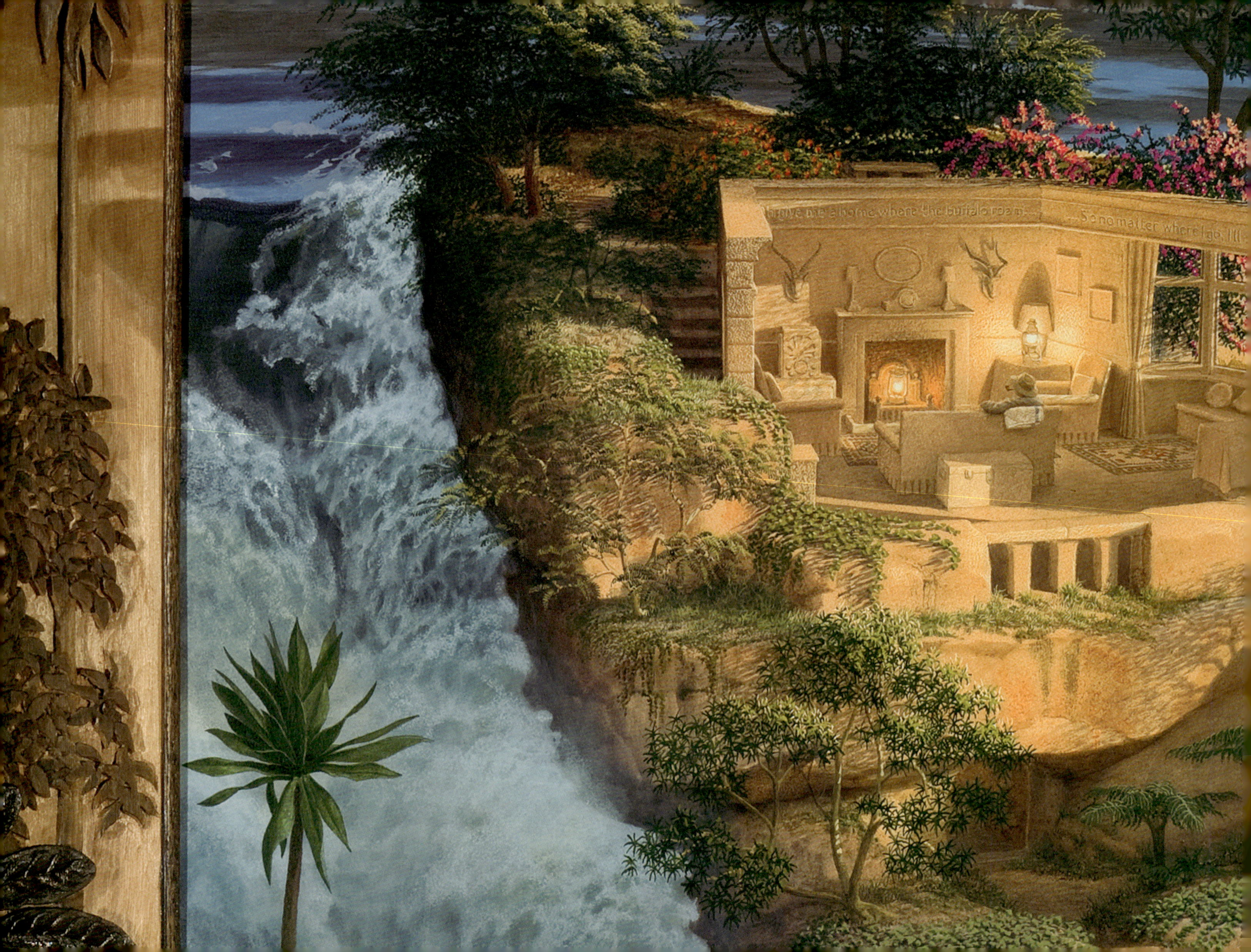

ive me a home where the buffalo roam...
...So no matter where I go,

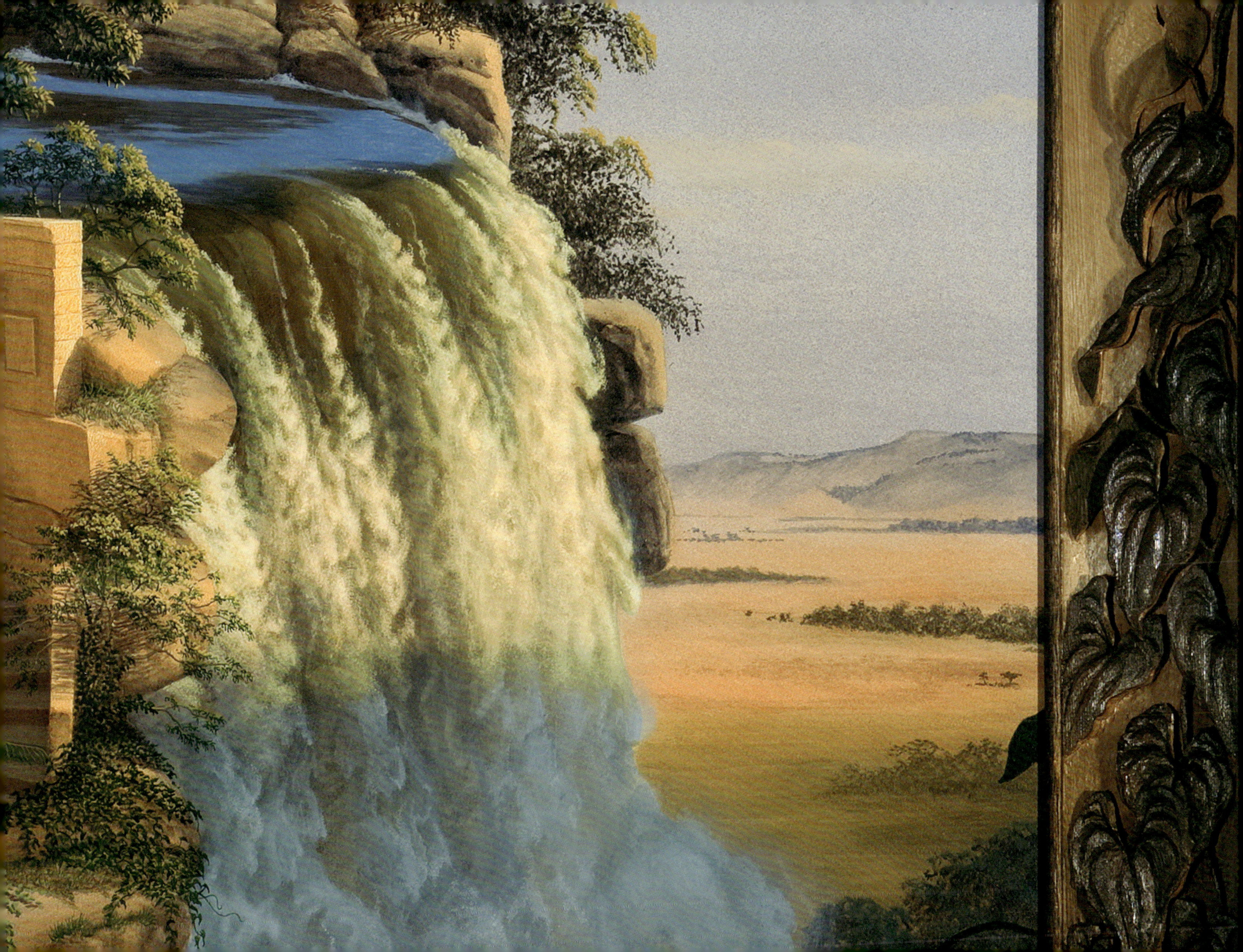

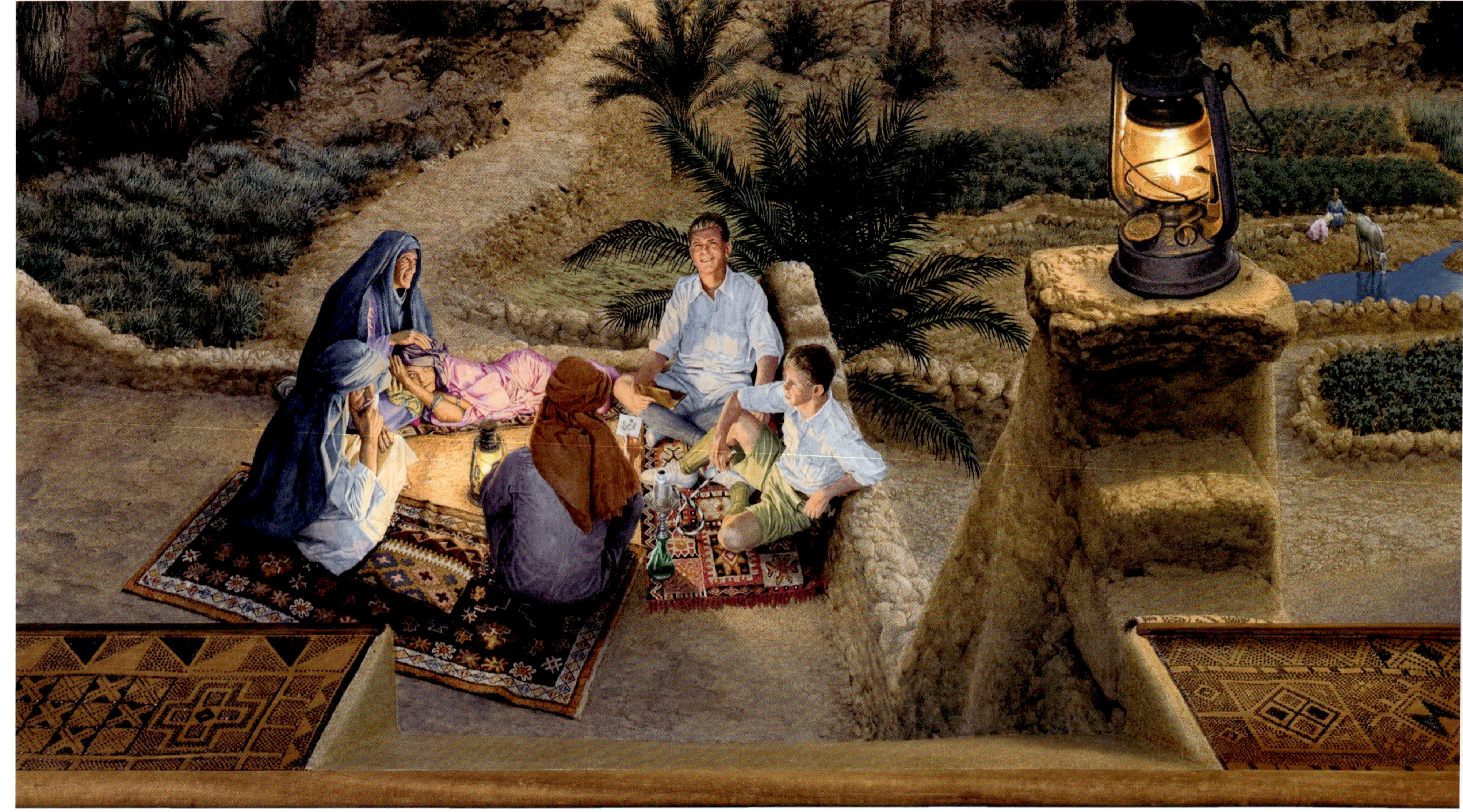

Morocco Bound
Acrylic & cedarwood, 127 x 206 cm framed, 2008/09
Exhibited: Everard Read Gallery, Johannesburg, 2009

Our North Sea magic carpet here moors to a rock above an oasis citadel. Warnings of marauding brigands make this a preferred option to the open desert and has the added advantage of replenishing supplies directly from below.

Part of the "shore leave watch" dine with a group of the locals, doing their best with sign language, family photos and party conjuring tricks.
The cast: far left, "looking local" – the artist.
Top right, - The artist's Grandfather, Walter Henry in his RAF tropical fatigues, facing the viewer.
His grandson, the artist, looking "local," on the left
and his great-grandson Alex on the right.

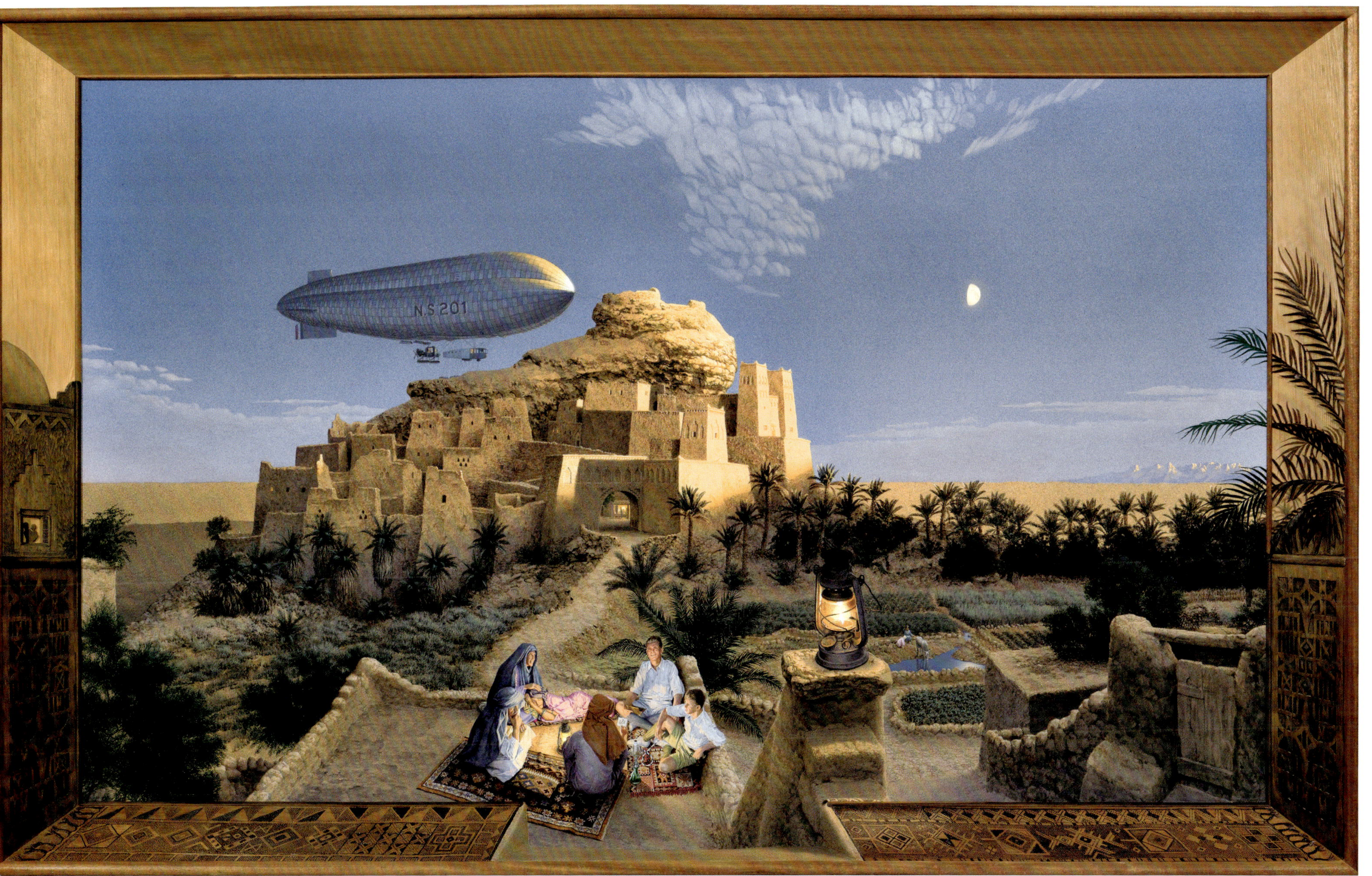
N.S 201

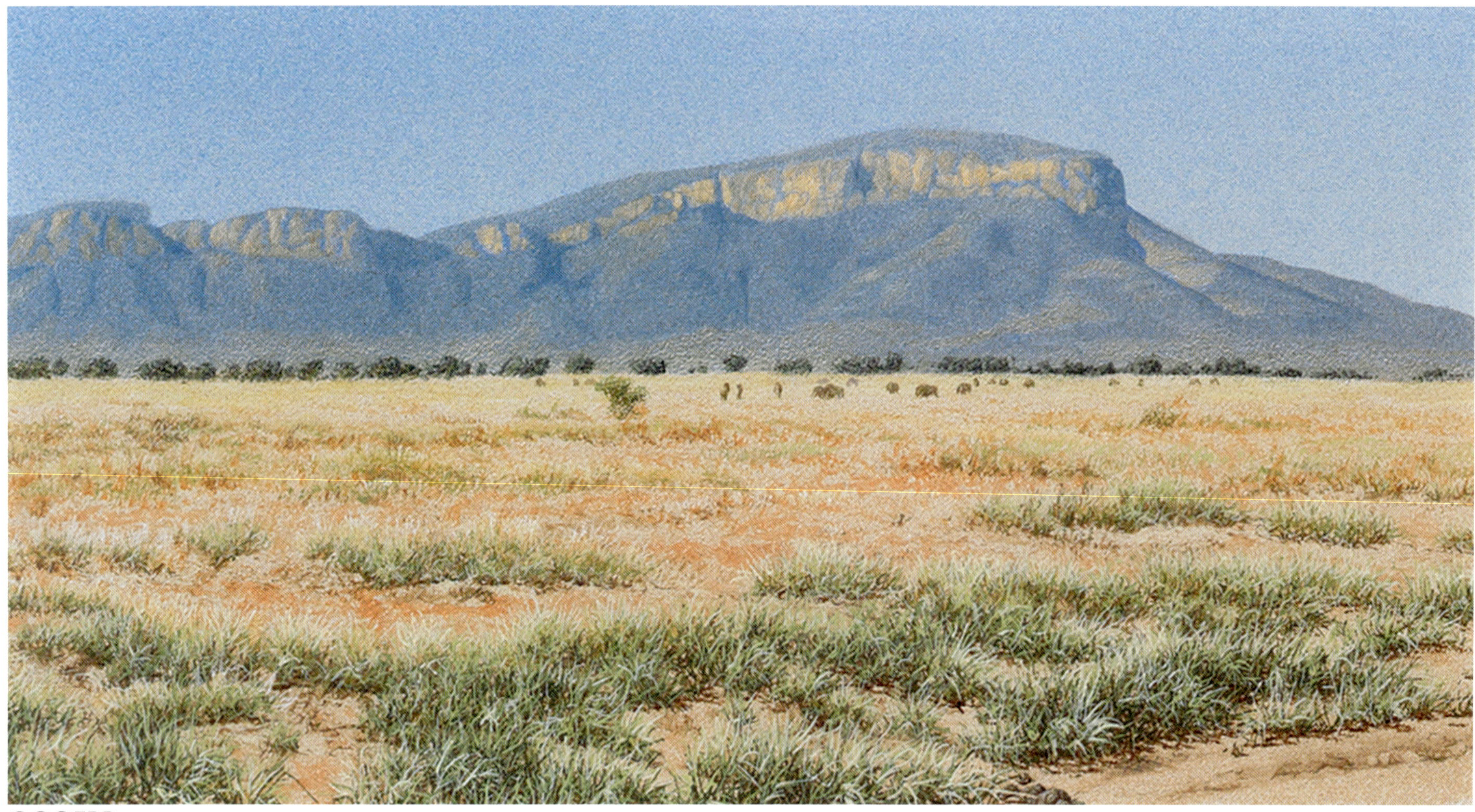

OOOERR

Acrylic & cedarwood, 95 x 157 cm framed, 2009
Exhibited: Everard Read Gallery, Johannesburg, 2009

The 1923 Austin Seven "Chummy".
Designed 1921-22 by Sir Herbert Austin and Stanley Edge as a real car alternative to the motorcycle combinations popular for those of modest means. (Such as the artist's grandfather). Carries two adults and two children – or two small adults in the back (or members of his tug-o-war team – who up-ended his on a hill).
Price new £165. Almost 300,000 made in 17 years of production.
Water cooled 4 cylinder, 747cc engine giving 10.5 bhp.
Top speed (in good conditions) 50 mph.

Lion. Panthera leo:
Height at shoulder 40 inches; length (without tail) up to 8 foot 4";
Weight 19¼ to 32 stone. Speed not exceeding 40 mph in short bursts. Roar carries up to 5 miles. (*"OOOERR"*).
Hunt by sight and sound, in prides. Sense of smell good.

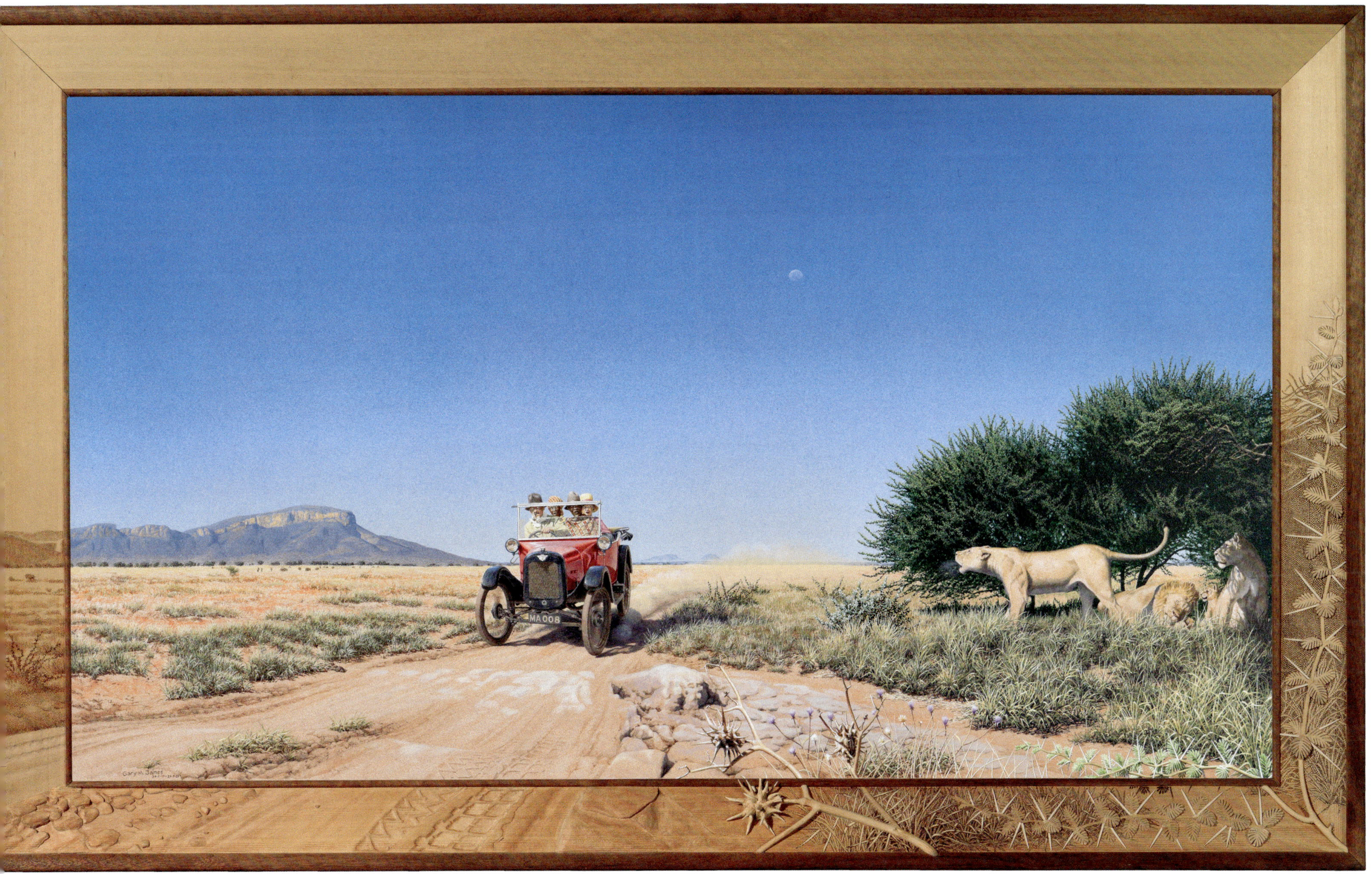
MA 008

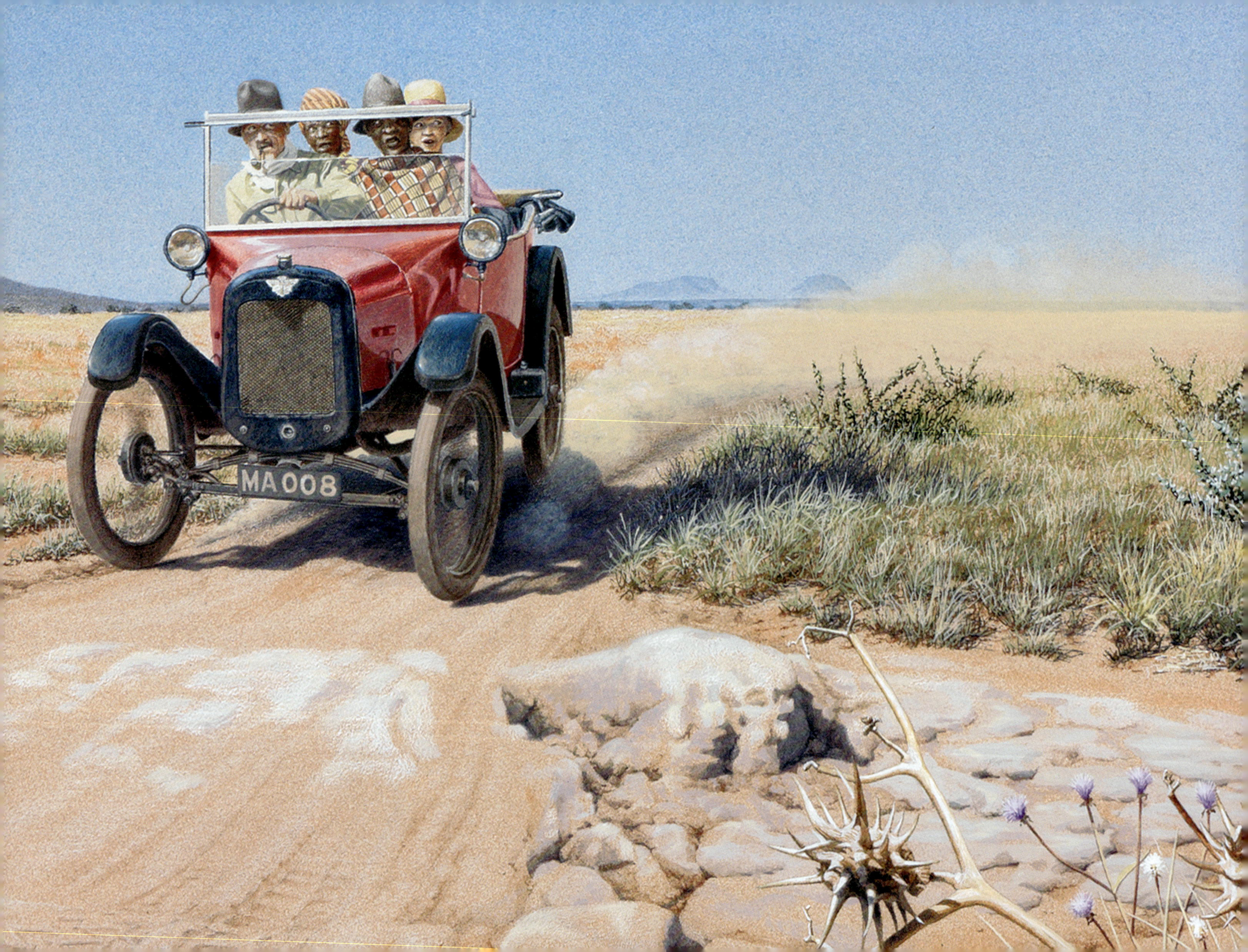
MA 008

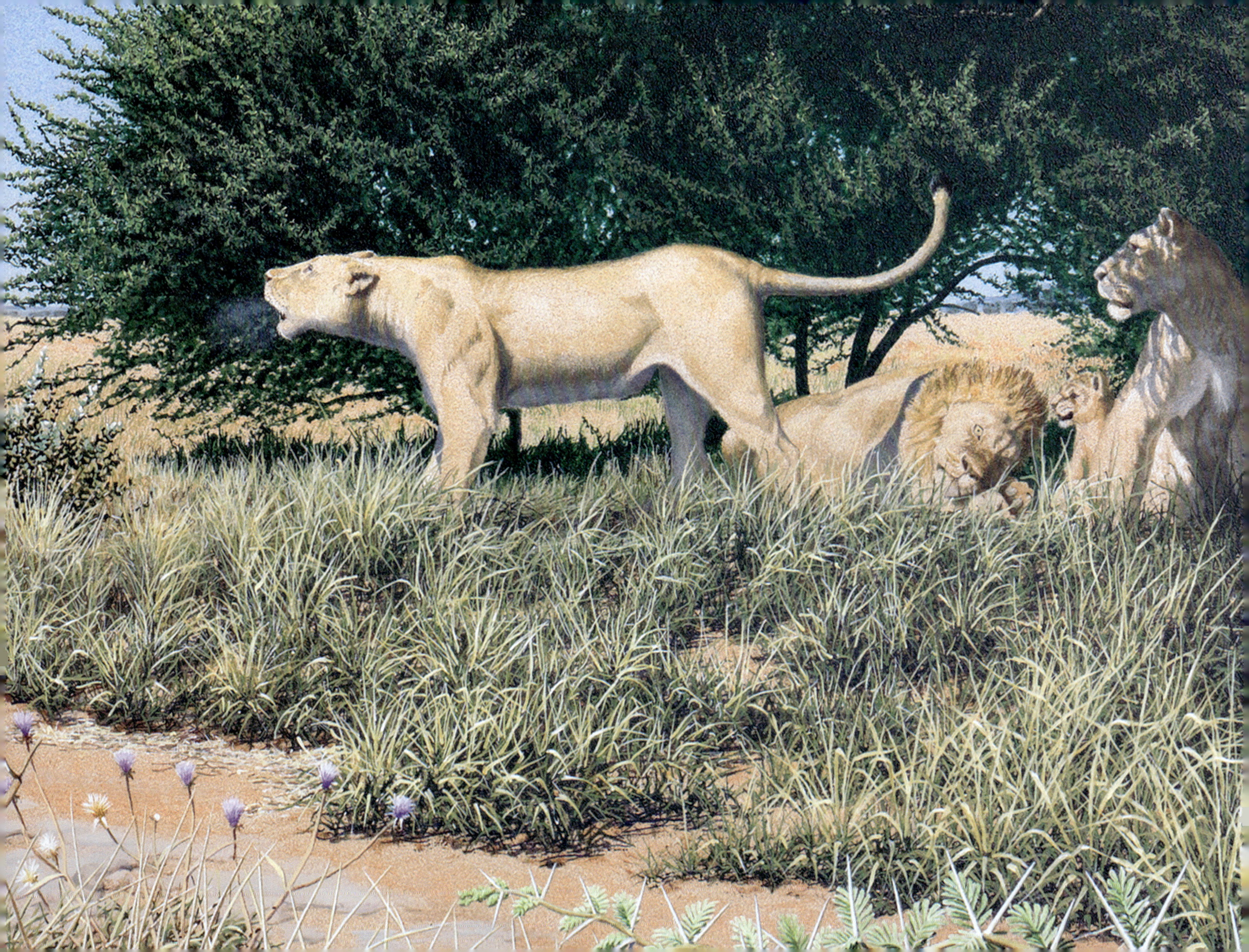

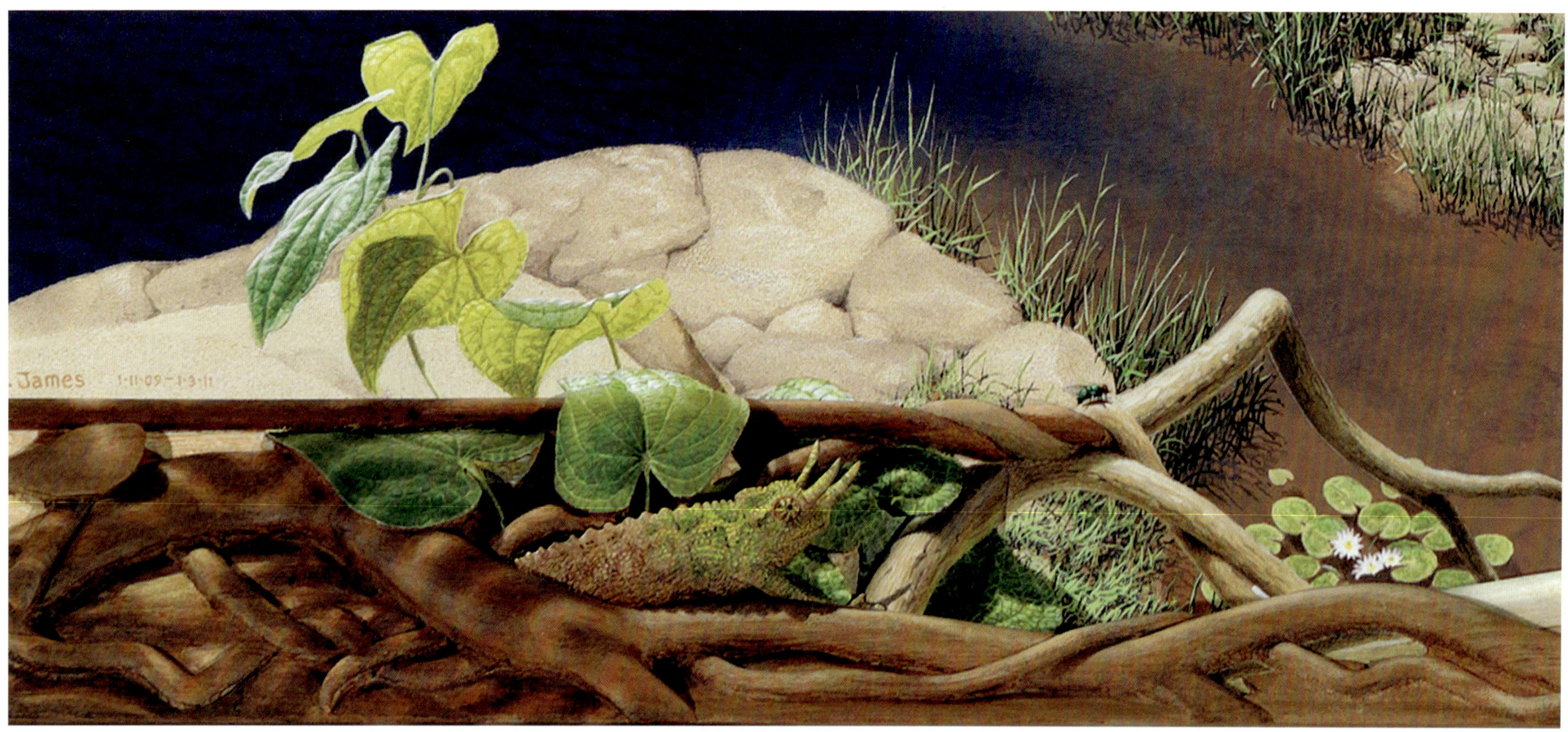

Pronouncement from the River Bed (RM 4)

Acrylic, cedar & pine wood & plastic clay, 127 x 187 cm, 2009/11

Exhibited: Everard Read Gallery, Johannesburg, 2011

True 'interfacing': The chameleon, his tail carved in the wood and his body modelled in 'plastic clay', lines up on his lunchtime fly – in the painting. It is keeping one eye on the viewer, the other on the fly.

A mwaguzi (soothsayer) famous for the accuracy of his predictions, takes to his rather novel podium and awaits the arrival of the local ruler in his flotilla. Unwittingly they have been preceded by Charlie and Rose Allnutt (now married) in the "sistership" of the "African Queen", lost as many will remember in the attempt to sink the German gun boat "Königin Luise" on Lake Wittelsbach-Nyanza during World War 1 (see C.S. Forester).
Once they have relinquished the V.I.P mooring the mwaguzi will deliver his pronouncements via a large speaking trumpet housed within a crocodile skin, punctuated by hoist puppet signifiers.

Rose's unfortunate missionary brother, the Rev. Samuel Sayer (deceased) would not have approved of this audience with "false prophets" and would most certainly have scorned the claim that there was to be another war fought by land, sea and air by the Wazungu at an unspecified date. Unfortunately the plague of locusts, also foretold, hits the area two days later.

The Mooning Boy...Sharp eyed observers may spot the small boy "mooning" at the royal barge (page 100) and have wondered at his future. The author would like to give reassurance that though the "courtiers" wanted him thrashed, Chief Freddy, wise to the ways of small boys had other ideas. He had stones put in the pockets of the boy's shorts, which were then tossed into the river. "They needed a wash" said he "and are now clean. You had better fetch them". Of course the children of those parts who made pocket money by diving for coins would have no problem in doing so.

The next time the Chief saw the boy he asked "are your shorts dry yet?" At which everyone laughed uproariously. In later years the miscreant, now a man, grew quite weary of relative strangers who would ask him "are your shorts dry yet?" In fact the saying became common parlance for anyone whose misdeeds had found them out.

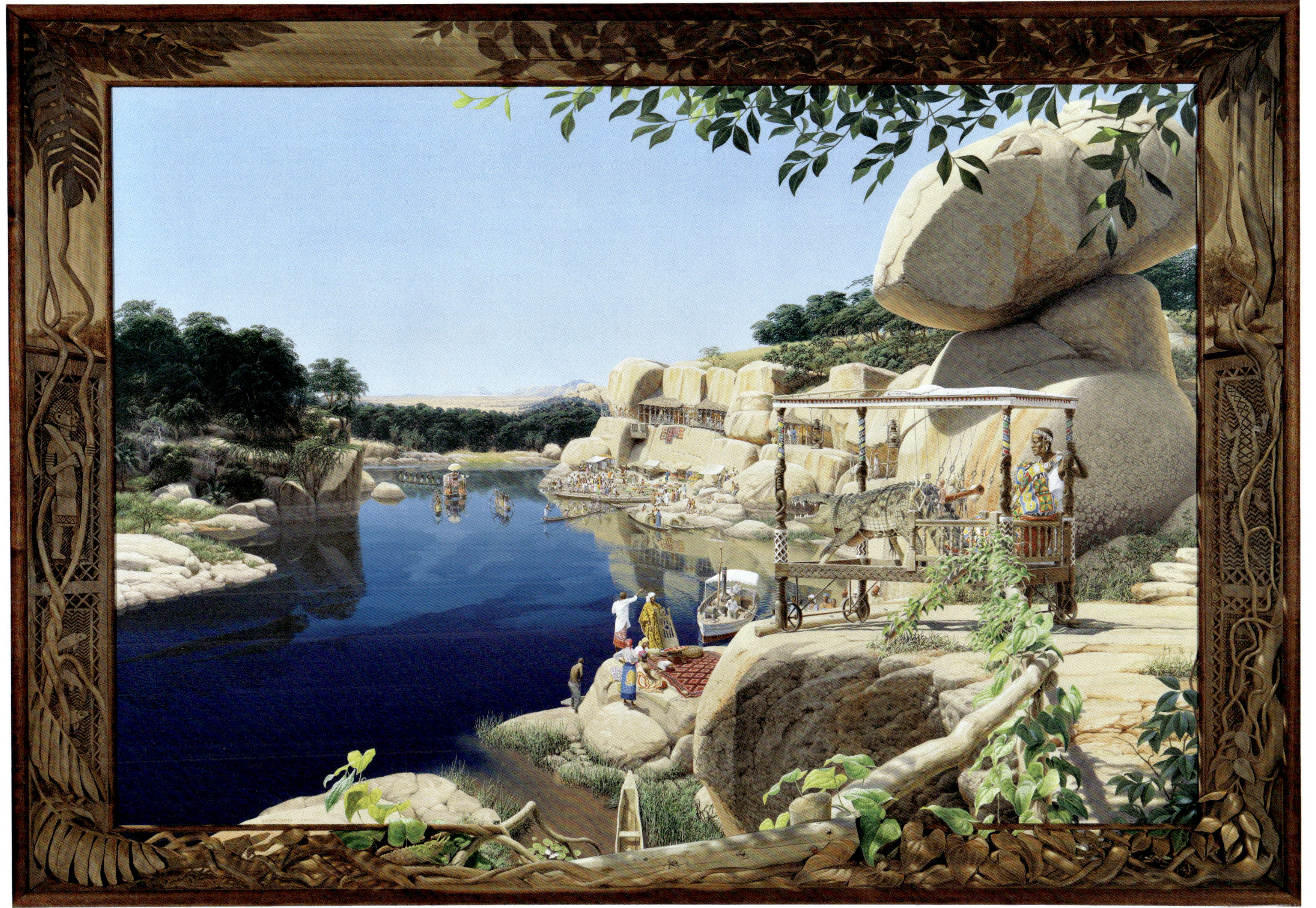

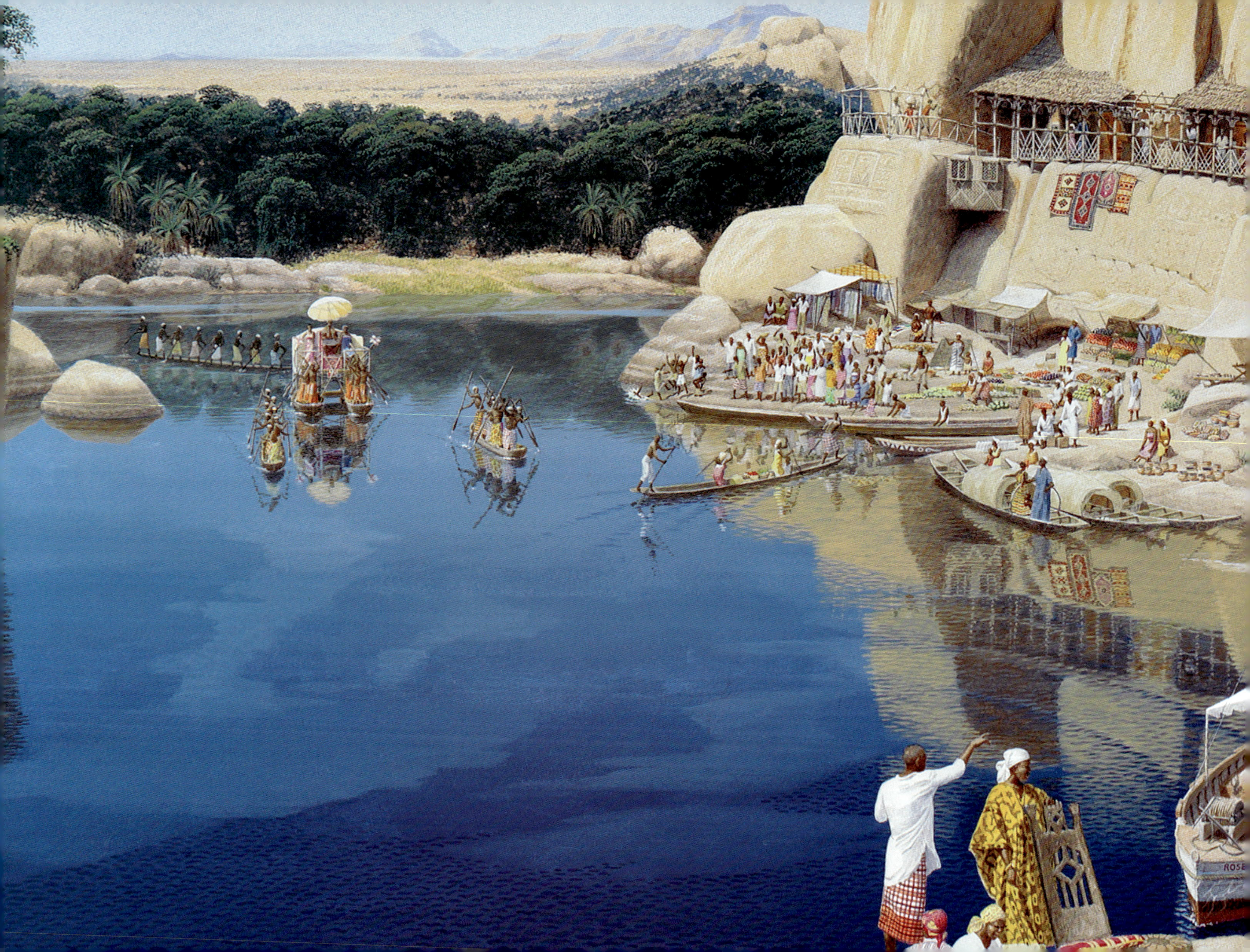

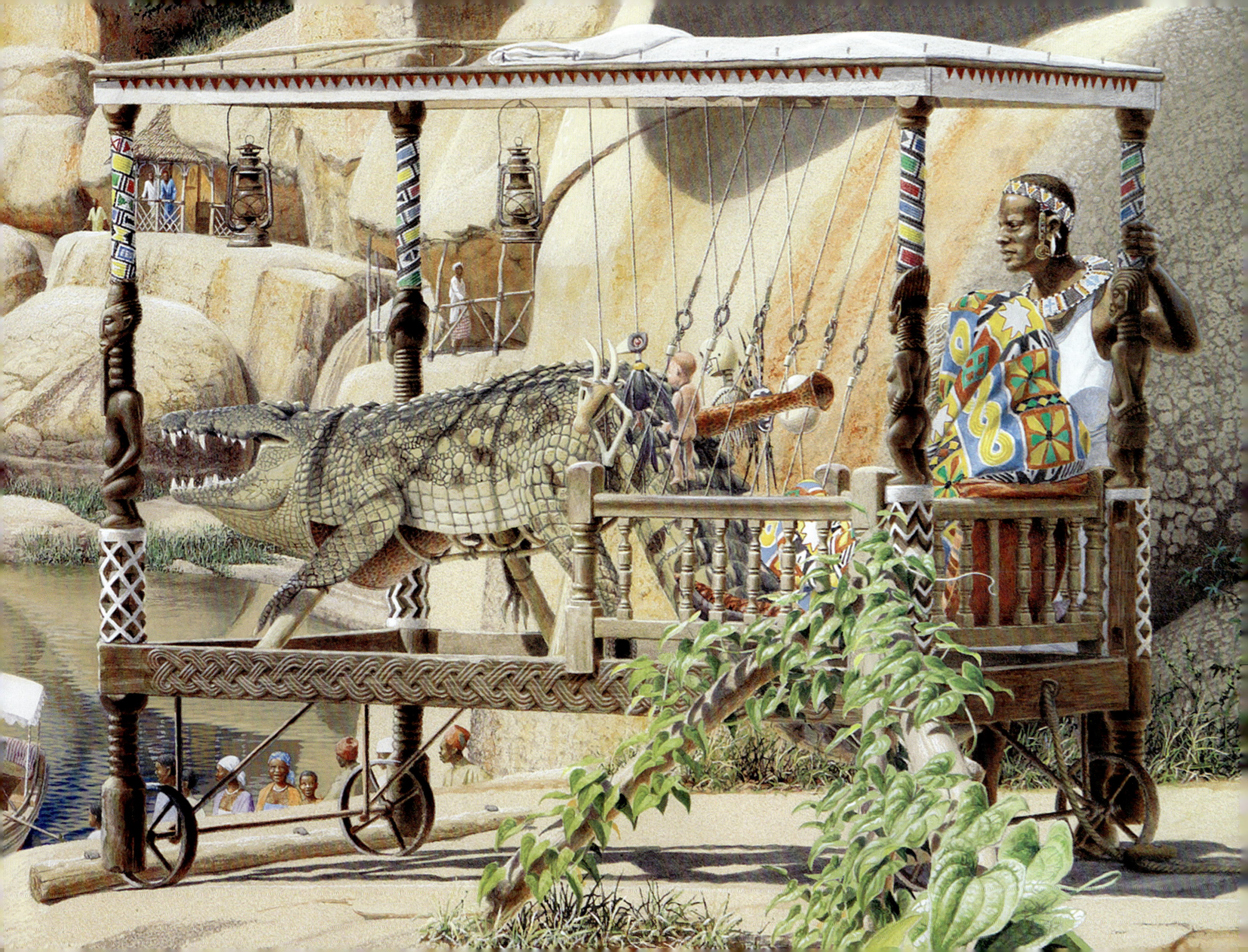

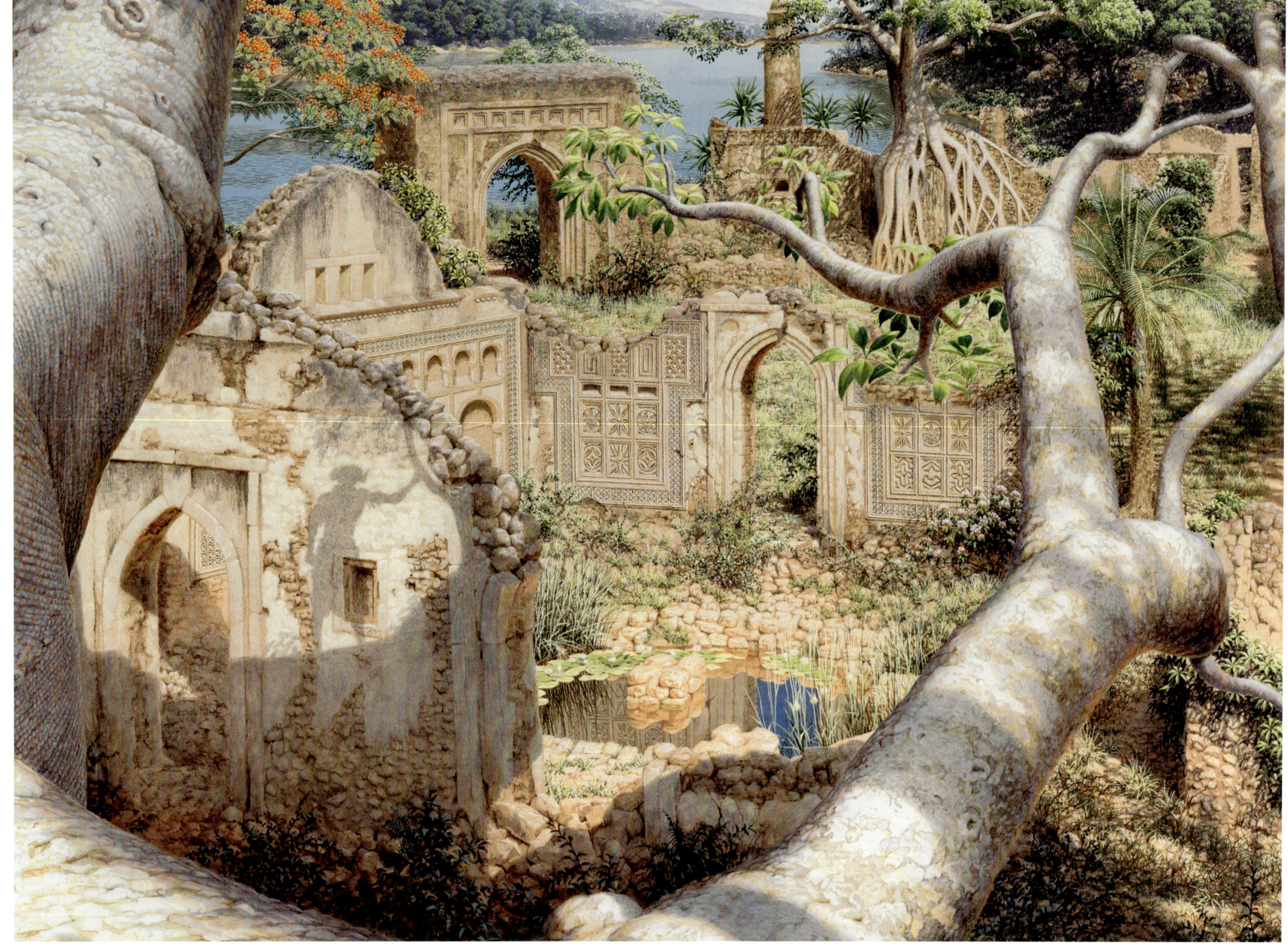

Overseer

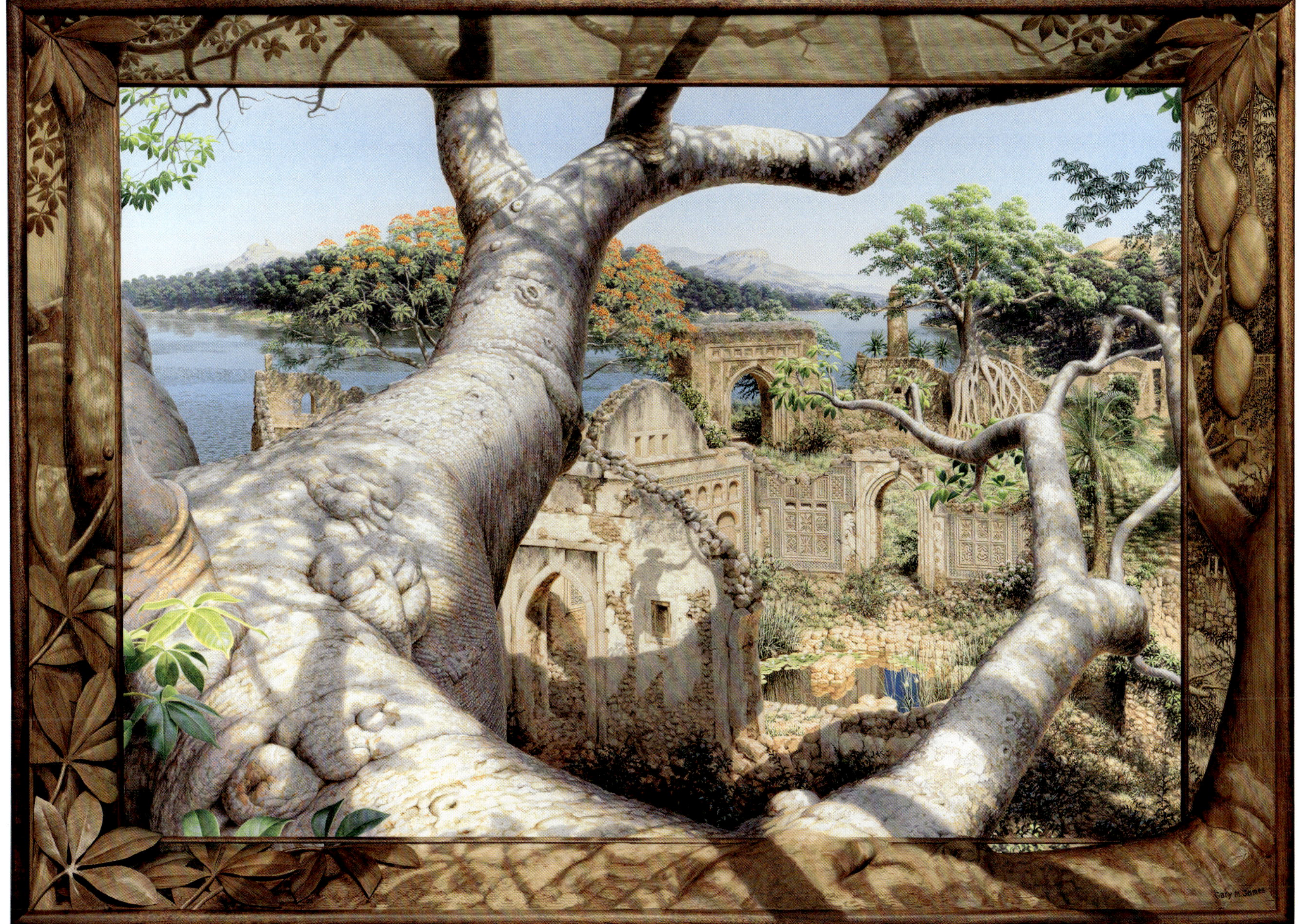

Overseer

Acrylic, cedarwood, 110.5 x 156.5 cm framed , 2011/12

Exhibited: Everard Read Gallery, Johannesburg, 2012

On a bend in the Simahali po pote, about a mile up river from River Market and half hidden in jungle, lie the ruins of an inland entrepôt of coastal traders. Once prosperous, dealing in gold, ivory and skins a change of regime saw the traders take to slaving. "Stocks" being depleted further upstream their depredations came closer to home, with the result of a regional uprising launched from the "Bird Rock" visible over the tree tops to the left. Cut off and besieged the slavers attempted to escape by boat, but running out of ammunition were rammed and sank. Thus they became a banquet for the crocodiles.

The giant baobab dominating the scene and perhaps as old as a thousand years, would have already been a mature tree during these events. Believed to be the haunt of a guardian spirit.

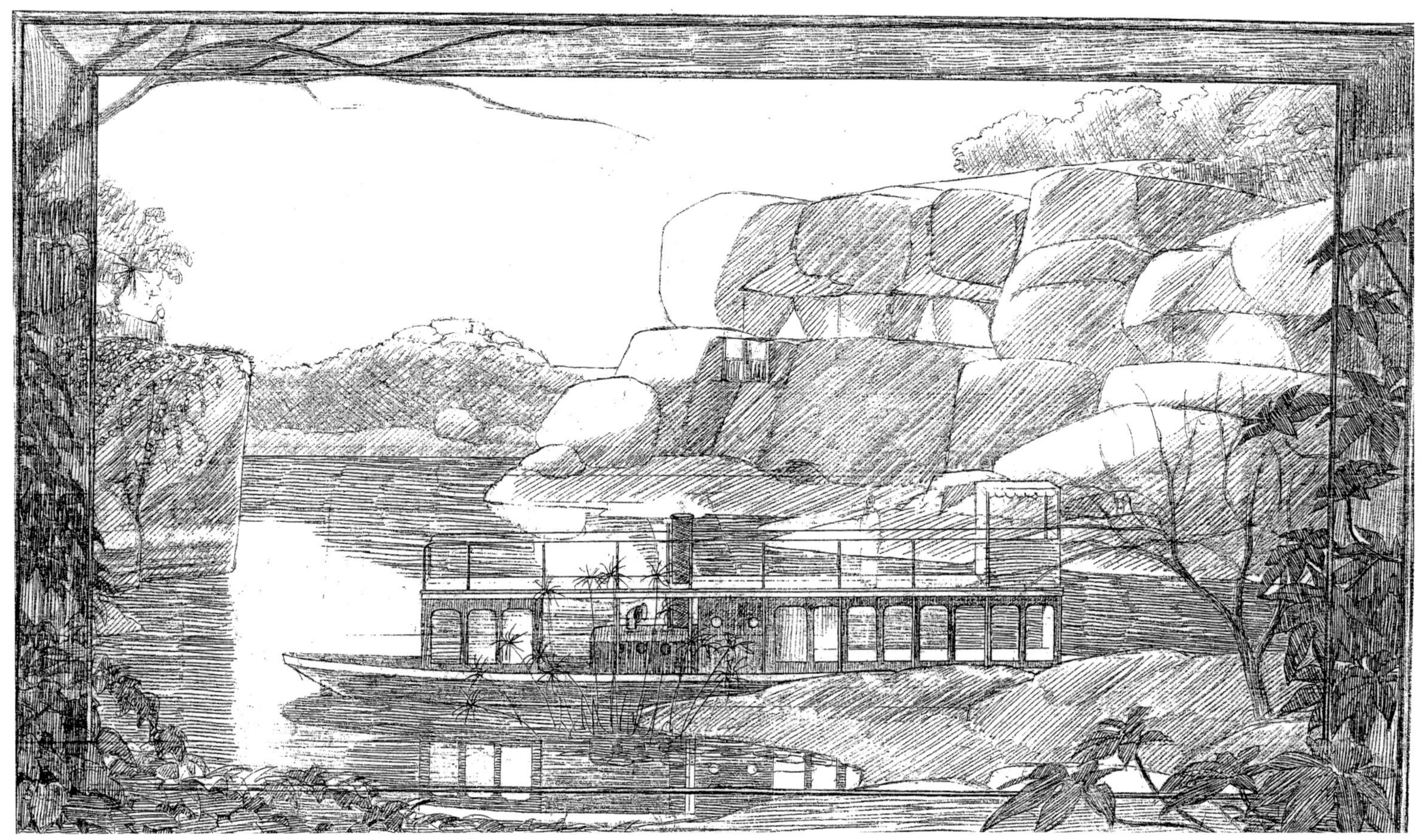

Preliminary A3 pencil drawing for
Sundowner (RM 5)

Before showing this painting the Reader may find it of interest to follow some of the processes involved in its production.

The following picture sequence outlines some of the stages without going into all technicalities.

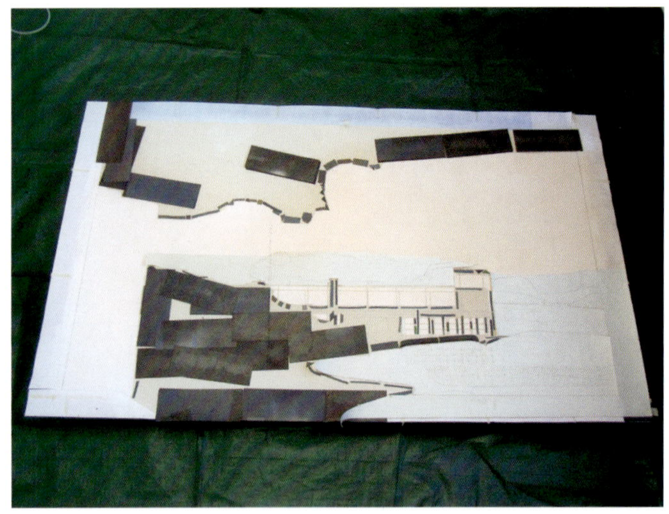

1. Paper mask weighted with metal plates and pieces of lead. Preliminary colours sprayed in using a sprayer made from a glass jar, aluminium and coronary artery catheter!

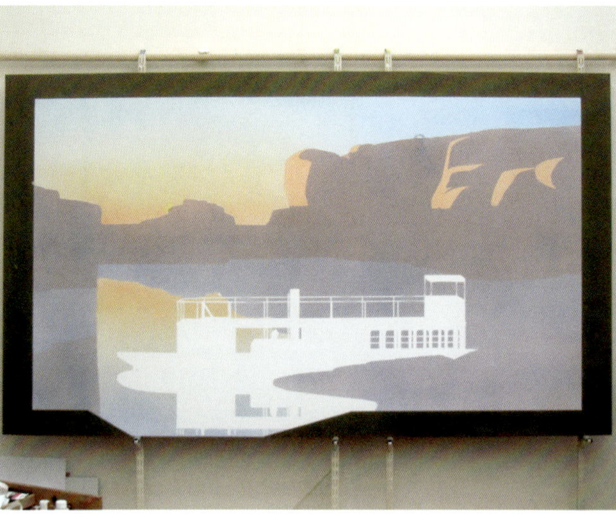

2. Preliminary colours completed. The dark margin left for frame backing – leaving an interfacing cut-away below

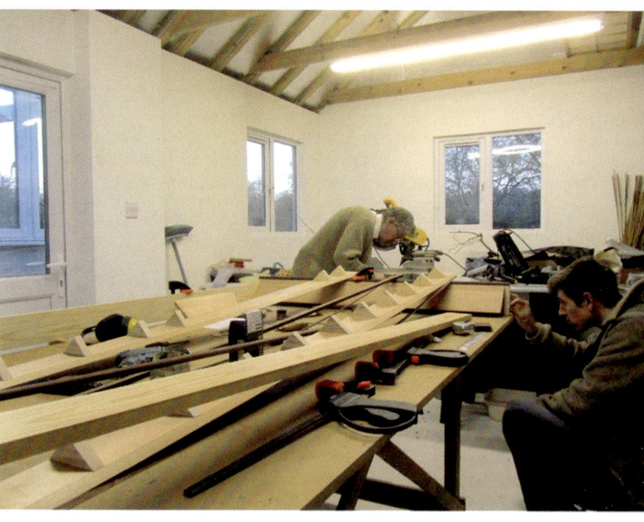

3. Constructing the basic frame in our workshop. (See page 30)

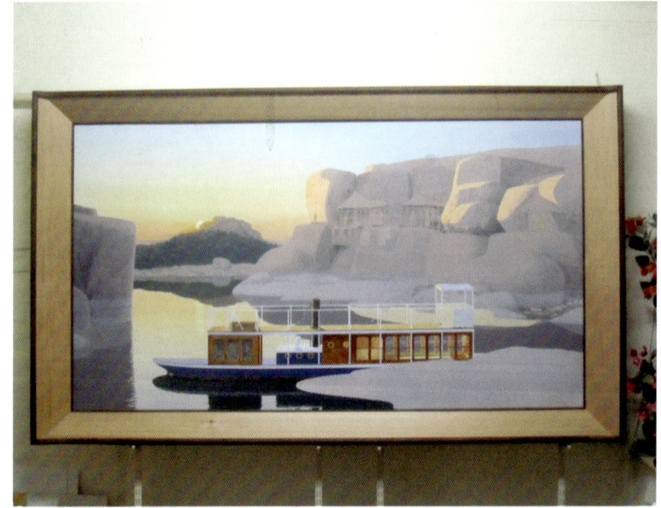

4. Panel fitted into basic frame. Note the slight flaring at the outer margins of the frame to allow deeper bracketing.

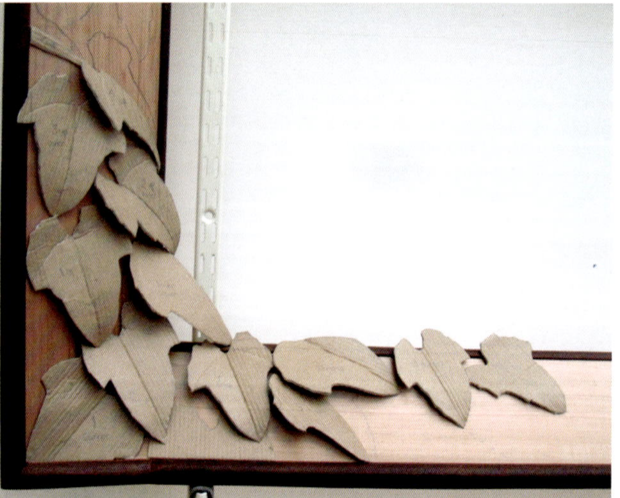

5. Cardboard cut-outs rehearse the carved cedar "glue-on" leaves to follow. Shallower relief carved directly into the cedar plank "facings".

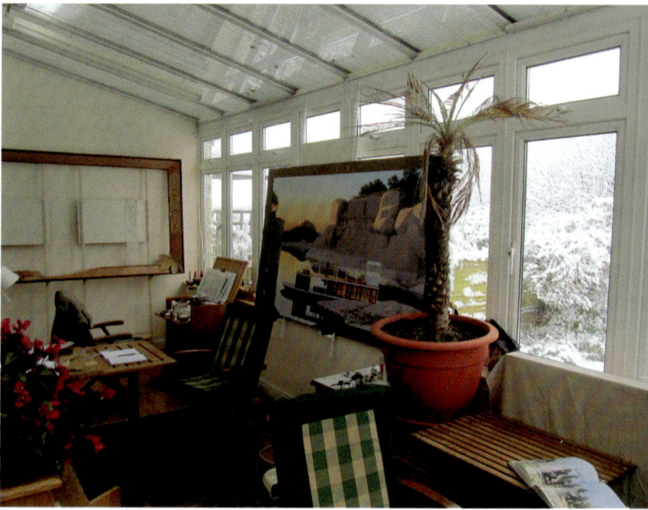

6. Painting sunny Africa in snowy England. Frame carving continues on the end wall rack.

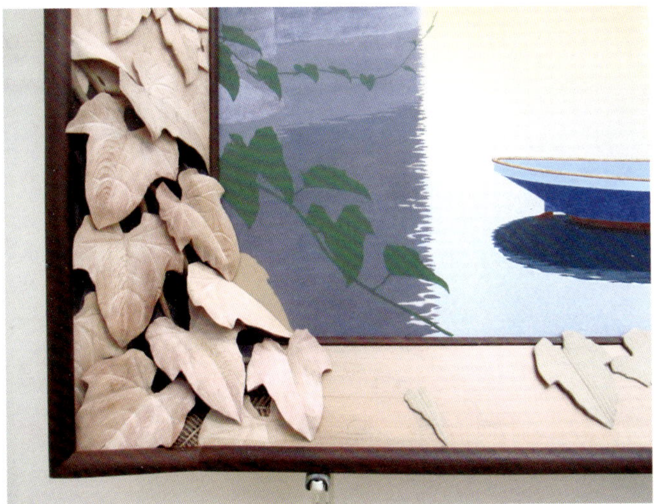

7. Cedar leaves replacing the cardboard.
Bracketing plants: L.H.S. – Ipomoea creeper ....
(Both plants found alongside the Telek River, Kenya).

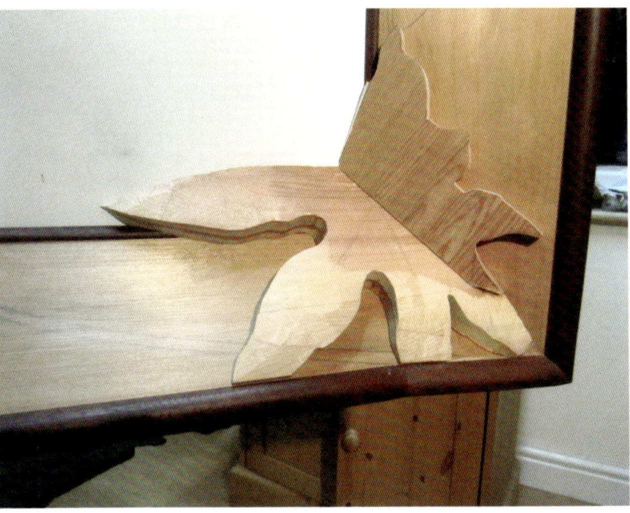

8. Preparing a block for the corner ricinus leaf. R.H.S. – Ricinus communis, or castor oil plant.
(Seeds provide the deadly ricin poison).

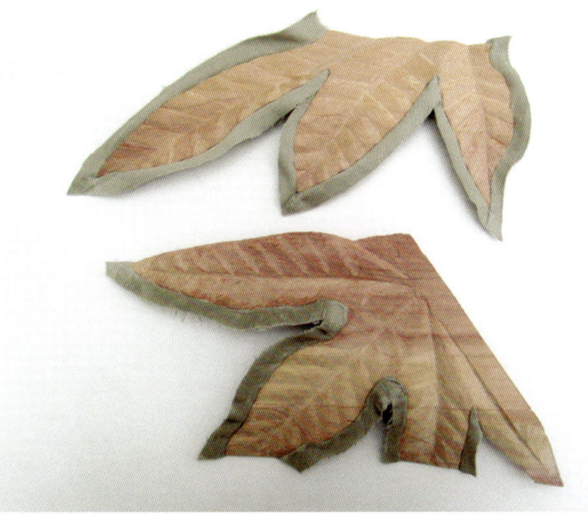

9. Cloth, wood glue and cedar dust edging added to the carved leaf blocks preparatory to cutting the finely detailed dentate leaf edge.

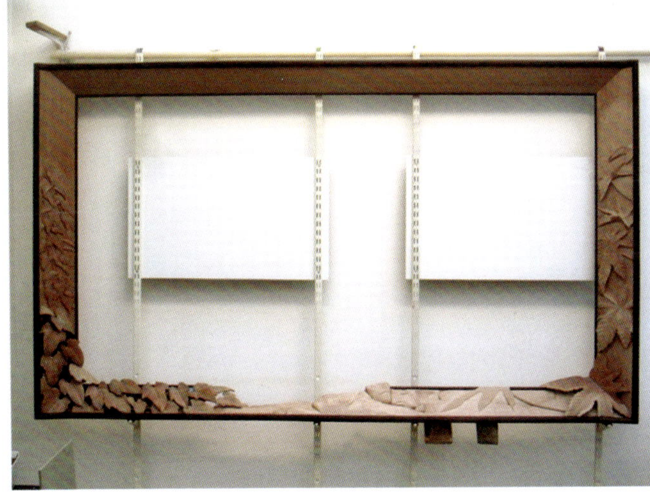

10. Working on wall racks in the studio, the carving approaches completion.

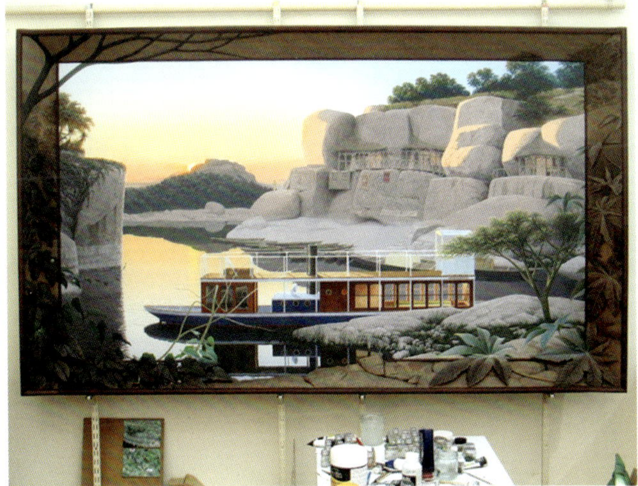

11. "Dusk" dark staining added selectively to frame. Cliff top vegetation stippled with a hot poker. Thin strip overhead acacia branches added. Painting recommenced.

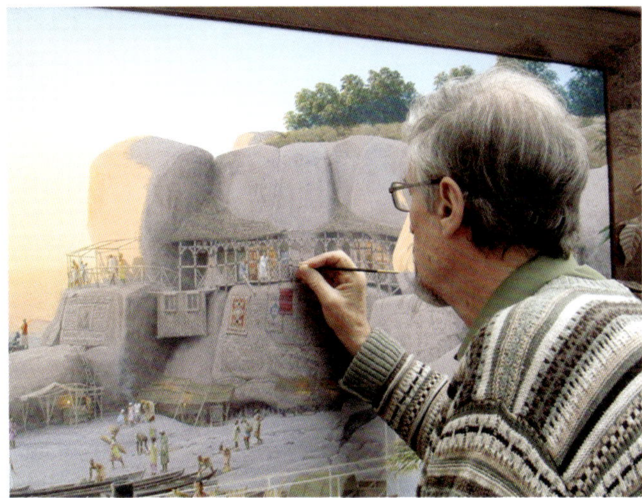

12. Revisiting the Cliffside gallery 24 years after its first "exploration". And yes, that is a "00" brush.

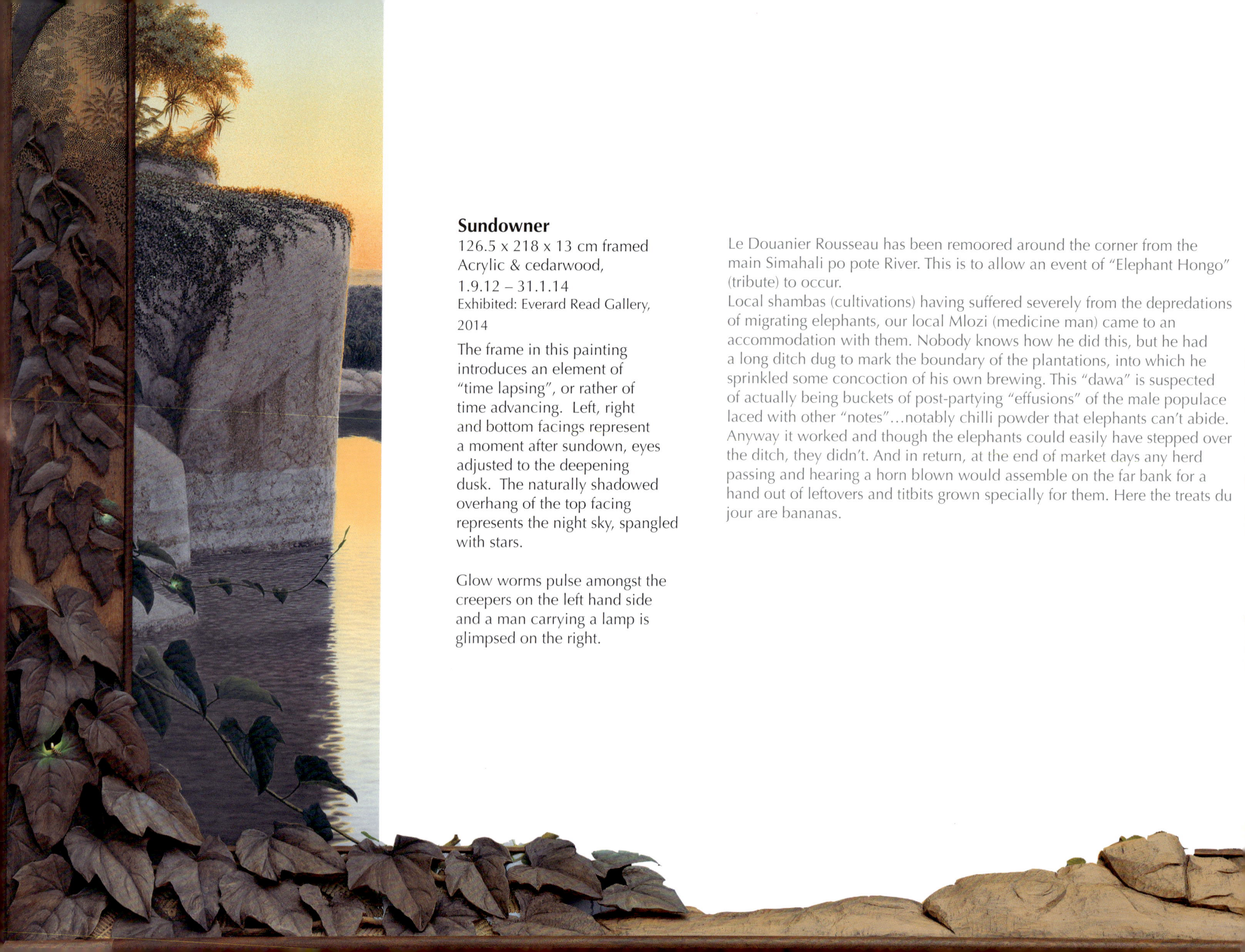

Sundowner
126.5 x 218 x 13 cm framed
Acrylic & cedarwood,
1.9.12 – 31.1.14
Exhibited: Everard Read Gallery, 2014

The frame in this painting introduces an element of "time lapsing", or rather of time advancing. Left, right and bottom facings represent a moment after sundown, eyes adjusted to the deepening dusk. The naturally shadowed overhang of the top facing represents the night sky, spangled with stars.

Glow worms pulse amongst the creepers on the left hand side and a man carrying a lamp is glimpsed on the right.

Le Douanier Rousseau has been remoored around the corner from the main Simahali po pote River. This is to allow an event of "Elephant Hongo" (tribute) to occur.

Local shambas (cultivations) having suffered severely from the depredations of migrating elephants, our local Mlozi (medicine man) came to an accommodation with them. Nobody knows how he did this, but he had a long ditch dug to mark the boundary of the plantations, into which he sprinkled some concoction of his own brewing. This "dawa" is suspected of actually being buckets of post-partying "effusions" of the male populace laced with other "notes"…notably chilli powder that elephants can't abide. Anyway it worked and though the elephants could easily have stepped over the ditch, they didn't. And in return, at the end of market days any herd passing and hearing a horn blown would assemble on the far bank for a hand out of leftovers and titbits grown specially for them. Here the treats du jour are bananas.

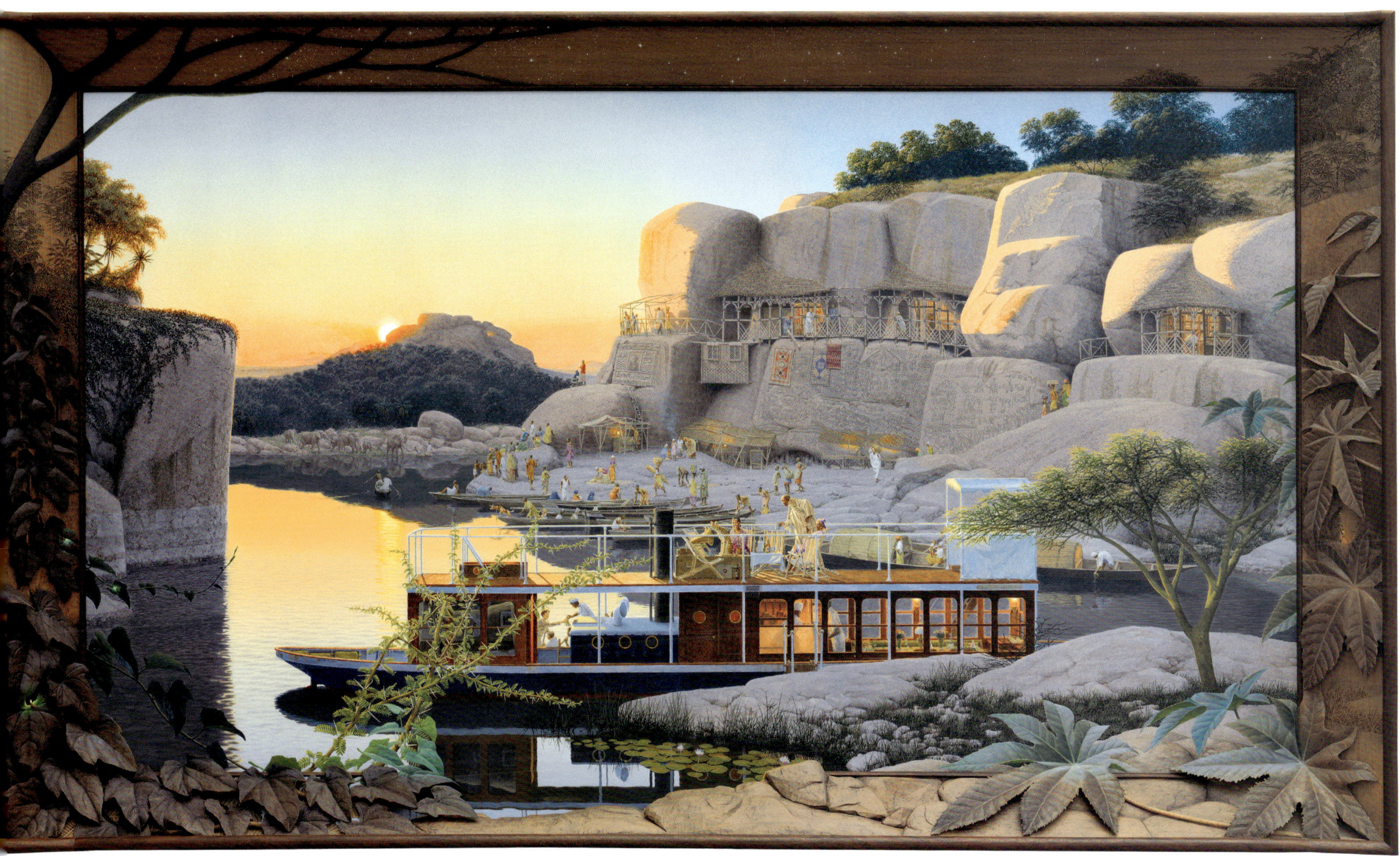

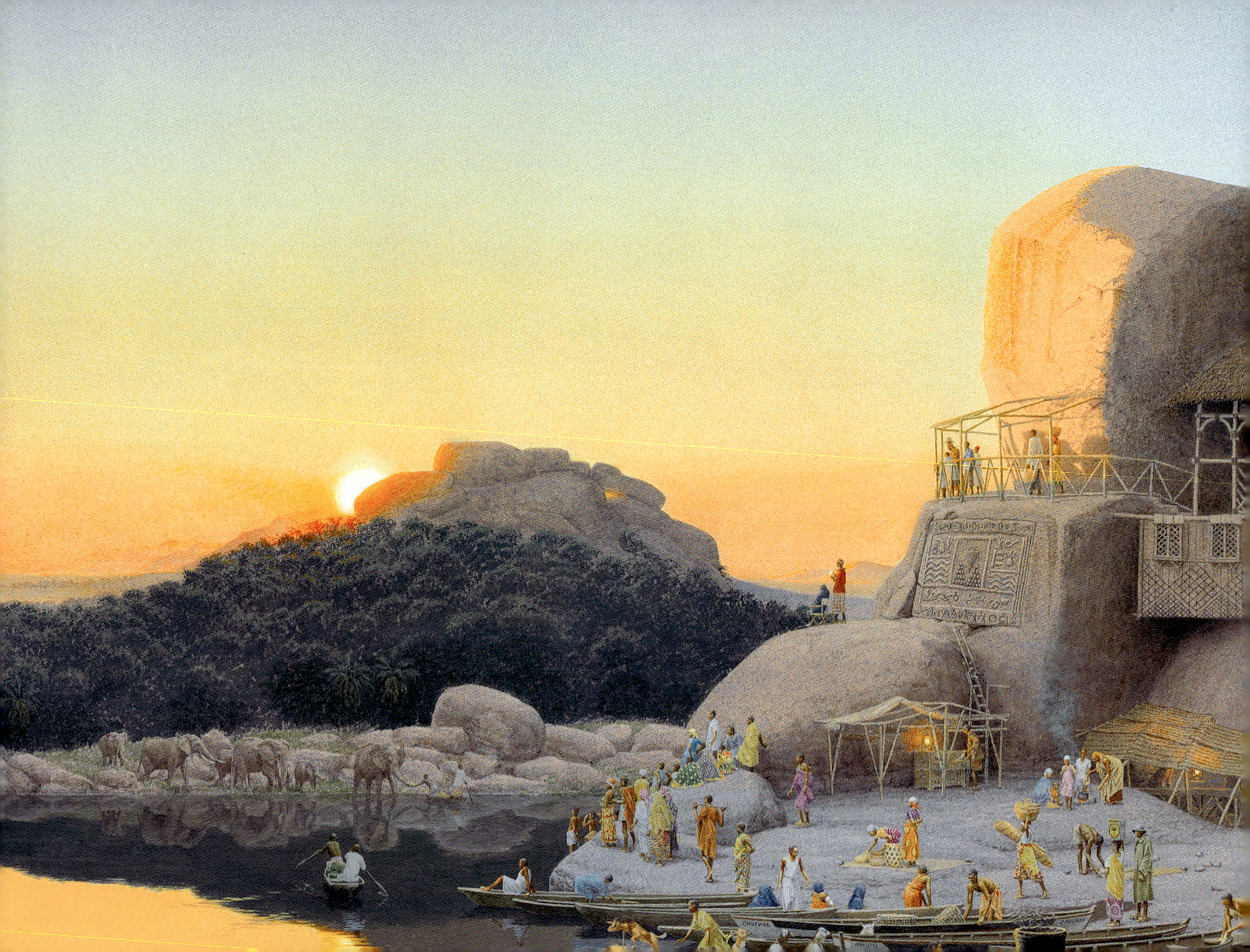

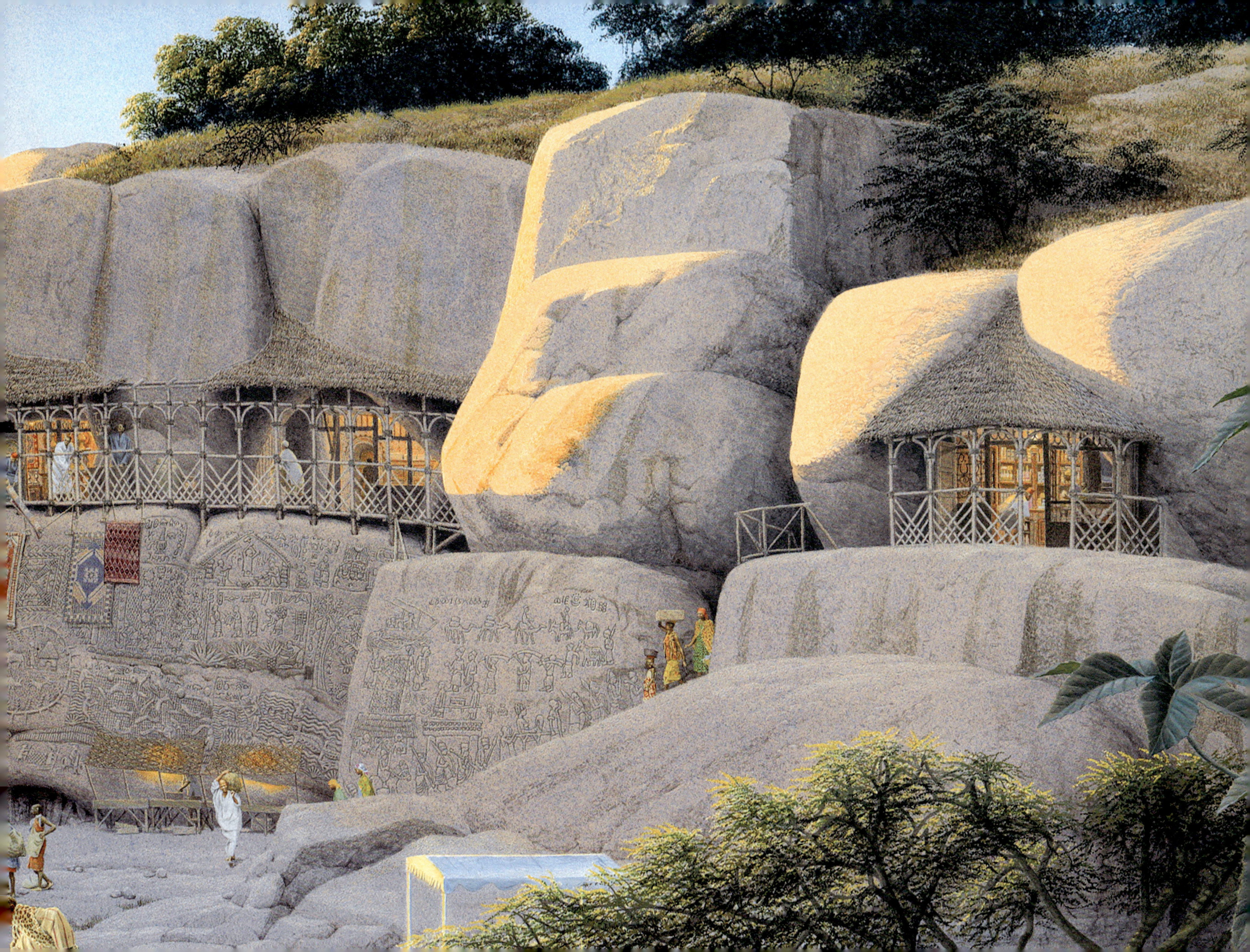

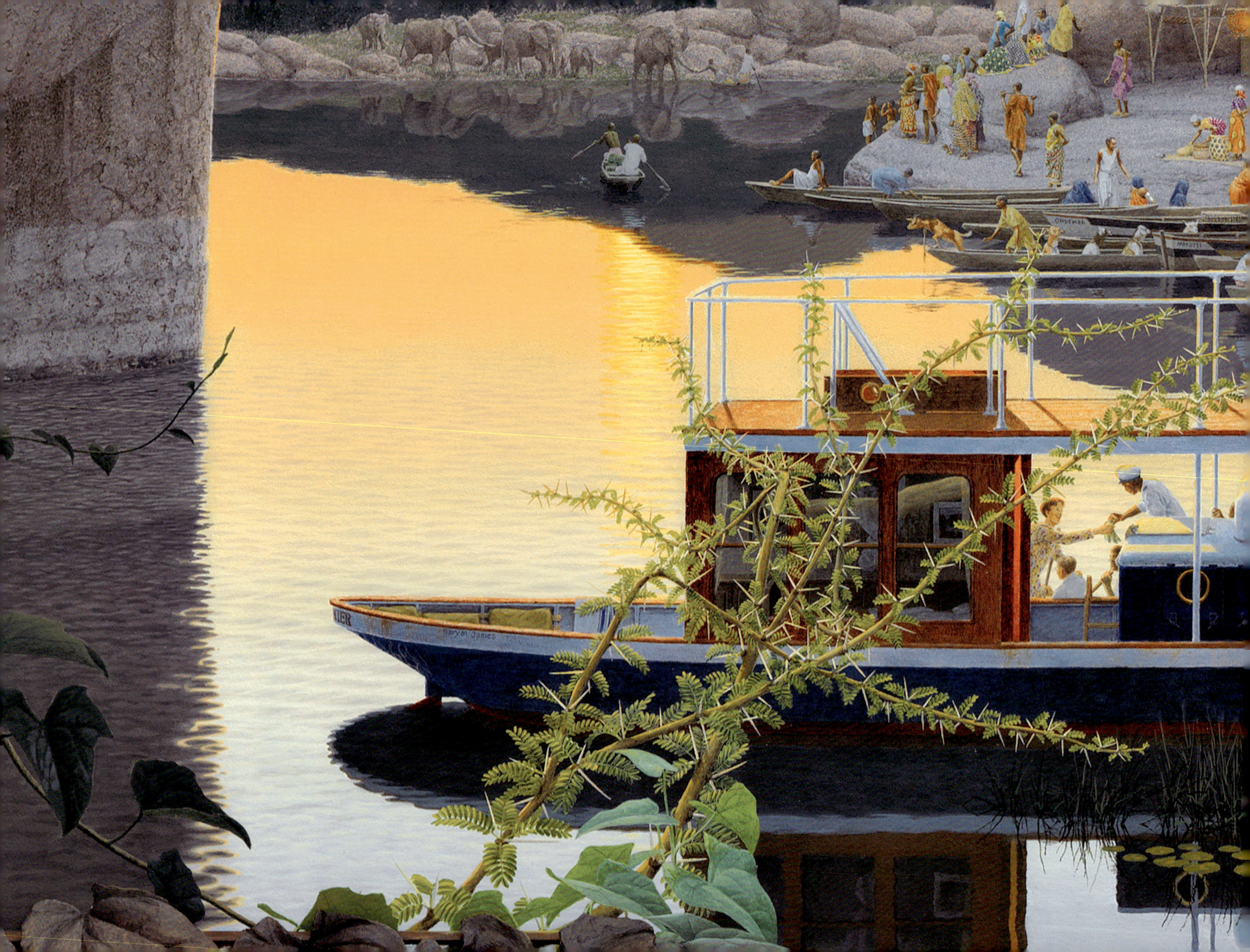
Gary M. James

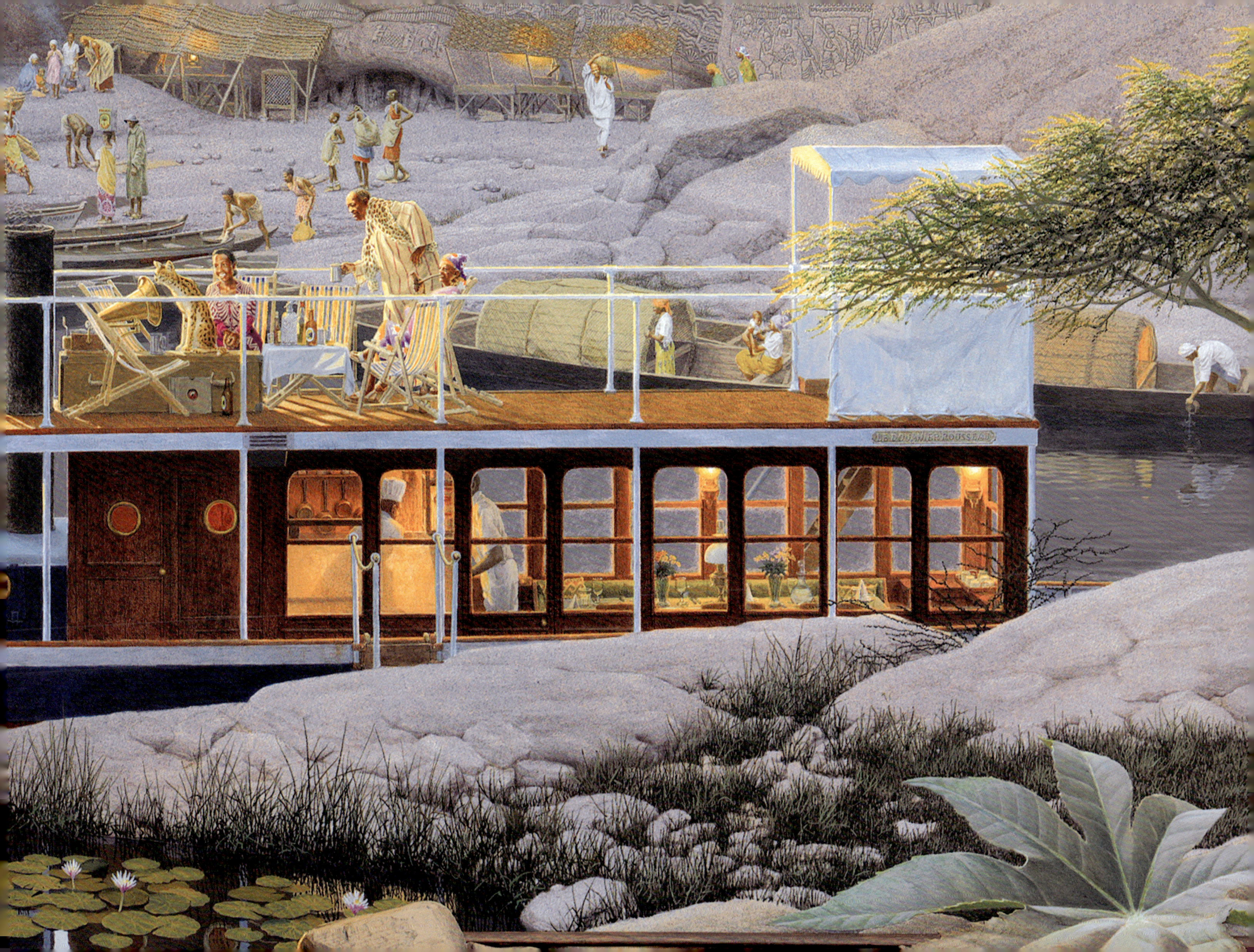

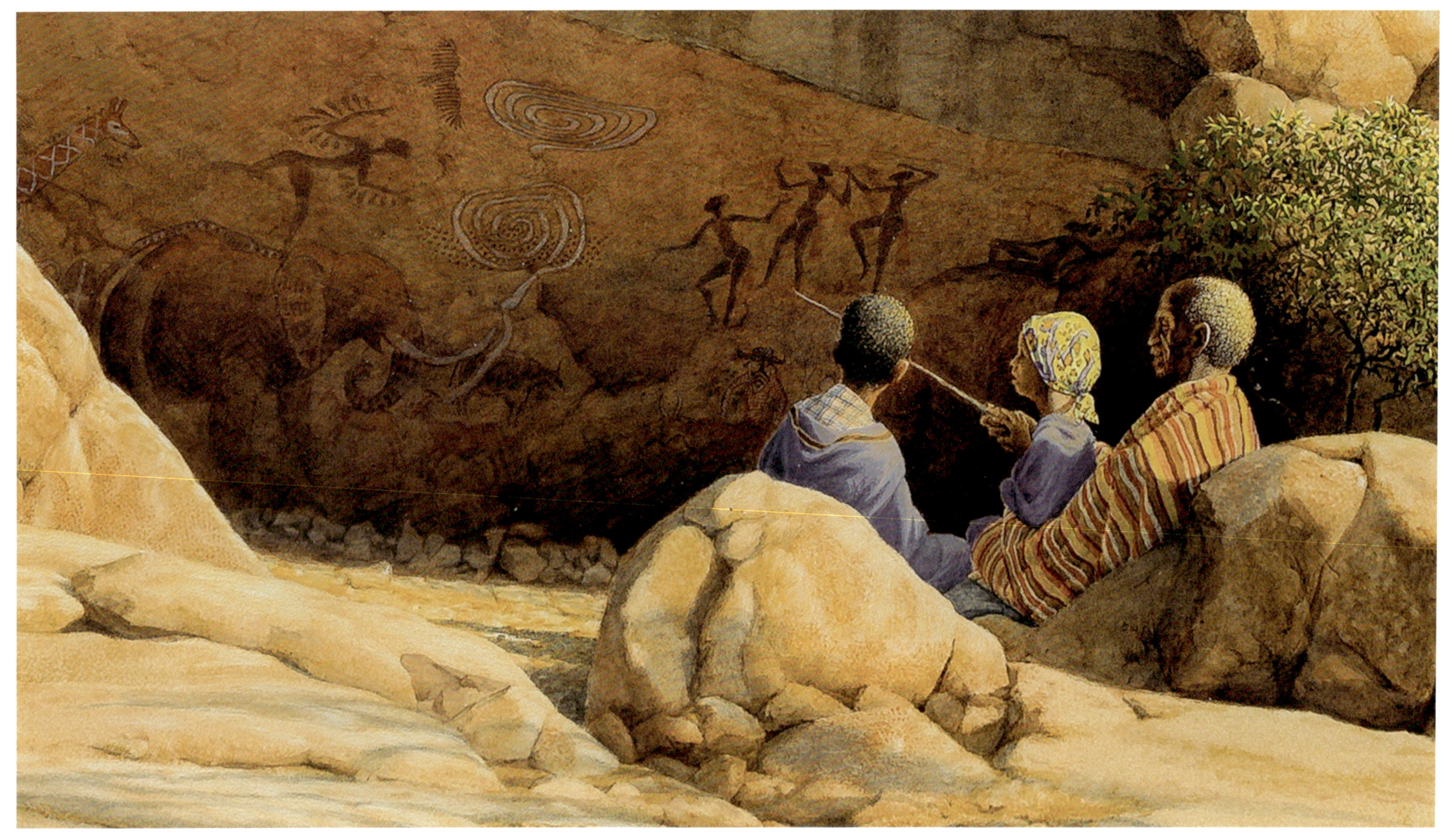

The Story of Nusu-nusu (Half and half)

126 x 186 cm framed, Acrylic & cedarwood, selectively carved, bleached, painted and poker-worked.
18.9.14 – 15.3.16
Exhibited: CIRCA Gallery, London, 2016

The title might equally be 'A Story of Art' given the millennia encompassed by the rock paintings depicted in this rendering.
Here they are the basis of a story handed down from generation to generation by grandfathers detailed off to keep the grandchildren amused whilst the parents have a lie-in.
This telling, as depicted here in poker work along the bottom 'facing' and up the tree, is long and rambling and could well last to lunch time.

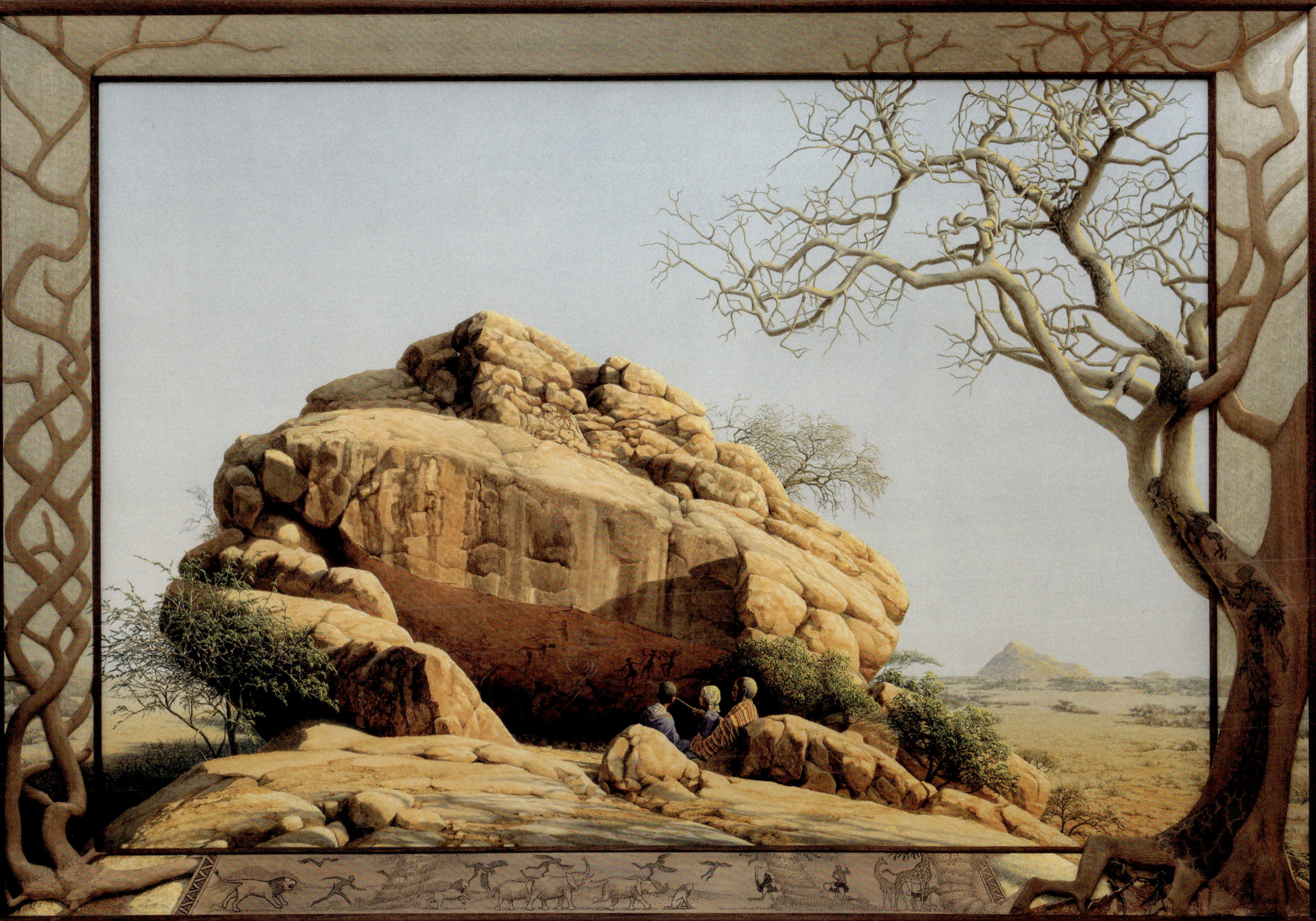

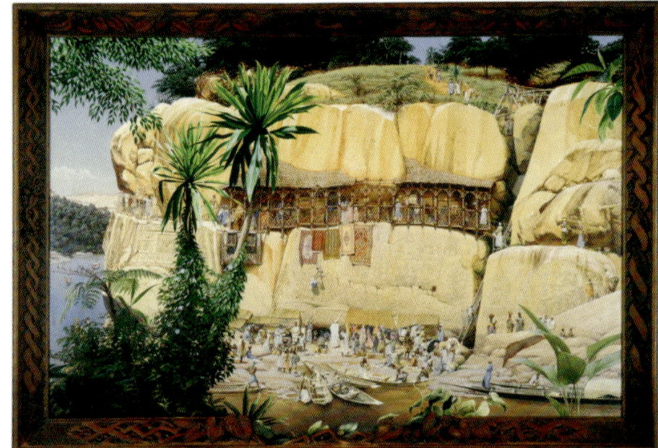

River Market Viewpoint 

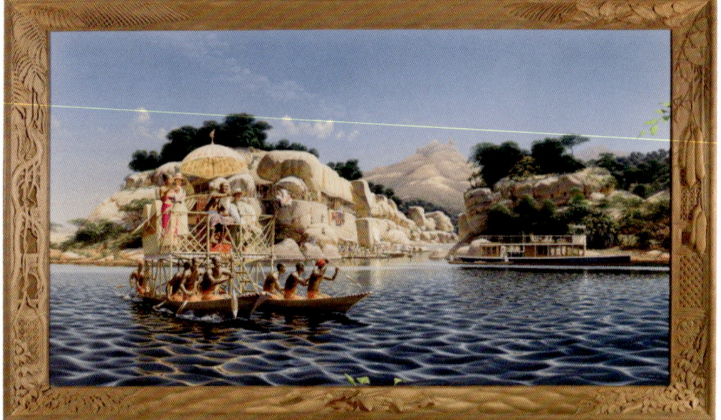

Return to River Market Viewpoint 

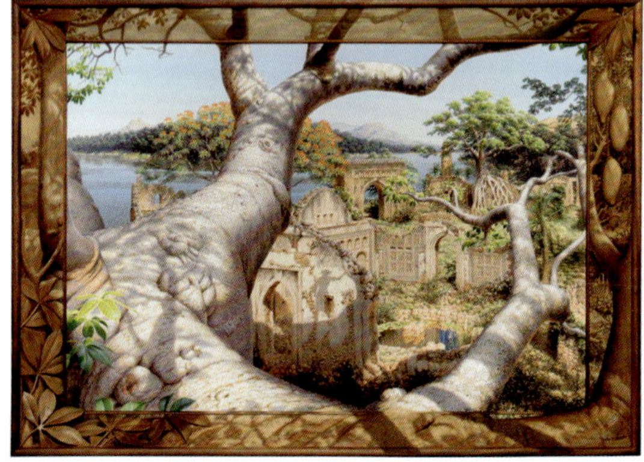

Overseer: The "Lost City" is about 1 mile upstream from here

The River Market Series

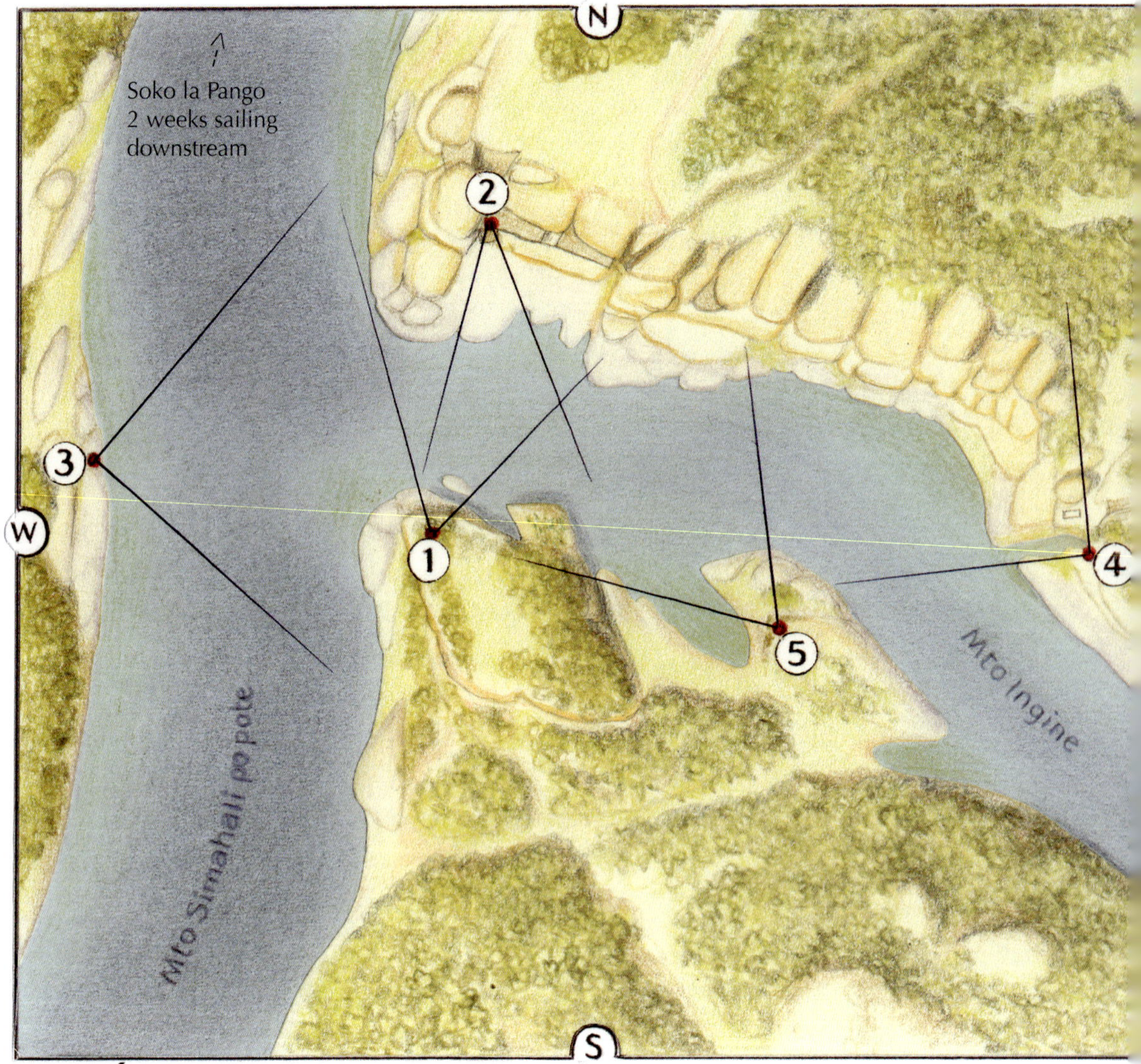

N

Soko la Pango
2 weeks sailing
downstream

2

3

W

1

4

5

Mto Simahali po pote

Mto Ingine

S

Numbers indicate the viewing point of each painting and the order of production. Fine black lines give the scope of each view.

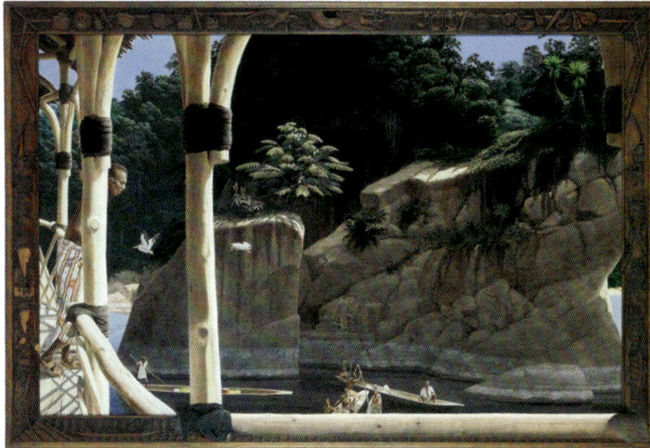

View from the gallery Viewpoint 

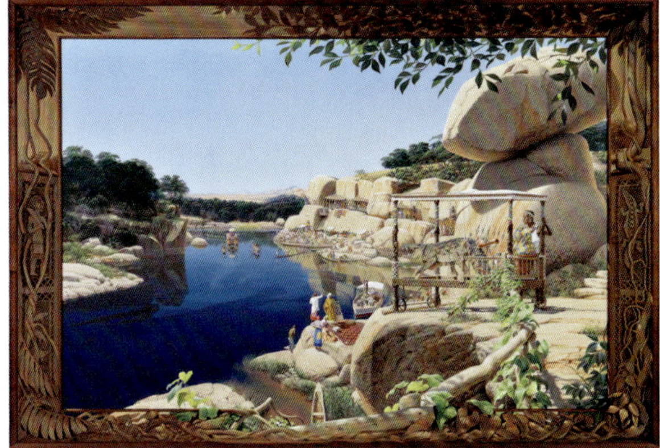

A pronouncement from the River Bed Viewpoint ④

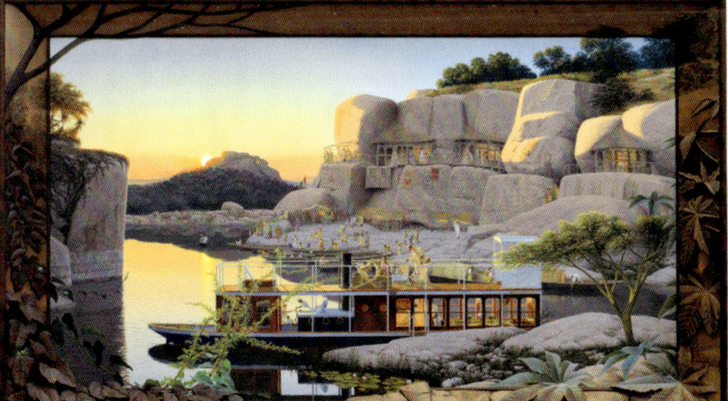

Sundowner Viewpoint 

Contents of Part 6
Paintings by Alexander James

Part 6: ALEX comes aboard....

Following travels to New York and Indo China, Alex worked on a series of paintings inspired by these destinations. Further travels to Egypt, Tunisia, Kenya and South Africa led to his joining the author to form Voyage Art Ltd.

The working relationship this developed has been invaluable to both and, whilst this book is intended to present a retrospective of the author's work, we couldn't close without including a selection of images, as a "trailer" for Alex's forays into an art and continent that is so important to us.

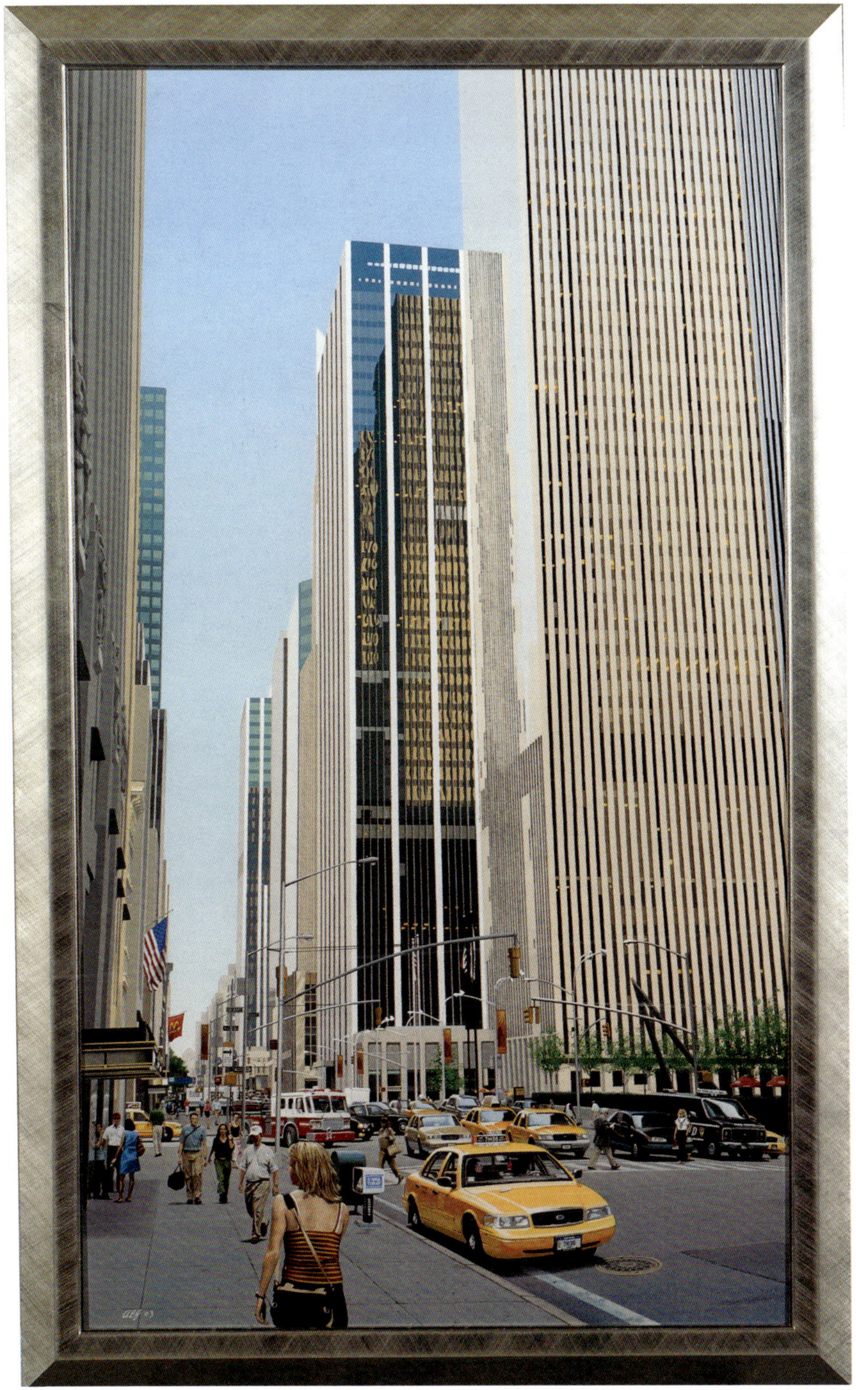

6th Avenue, New York

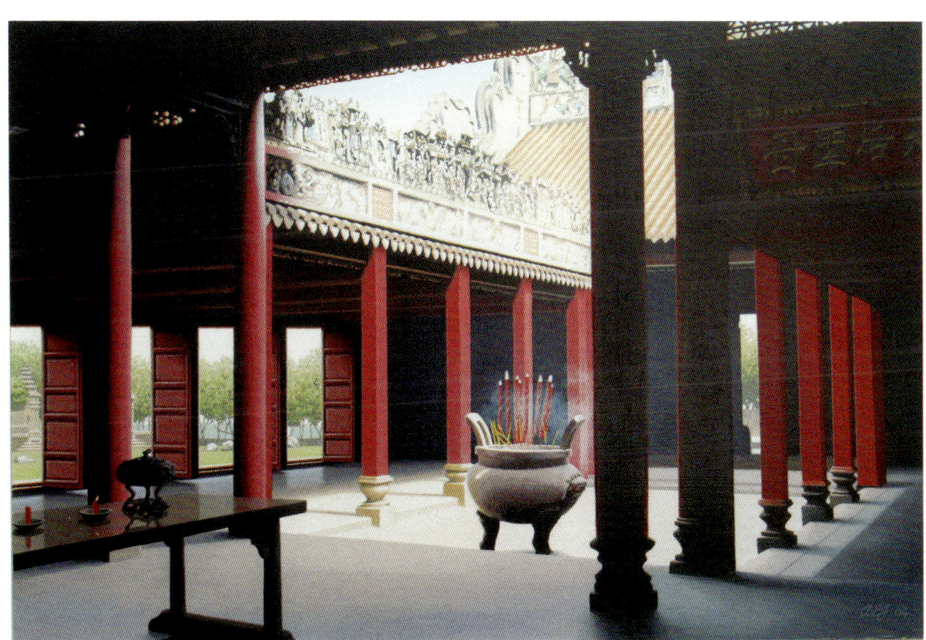

Vietnamese temple

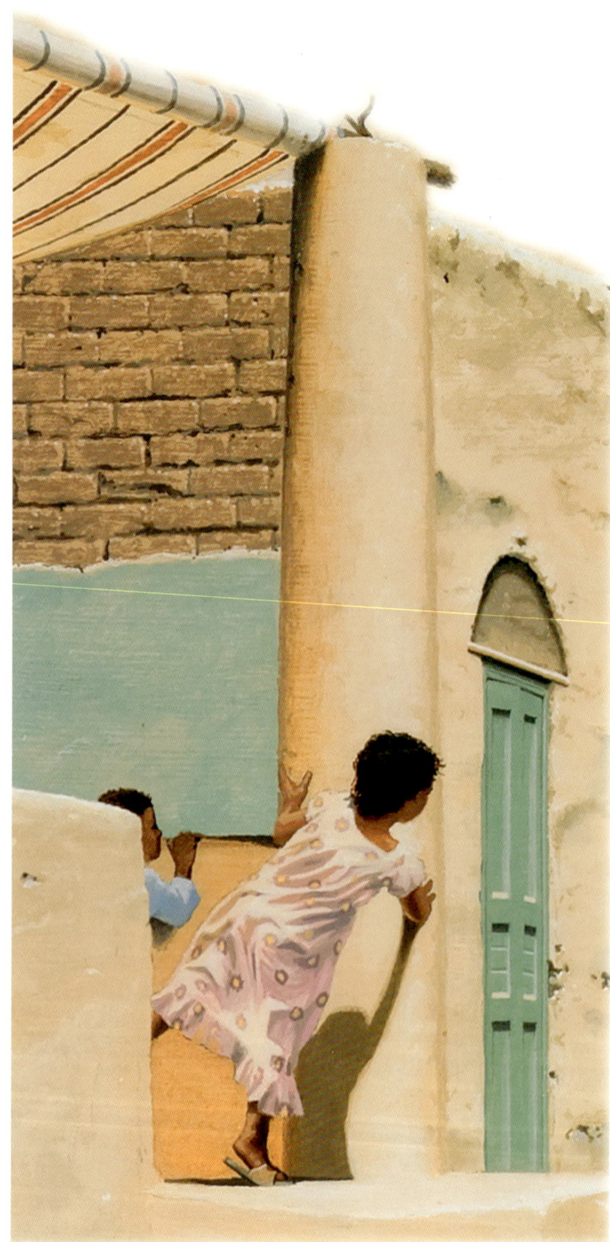

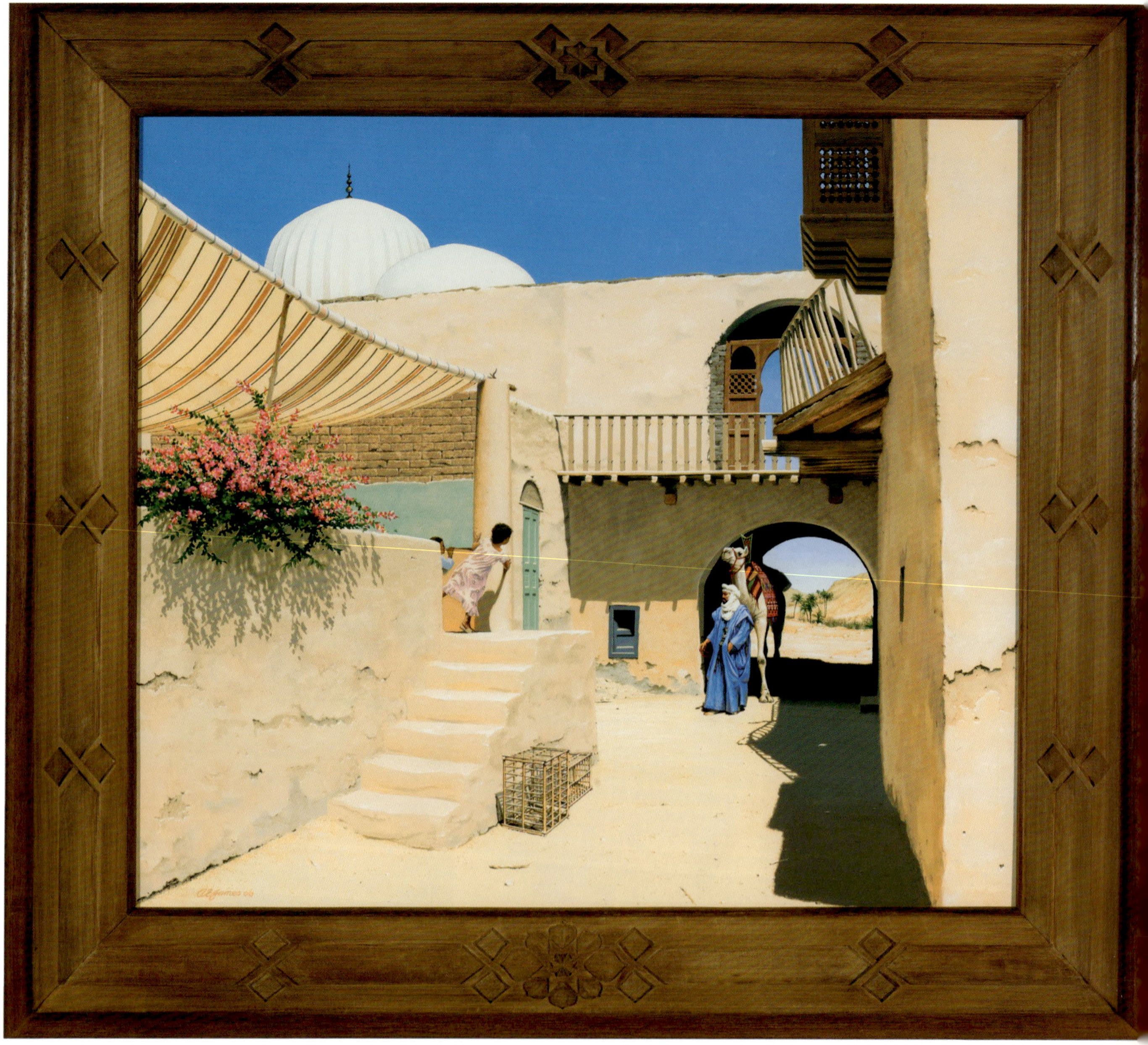

Salt Seller
79 x 88 cm framed, 2006
Exhibited: Everard Read Gallery, Johannesburg, 2008

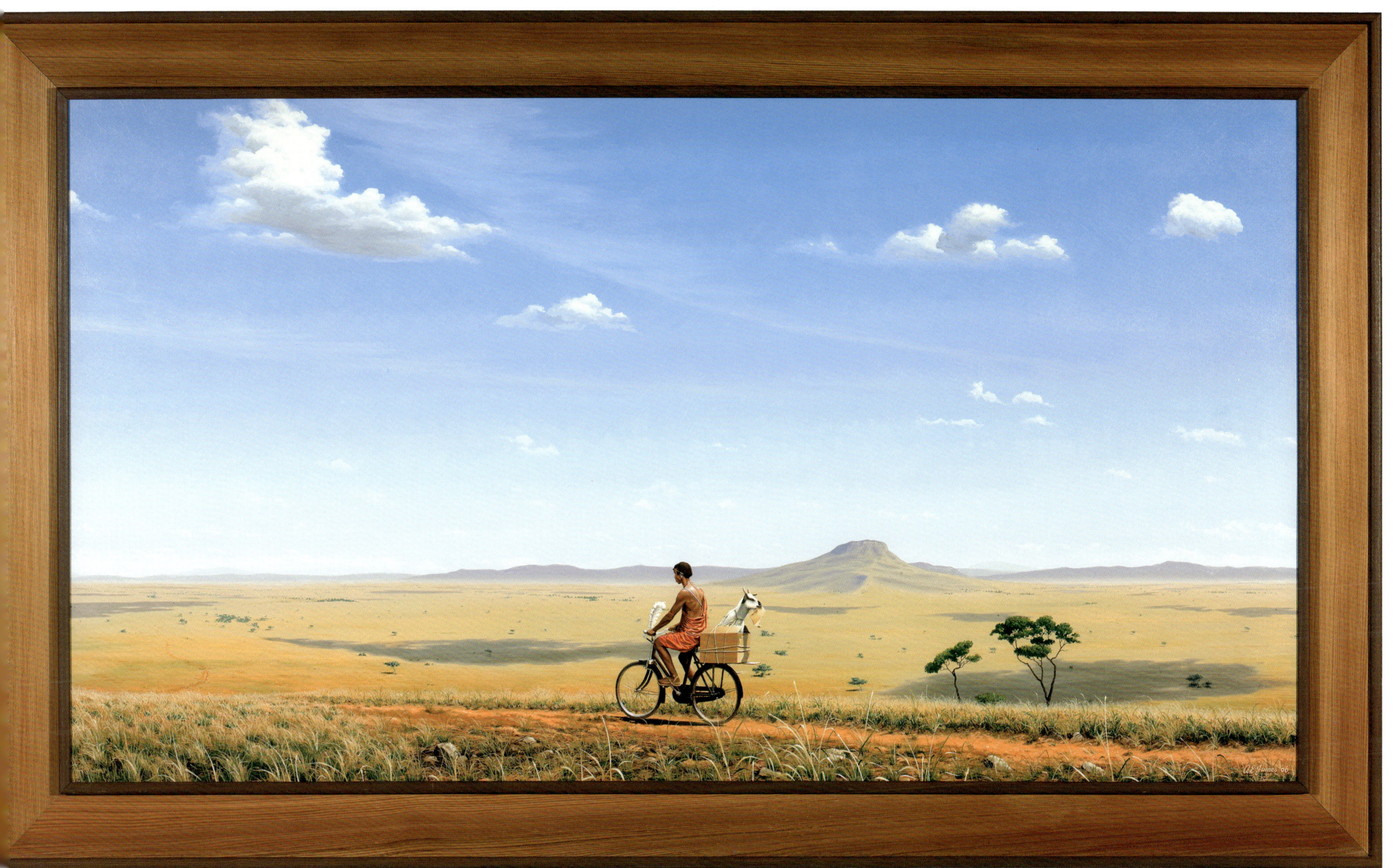

The goat between
82 x 138 cm framed, 2006
Exhibited: Everard Read Gallery, Johannesburg, 2008

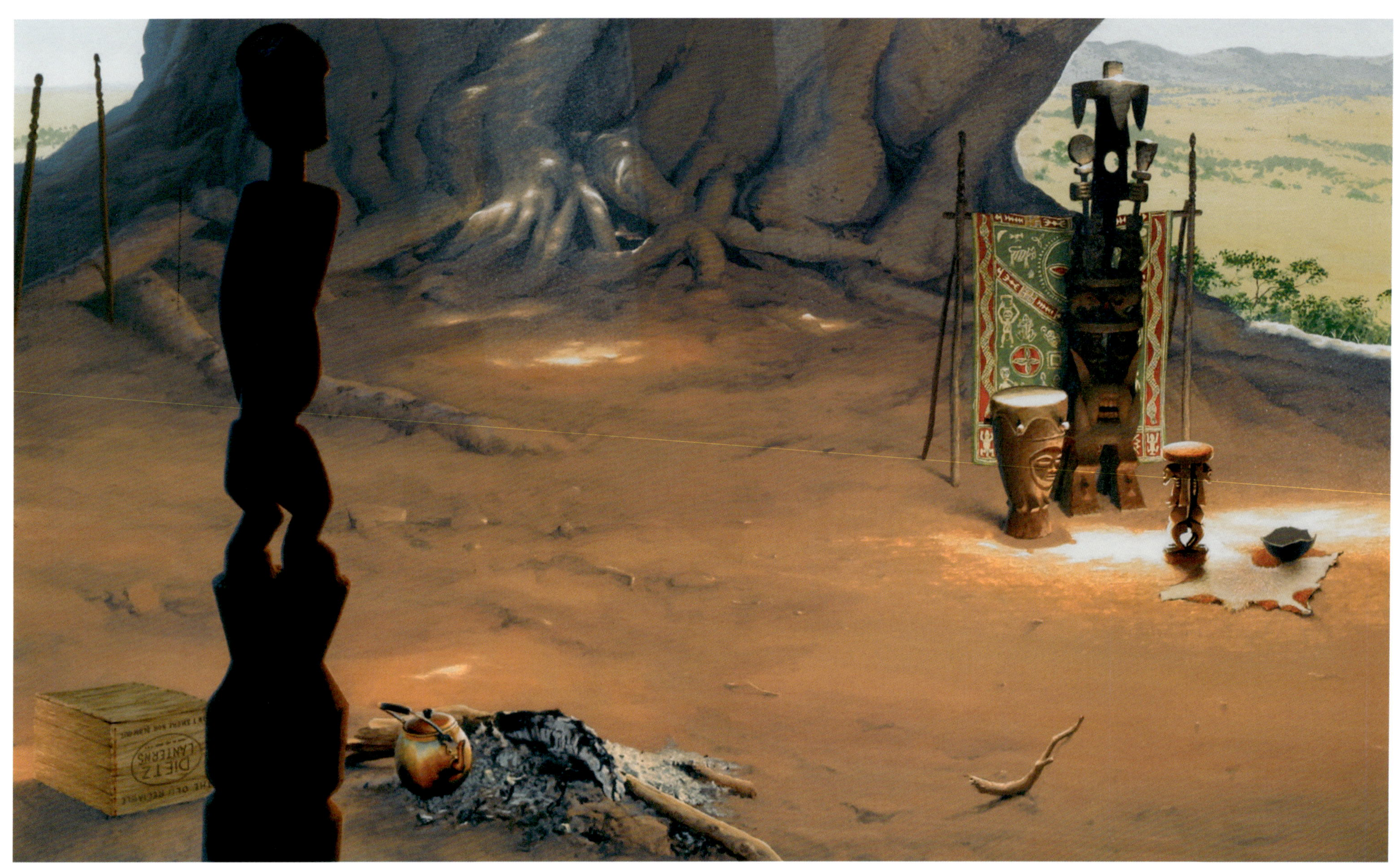

A Wayside Oracle 2
90 x 170 cm (approx), 2008/09
Exhibited: Everard Read Gallery, Johannesburg, 2009

Our breakfast campfire
El Kharga Oasis, Egypt 2006

Drums and totems

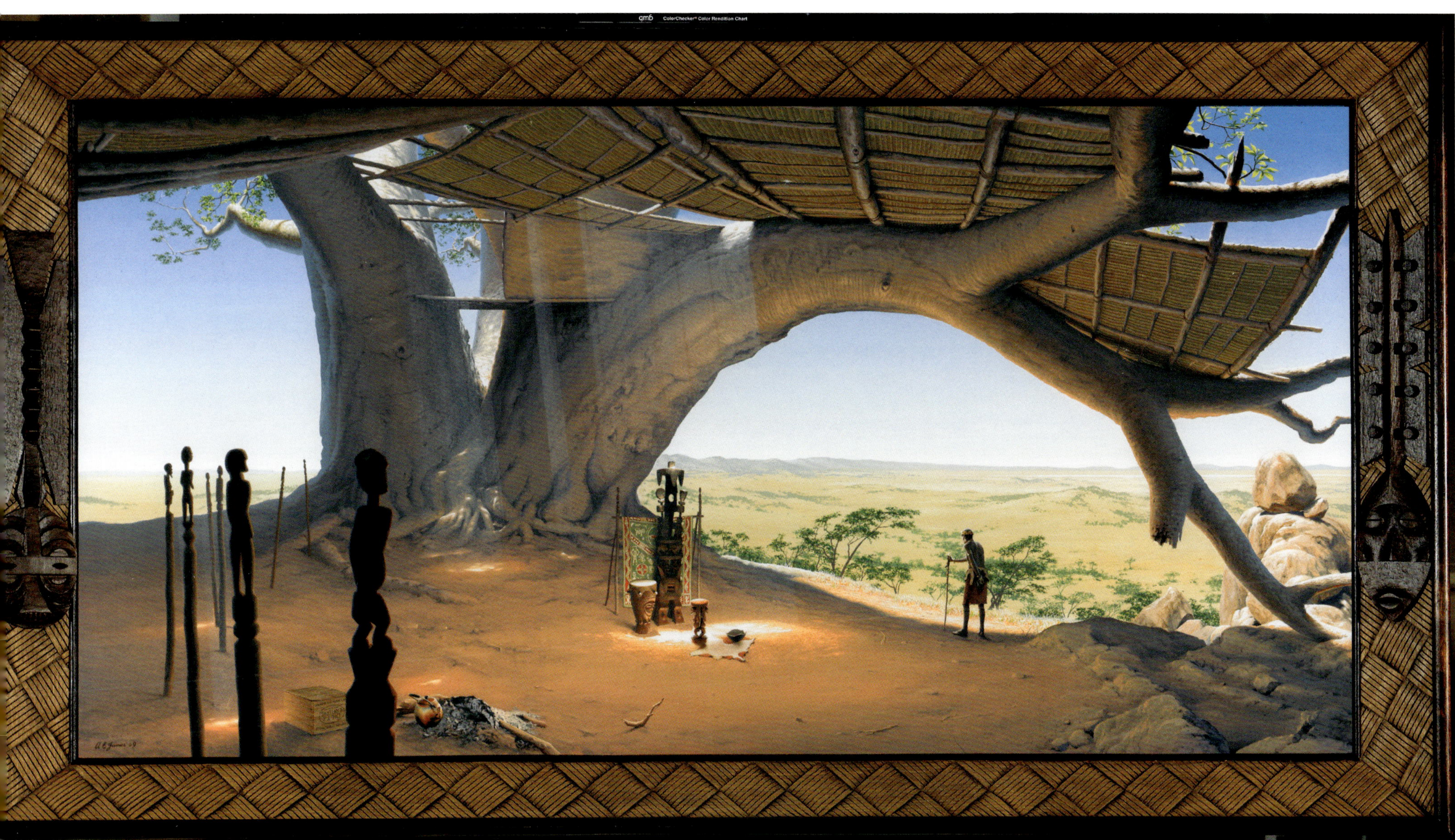

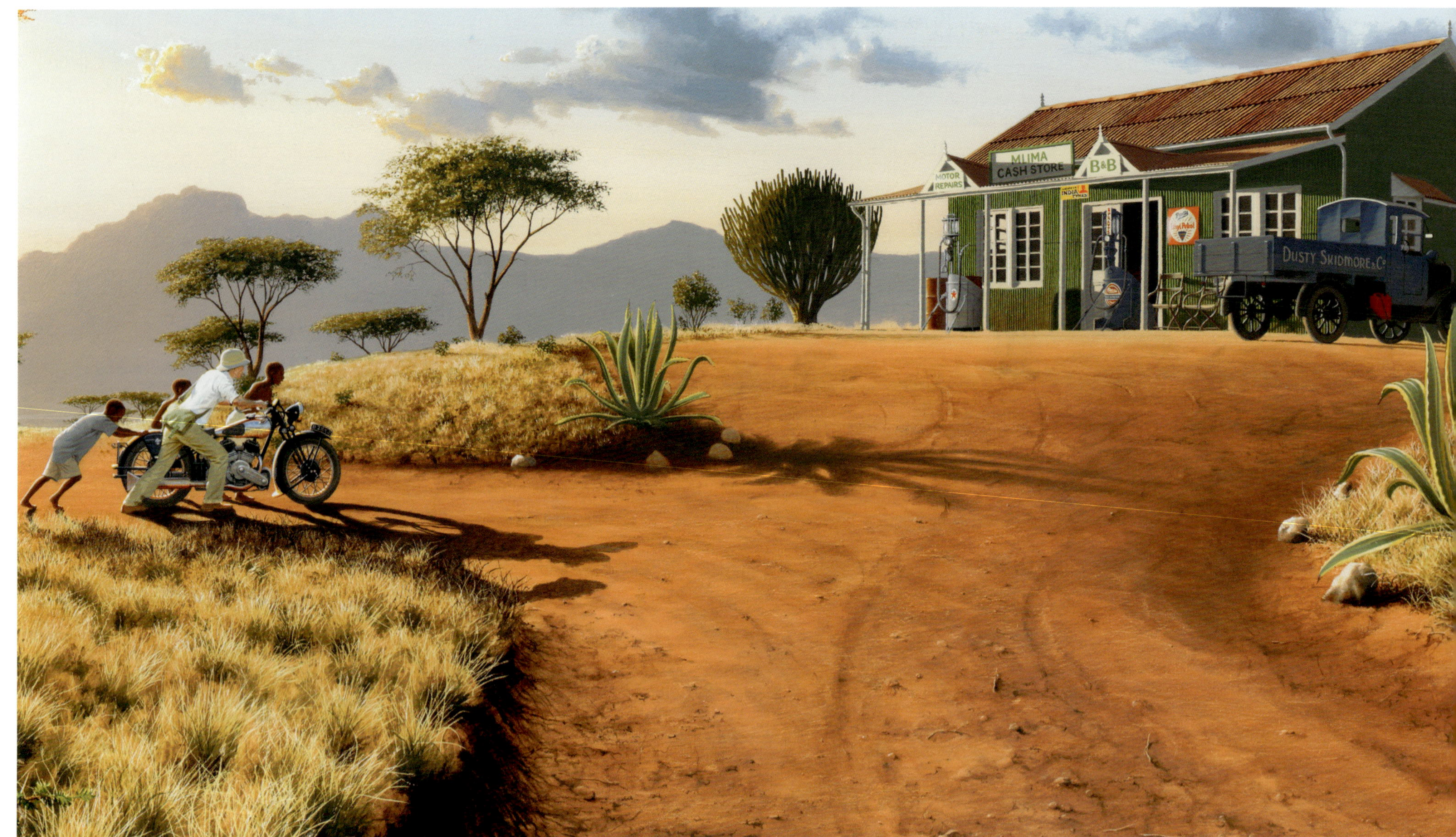

Mlima

(Swahili: a high hill or long, steep ascent.)

80 x 120 cm - approx. 2009

Exhibited: Everard Read Gallery, Johannesburg, 2009

The motorcycle is a Brough Superior

Brough Superior motorcycles, sidecars, and motor cars were made by George Brough in his Brough Superior works on Haydn Road in Nottingham, England, from 1919 to 1940. The motorcycles were dubbed the "Rolls-Royce of Motorcycles" by H. D. Teague of The Motor Cycle newspaper (Wikipedia).

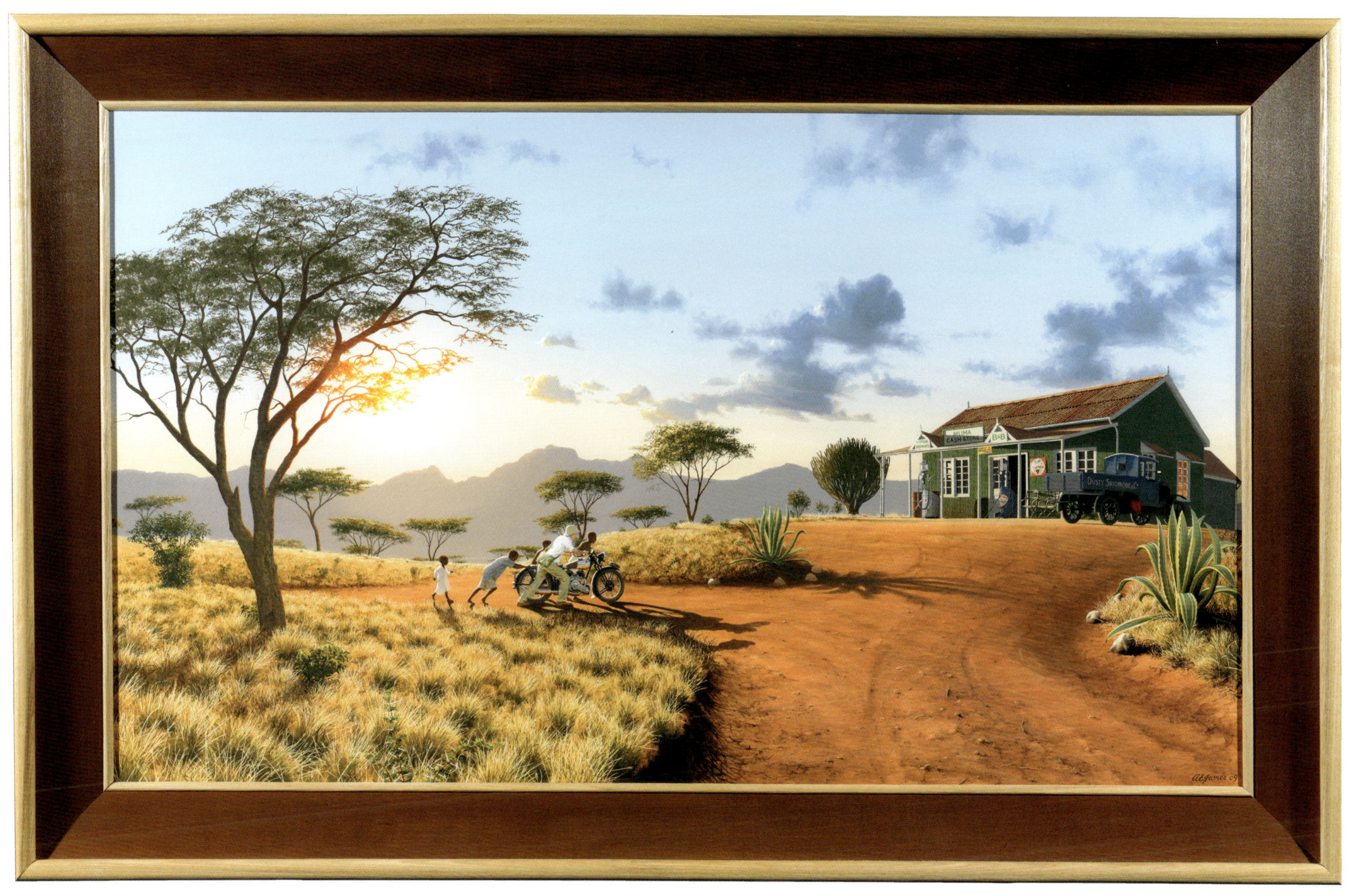
MUMA
CASH STORE
B&B

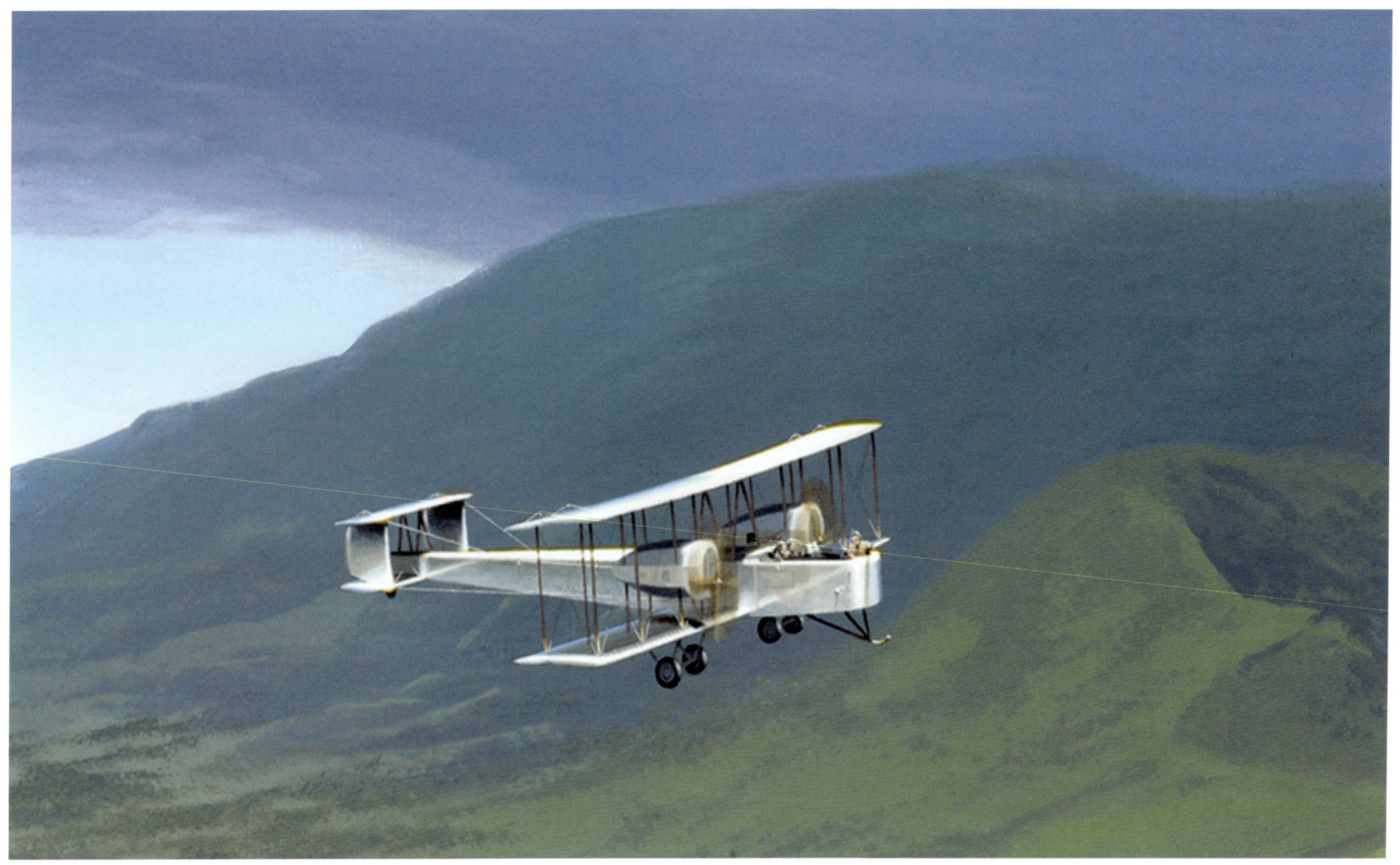

Silver Queen 1920
113.5 x 133 cm framed 2009
Exhibited: Everard Read Gallery, Johannesburg, 2009

In 1920 the first flight from England (Brooklands) to Cape Town was made by two South Africans, Pierre van Ryneveld and Quintin Brand. Flying a Vickers Vimy the journey took 45 days. "Silver Queen I" was wrecked at Wadi Halfa and the journey continued in "Silver Queen II" another Vimy, via East Africa – until it too crashed on take off at Bulawayo. The flight was completed in a borrowed South African Air Force plane.
Van Ryneveld & Brand were knighted but were awarded only half the £10,000 prize offered by the Daily Mail as the trip had not been completed in the original aircraft.

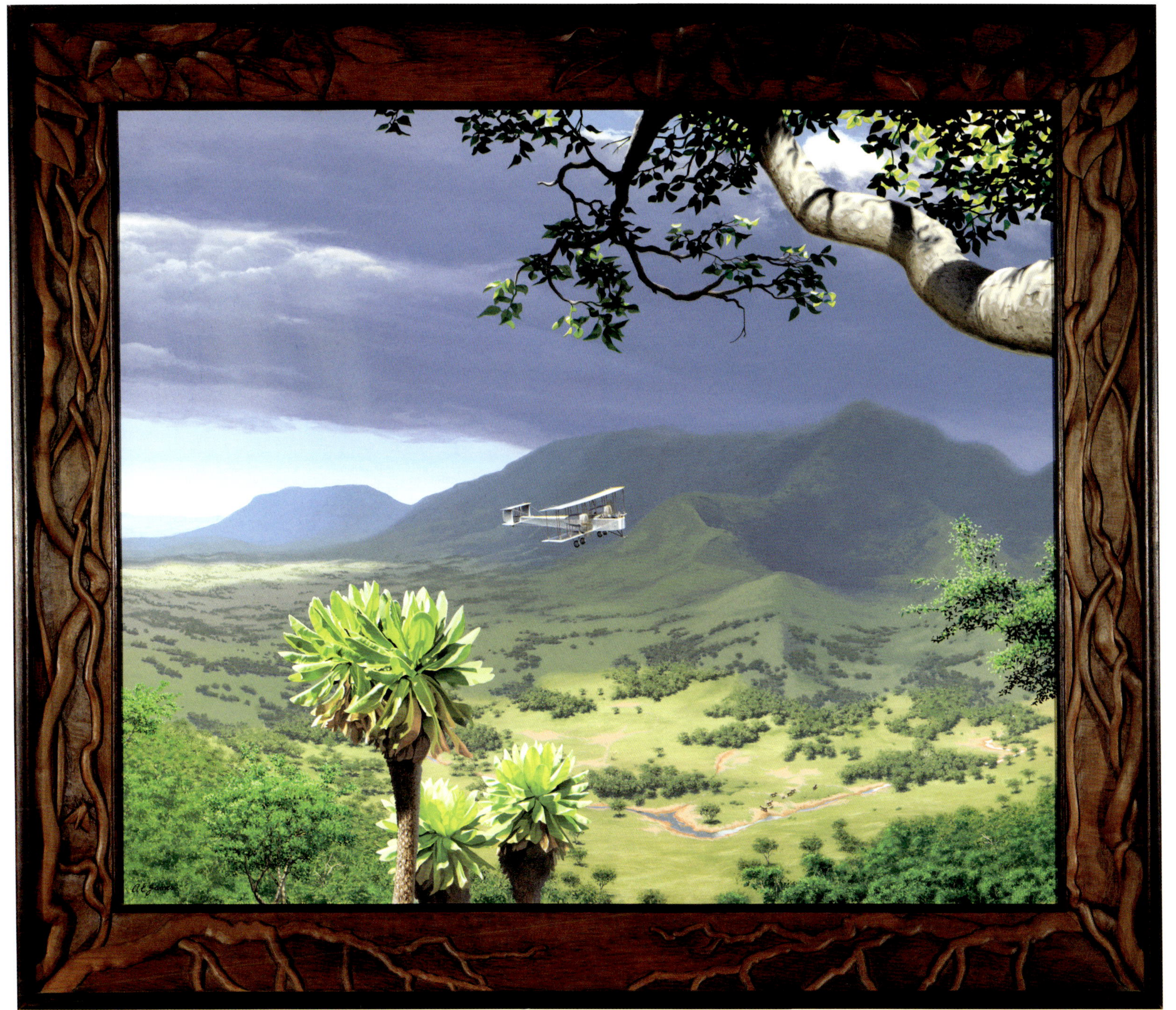

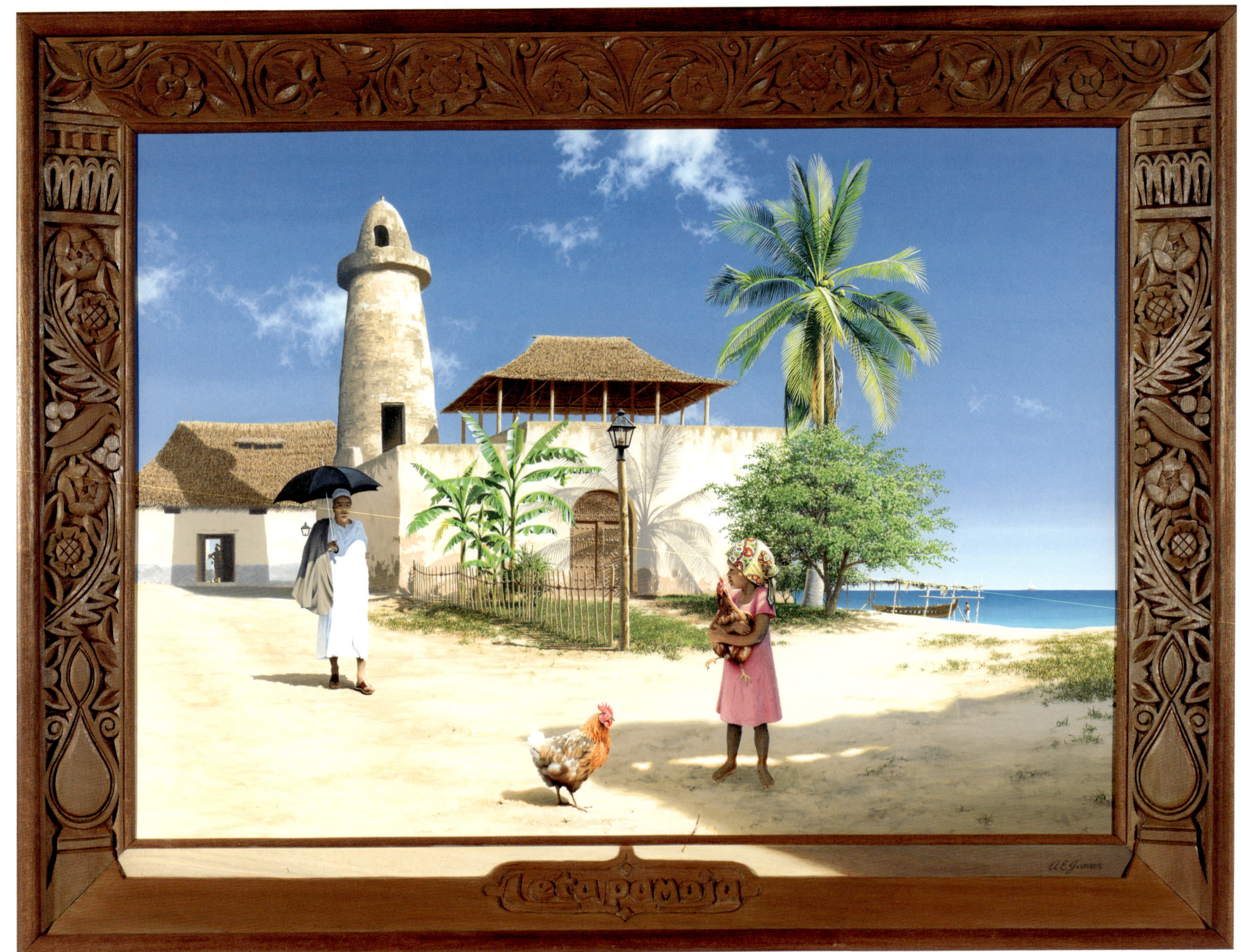

Roundup (Leta pamoja)
83 x 110 cm framed 2010
Exhibited: Everard Read Gallery, Johannesburg, 2013

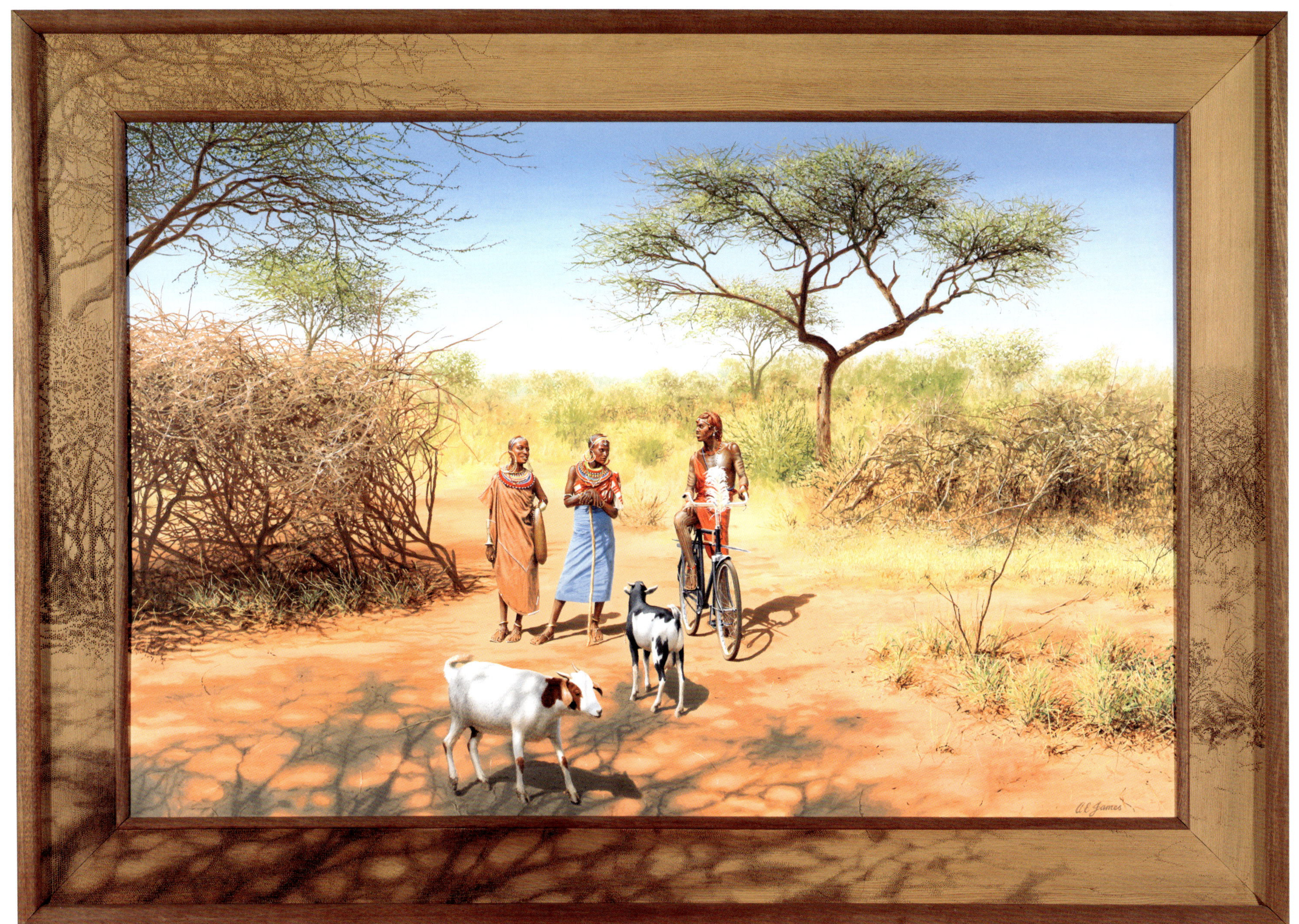

The Dude
75.5 x 108 cm framed, 2011
Exhibited: Everard Read Gallery, Johannesburg, 2013

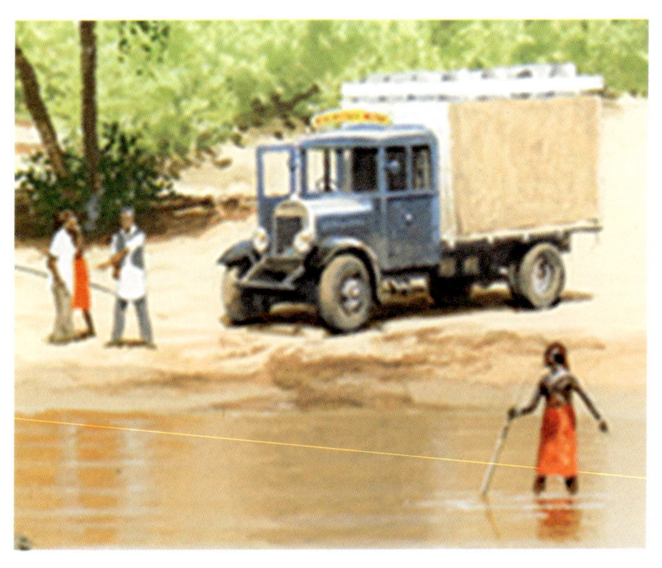

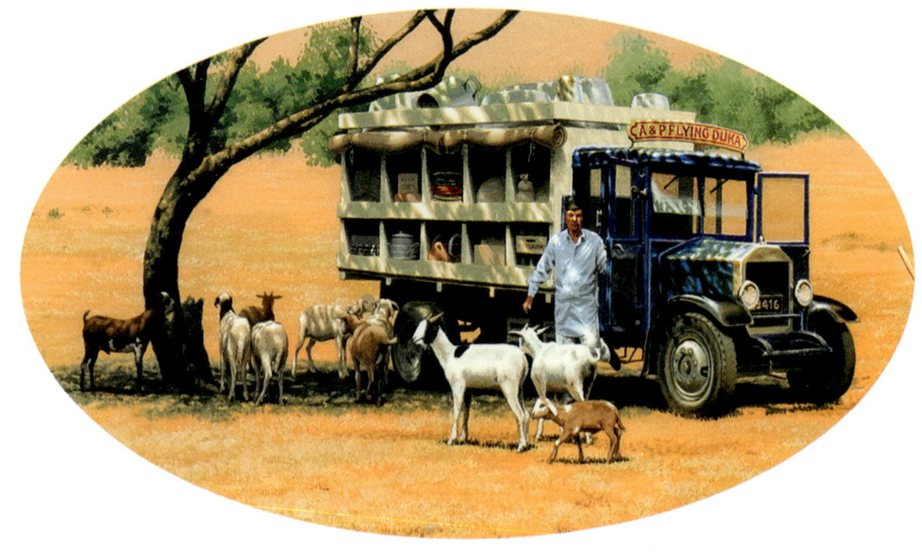

Knee high
79 x 139.5 cm framed, 2012
Exhibited: Everard Read Gallery, Johannesburg, 2013
A Samburu, braving crocodiles, tests the depth of the Uaso Nyiro River, swollen by the monsoon rains. Can the "Flying Duka" make it across without getting stuck and having to hire a team of oxen?

The "Flying Duka"
from another painting of that name.

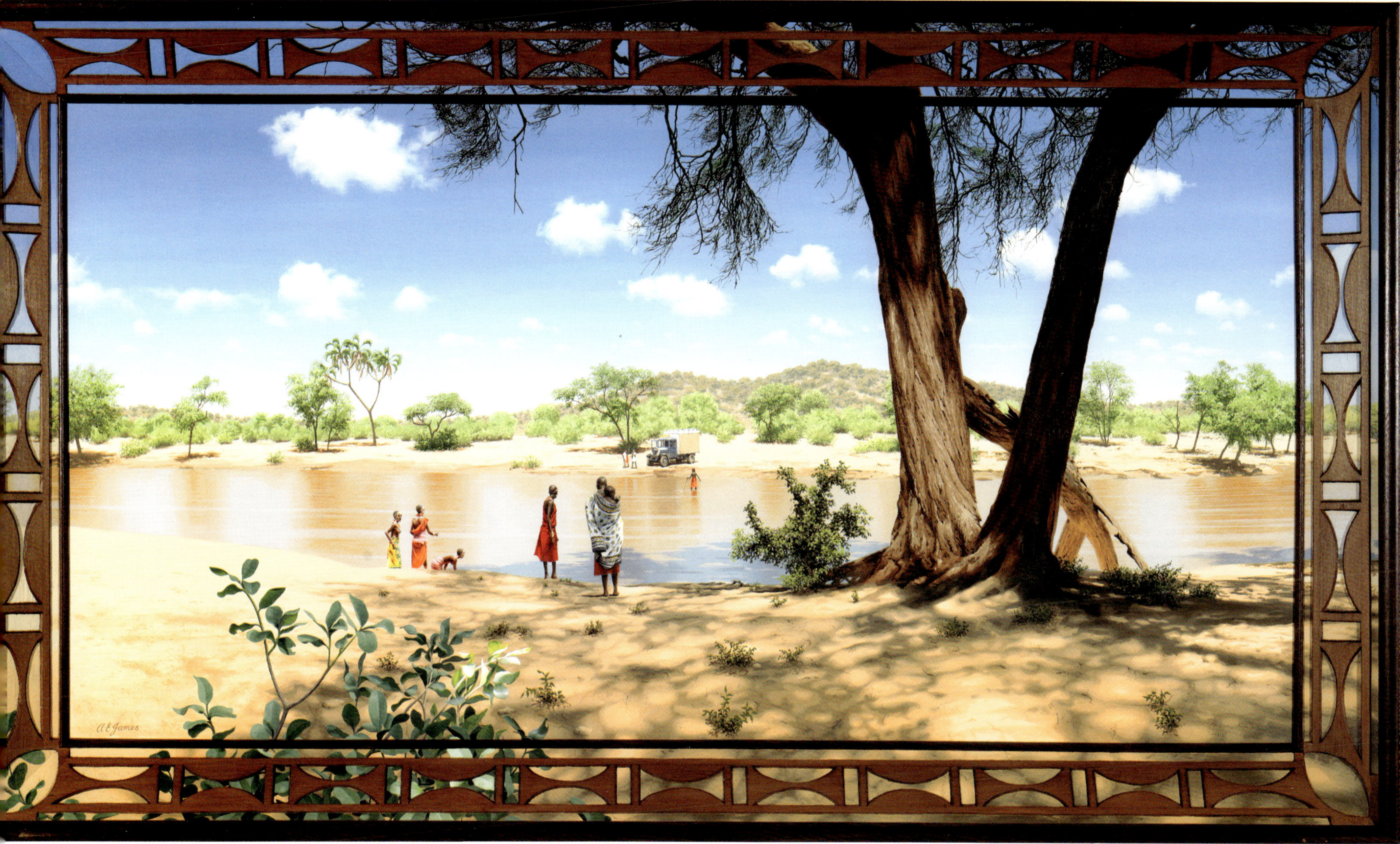

Knee high

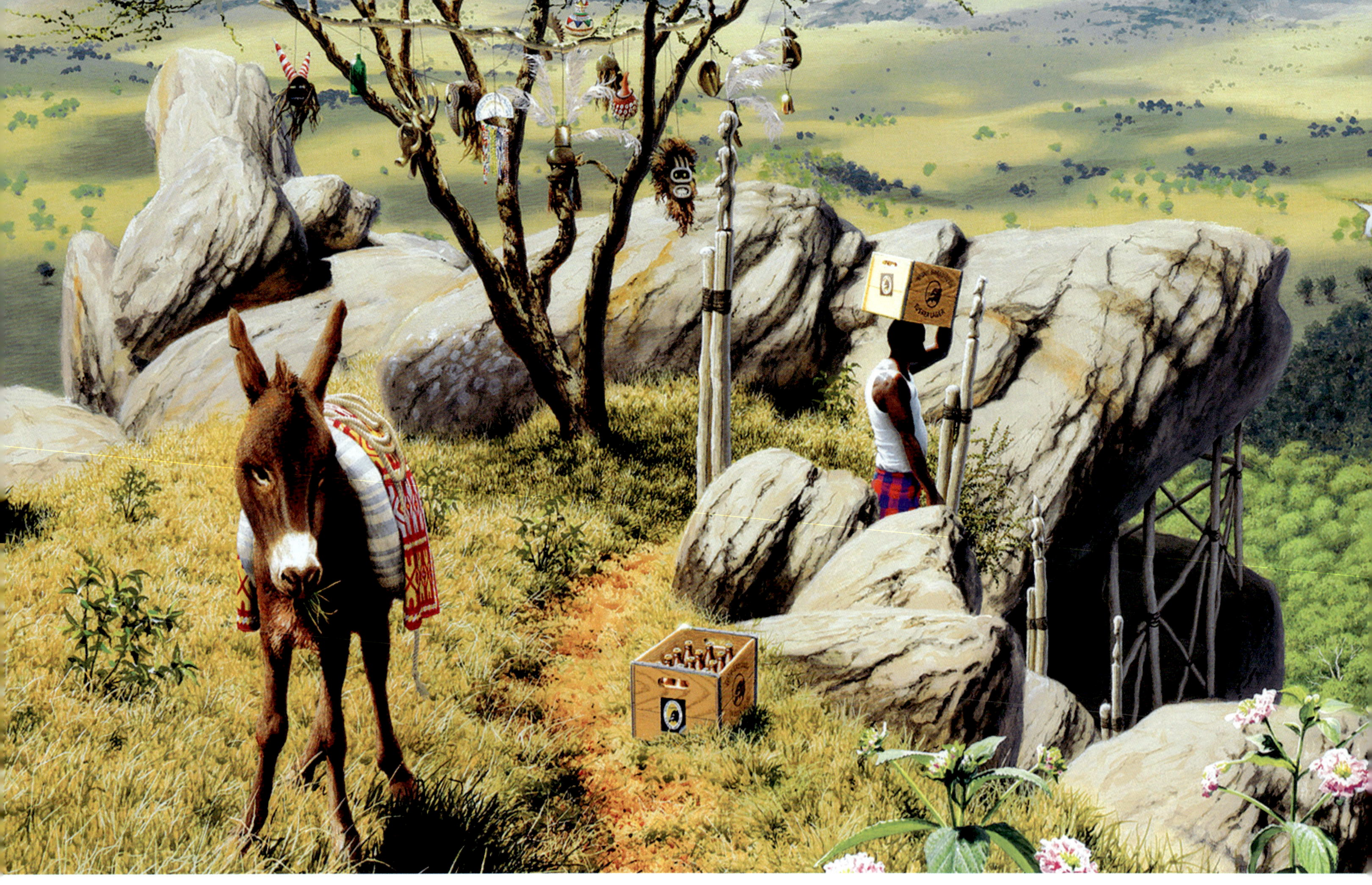

Beers for a baraza 107.5 x 145 cm framed 2013

("Baraza", Swahili for a meeting)
Exhibited: Everard Read Gallery, Johannesburg, 2014

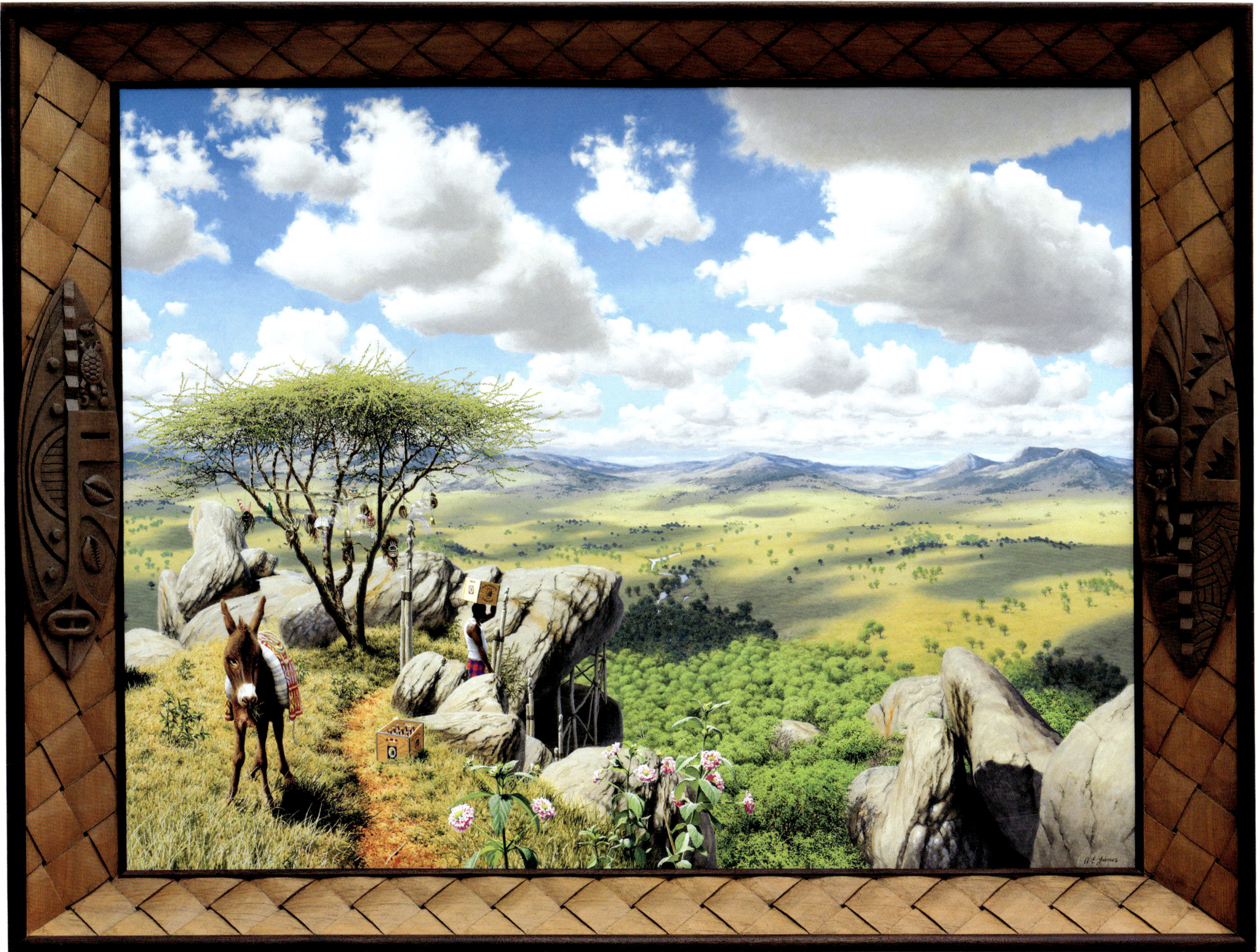

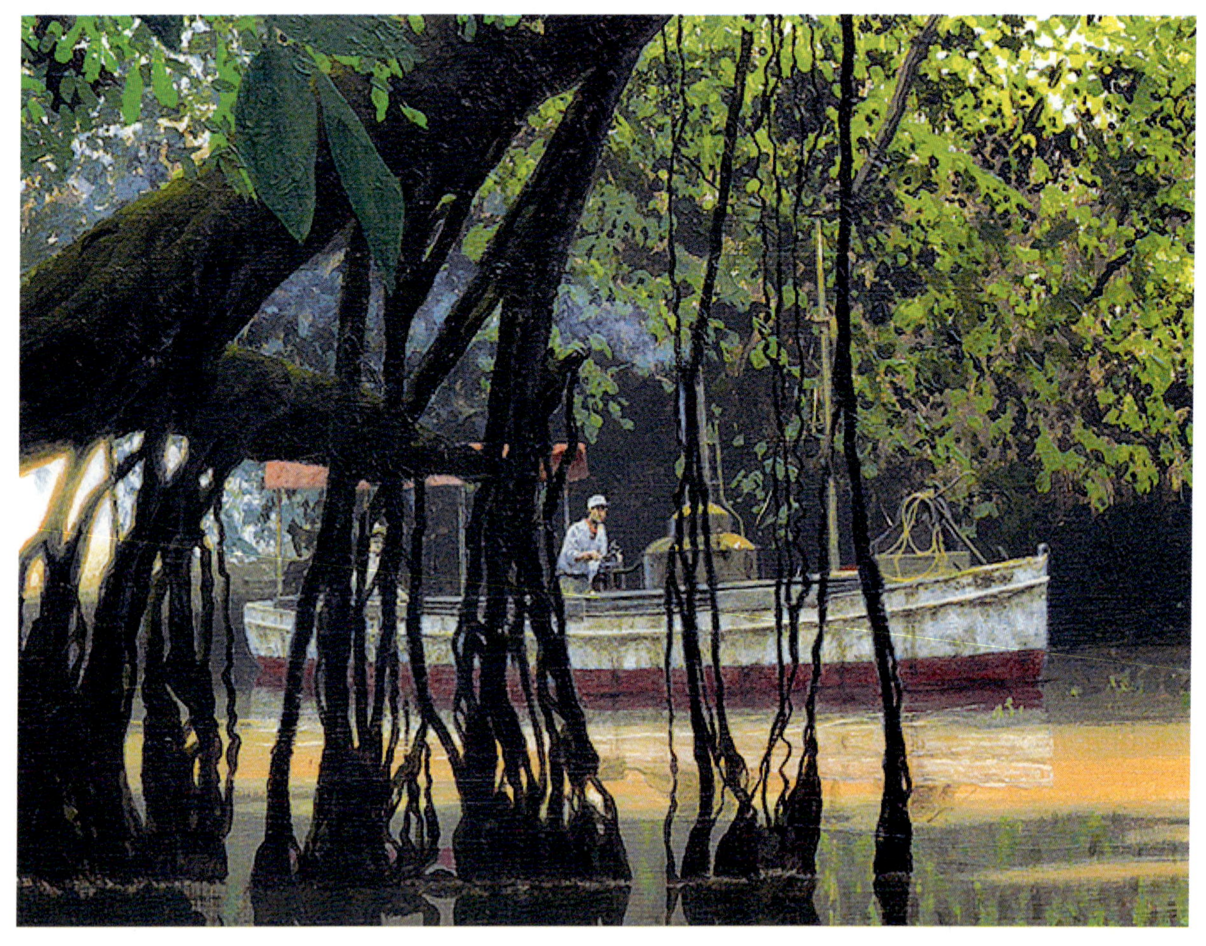

A surprise encounter

93 x 119.5 cm framed, 2013
Exhibited: Everard Read Gallery, Johannesburg, 2014

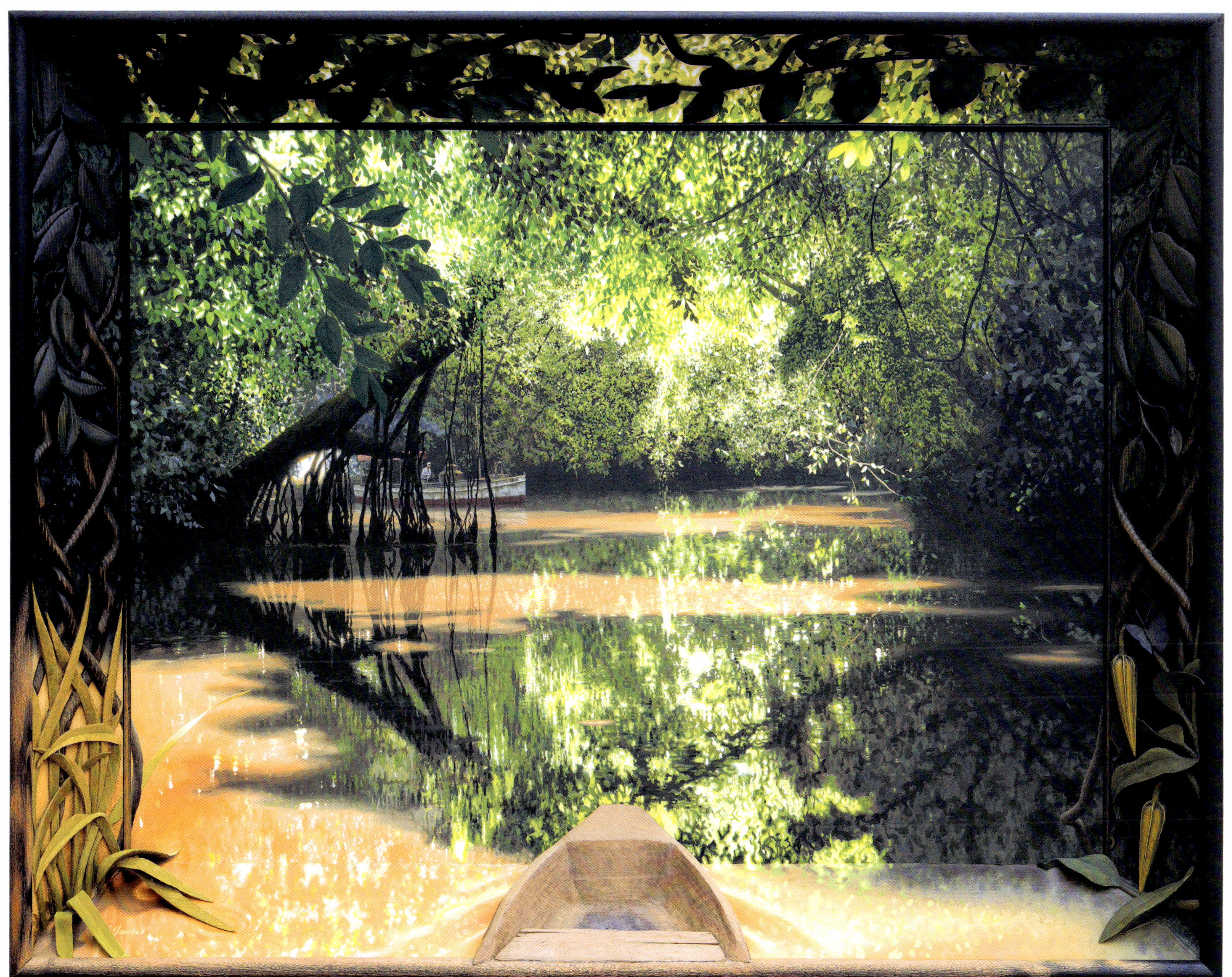

Pirogue prow (carved) enters the painting.

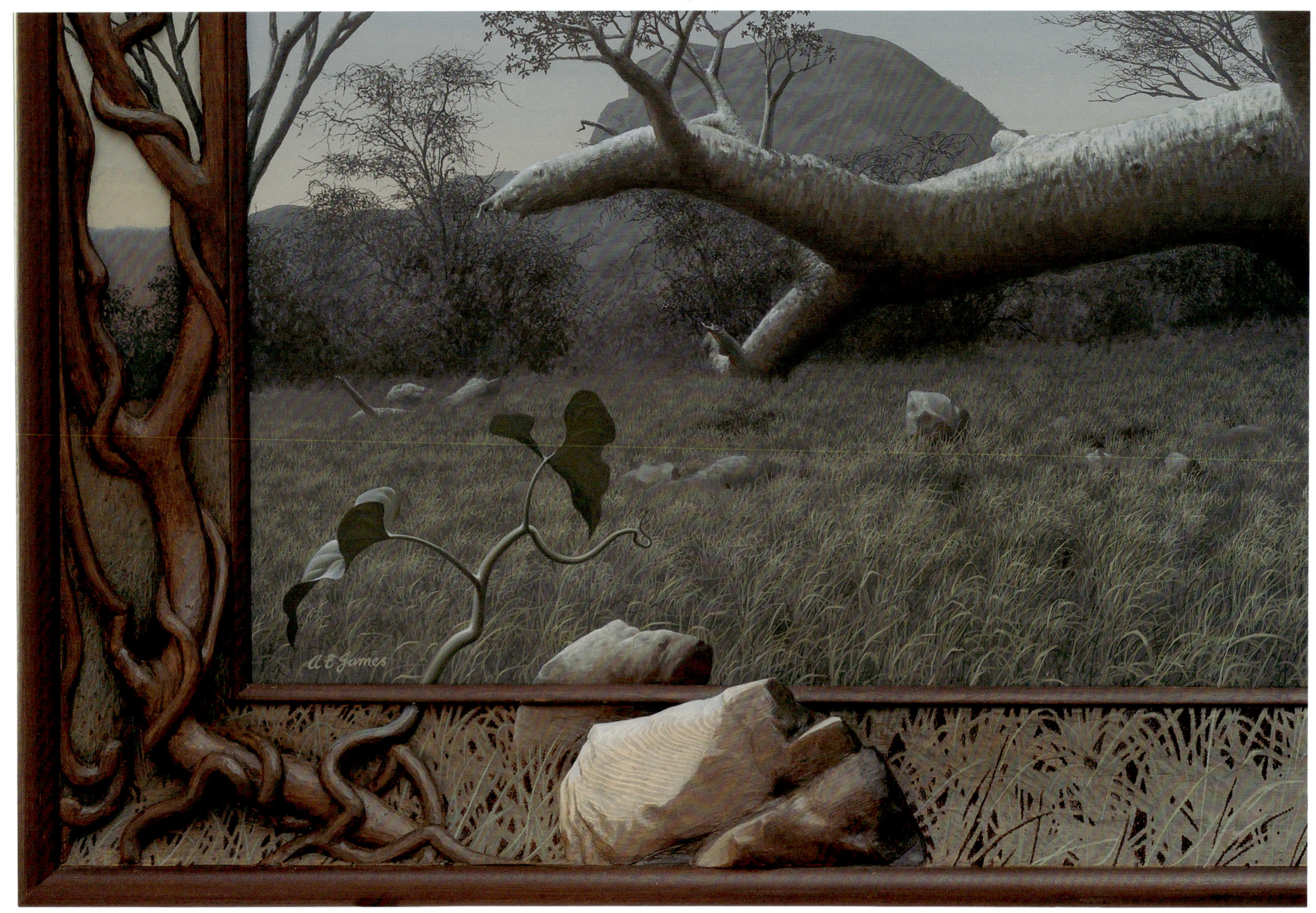

Fading Light
Acrylic & cedarwood, carved, painted and poker-worked.

102 x 140 cm framed, 2014-2016.
Exhibited: Circa Gallery, Chelsea, 2016.

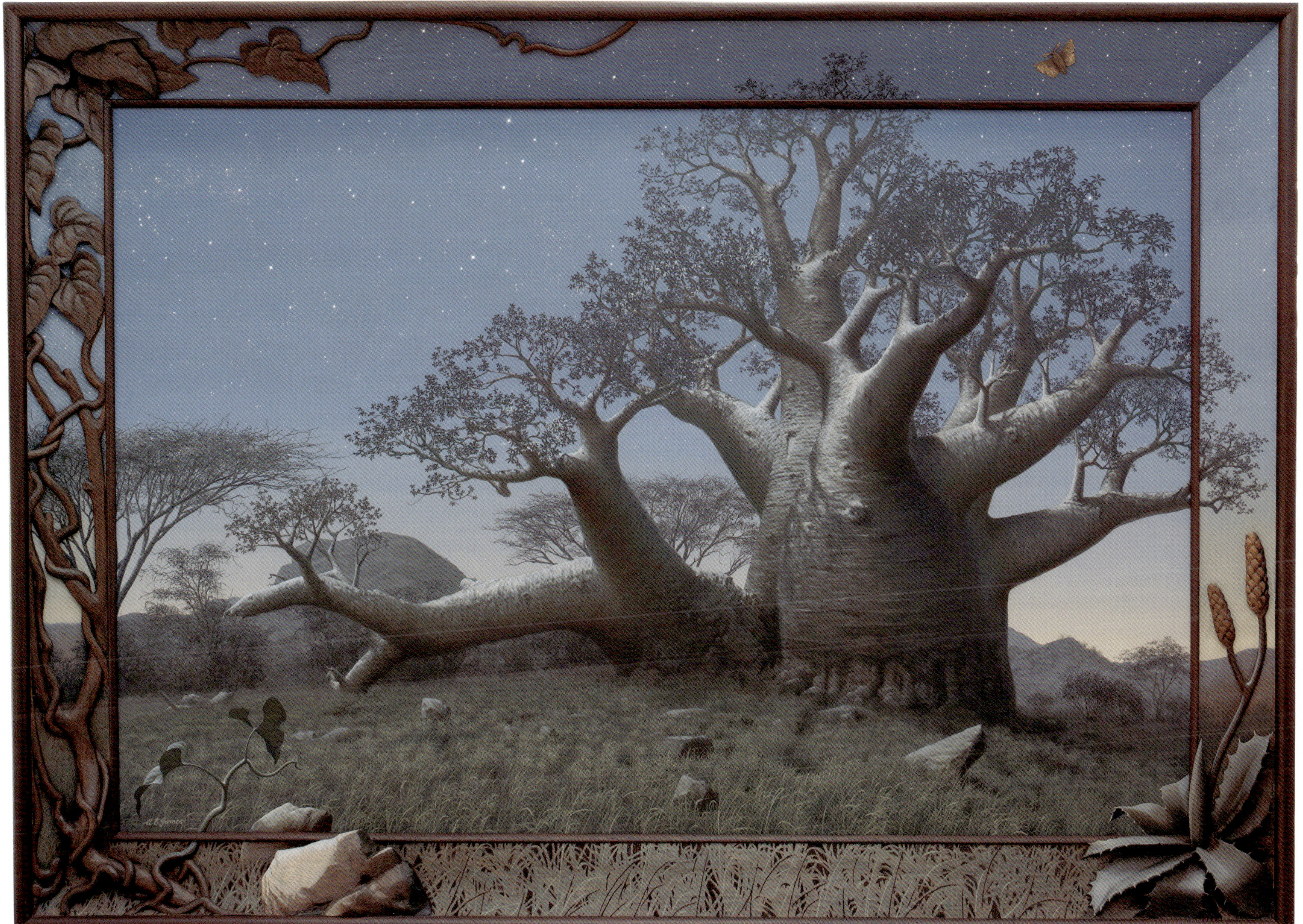

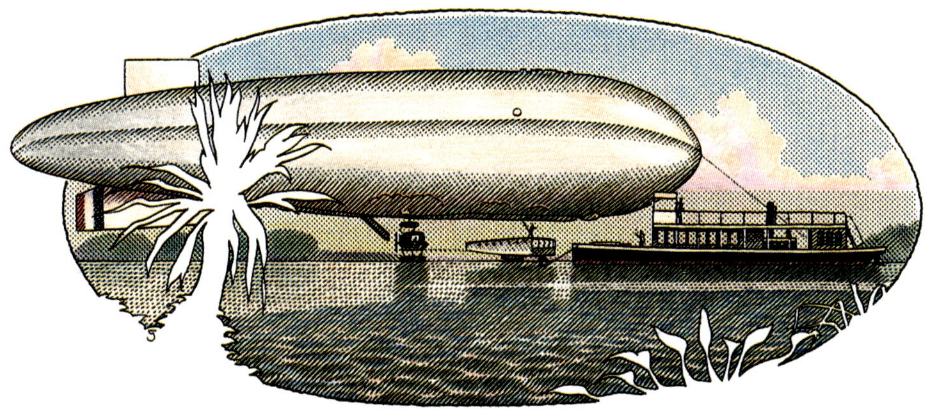

THE VOYAGE CONTINUES....

... but in the meantime you may wish to purchase an Art Print of one or more of our paintings or a copy of the British Time Scale (see pages 13-15).

Carnival Digital Graphics in Bristol, England, offer a bespoke printing service with our full support and approval. They will be happy to discuss and supply your requirements for art prints.

You can contact them directly:
E: paul@carnivalgraphics.com
T: +44 (0) 117 978 1731

The British Timescale is available from Clinical Press Ltd.
Redland Green Farm
Redland
Bristol
BS6 7HF
www.clinicalpress.co.uk
loisgoddard@mac.com

The artists are available on their own websites
Gary M James: www.voyagetotheinterior.com
Alexander James: www.alexedwardjames.com

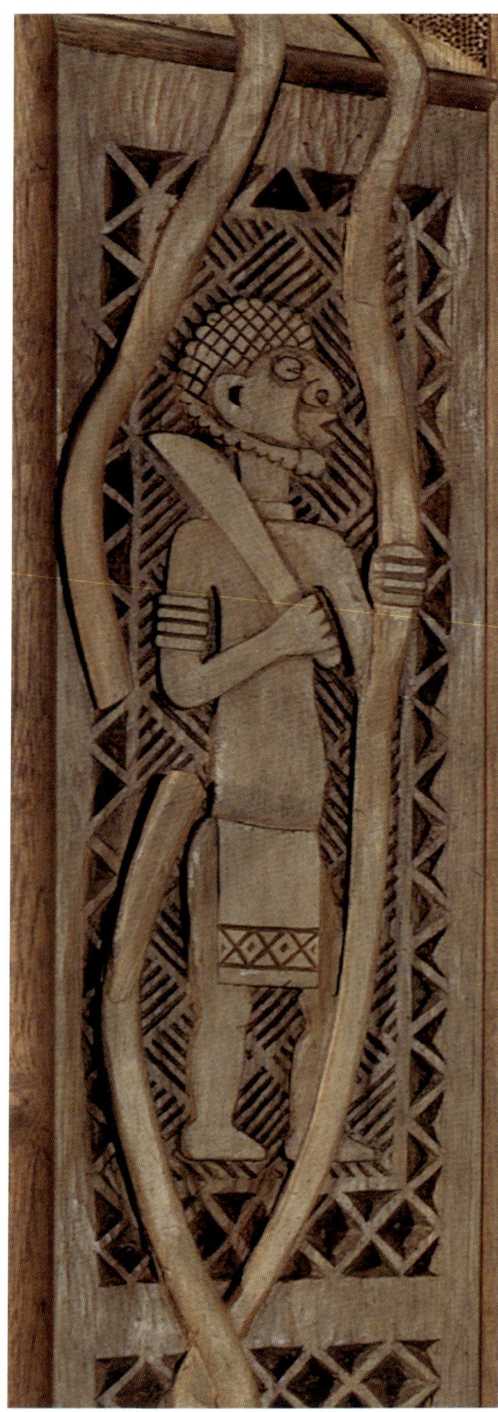

The Paintings of **Gary M. James**

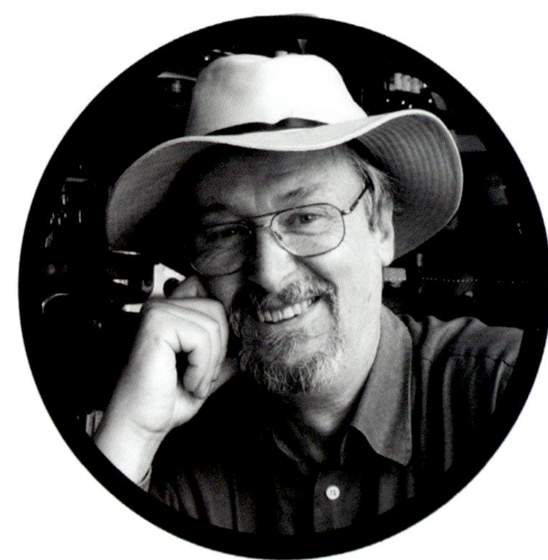

Gary M. James

In an art world dominated by the cult of celebrity, in which only one painter in two hundred is estimated to make a living solely from their art, how can an erstwhile medical artist come to challenge a whole academy's commissions on the strength of his one painting a year?

An upbringing in Kenya played its part, but the artist/author maintains that his unusual "success" was achieved by ignoring all contemporary art fashions and concentrating on the timeless language of figurative art. In these, skill and imagination can take wing.

Here painter and sculptor come together in one to elevate the frame from afterthought to magic portal.

From the Foreword by **Mark Read**

"A creator of unique visions"
"This publication succeeds completely in telling a tale which has evolved over decades"

Also introducing the art of **Alexander E. James.**
Alexander is the artist son and working partner of Gary M. James.

This book is available from the publishers Clinical Press Ltd.

loisgoddard@mac.com
www.clinicalpress.co.uk